Elijah Muhammad and Islam

Elijah Muhammad and Islam

Herbert Berg

NEW YORK UNIVERSITY PRESS

New York and London

NEW YORK UNIVERSITY PRESS
New York and London
www.nyupress.org

Library of Congress Cataloging-in-Publication Data
Berg, Herbert.
Elijah Muhammad and Islam / Herbert Berg.
p.   cm.
Includes bibliographical references and index.
ISBN-13: 978-0-8147-9113-4 (cl : alk. paper)
ISBN-10: 0-8147-9113-1 (cl : alk. paper)
1. Elijah Muhammad, 1897-1975. 2. Black Muslims—Doctrines. 3.
Black Muslims—Relations—Islam. 4. Islam—Relations—Black
Muslims. 5. Islam—United States—History. 6. African American
Muslims—United States—History.   I. Title.
BP223.Z8E414 2009
297.8'7092—dc22   [B]   2008042973

New York University Press books are printed on acid-free paper,
and their binding materials are chosen for strength and durability.
We strive to use environmentally responsible suppliers and materials
to the greatest extent possible in publishing our books.

Manufactured in the United States of America

10 9 8 7 6 5 4 3 2 1

To H.H., M.P., S.J., and C.B.C.P.,
each of whom cried to me,
"Hey, why not ask for more?"

Contents

Acknowledgments

I wish to acknowledge my indebtedness to all those institutions, scholars, and friends without whom I would not have had the wherewithal to complete this study. Much of my early research was supported by a postdoctoral fellowship from the Social Sciences and Humanities Research Council of Canada, a summer research stipend from the University of North Carolina–Wilmington, a summer stipend from the National Endowment for the Humanities, and a research grant from the American Academy of Religion.

I am grateful to colleagues and friends who were so generous with their time and support over the years: Drs. William E. Arnal, Willi Braun, Walt Conser, Matt Eshleman, Russell McCutcheon, Diana Pasulka, and Tom Schmid. Although they may not realize it and may even deny it, some of them have shaped me as a scholar and some have given me advice and encouragement at just the right time. Thank you also to Jennifer Hammer (my editor at NYU Press), Stephanie Smith, and the two anonymous readers who read the manuscript and whose valuable suggestions significantly improved this book.

Finally, I would like to thank my friends Steve, Bill, Darlene, Willi, Johannes, Helen May, Stephanie, Josh, and Sarah. Without their love and friendship this study and much else would not have been possible or worth it.

Introduction

In early 1972 Elijah Muhammad granted a rare interview. Although at the time he seemed to be at the center of a movement beset by inner power struggles and external opposition, the frail and dignified leader of the Nation of Islam sat calmly, allowing sixteen journalists to ask whatever they wished. With poise and in his awkward English, Elijah Muhammad answered their questions about God, Islam, Blacks, Whites, and his mission as the Messenger of Allah:

> For forty years I have been a target for assassination, but I do not pay any attention to that kind of talk. That does not annoy me, because I know God is on my side to protect me, Who Came in the Person of Master Fard Muhammad To Whom Praises Is Due forever.
>
> A good Muslim is one who observes and obeys the laws of the Religion of Islam, designed by God, Himself. . . . [There] will be a New Islam to what the old Orthodox Islam is today. It will be altogether a New One. . . . The Old Islam was led by white people, but this one will not be. This Islam will be established and led by Black Muslims only. . . . Islam in America is to reclaim our people and put them in their own. This is the Resurrection of our people in America.
>
> This is the Resurrection I refer to of our Black people in America. And this is the place that they must come up first. They are in the "crossroads" here and they have to be pointed out the right way to go out. I do not mean to say they go out of America, but out of the evils of America. . . . They were made unrighteous by the slavemasters. They are not even charged with it. You are forgiven everything of evil, on your accepting Islam—your Own. That is all God Asks you to do today, go back to your Own. You are forgiven for everything, because all the evil you did in the past, it was not you, it was the slavemaster who made you do evil.
>
> Yes, they [slave owners] were, by nature, made unrighteous. Their nature was that. . . . That included all white people then and all white

people now. They were made unrighteous. . . . Whether they are actually blue-eyed or not, if they are actually one of the members of that race, they are devils.

I did not choose myself. God chose me . . . I do not have visions, but I do have voices, at times. . . . I know God. I was with Him about three and about four or five months. I know His Voice. And when He Speaks, I know it. . . . It was [from] Him that I have learned all that I am now teaching. I do not know anything of myself. It is what He Has Given me. . . . I would only want to be remembered for the work that I do in the Name of Allah. That is what I want to be remembered for.[1]

Elijah Muhammad's answers highlight the problematic and dichotomous nature of Islam as he understood it. His commitment to Islam as a religion was personal, genuine, and momentous. His understanding of Islam was racial, provocative, and anomalous. Critics have always tended to fixate on the latter characteristics at the expense of the former. If we are to fully understand Elijah Muhammad, his Nation of Islam, and the rebirth of Islam that he spearheaded in America, this dual nature of his formulation of Islam cannot be neglected.

Moreover, in light of ongoing concerns about a clash between Western and Islamic civilizations,[2] it is ironic that hundreds of thousands—if not millions—of Muslims living in the United States were directly or indirectly converted to Islam via the uniquely American formulation of this religion by Elijah Muhammad. Approximately 30 percent of the United States's six to eight million Muslims are African American,[3] making Islam the second most popular religion among African Americans. Although the vast majority of these African American Muslims are now Sunni Muslims, many (or perhaps their parents or grandparents) were introduced to Islam through the Nation of Islam, a movement that was exclusively Black, segregationalist, and militant. Its leader for over forty years, Elijah Muhammad, was therefore arguably the most important person in the development of Islam in America, eclipsing other prominent figures such as Noble Drew Ali, Wali Fard Muhammad, Malcolm X, Louis Farrakhan, and Warith Deen Mohammed (originally known as Wallace D. Muhammad).

Despite his unrivaled prominence, Elijah Muhammad is rarely treated as a major figure in Islam. Quite rightly, he has been examined for his influence in the transformation of African American politics, economics, and psychology. But this book is unique in focusing exclusively on Elijah

Muhammad as a religious figure and, in particular, on his relationship with Islam and other Muslims. The hitherto limited scholarly attention given to Elijah Muhammad—at least from scholars of religion and scholars of Islam—especially when compared with, for example, that given to his Egyptian contemporary Sayyid Qutb (d. 1966), who is the ideologue of many contemporary Islamist groups, is due in part to the general perception of many Muslim and Western scholars that Elijah Muhammad was not "truly" a Muslim.[4] Most other Muslims believe in the absolute oneness and uniqueness of God (which precludes God taking any human form), the termination of prophethood with Muhammad (d. 632 C.E.), and the oneness of all humanity. Instead, Elijah Muhammad taught that Fard Muhammad, the founder of the Nation of Islam, was the incarnation of Allah and that he himself was Allah's Messenger, and he preached about the depravity of the "white devil" and advocated the physical separation of Whites and Blacks. At times Elijah Muhammad certainly helped foster the opinion that his movement was simply a sociopolitical one, with statements such as, "It is far more important to teach separation of the Blacks and the Whites in America than prayer."[5] And yet, his followers called their god "Allah," saw Muhammad as his prophet, prayed five times a day, looked to the Qur'an for the basis of their beliefs and practices, and, most significantly, called themselves Muslims.

What this book does not do is answer the question, "Was Elijah Muhammad a Muslim?" This seemingly simple question may be read in at least three overlapping ways. (1) It may be asking whether Elijah Muhammad was "one who was submitted" (that is the literal translation of the Arabic word "*muslim*") to Allah. If by "Allah" one means Wali Fard Muhammad, then he was most certainly a Muslim. Even if by "Allah" one means a deity generally believed to eschew human form, he may still have been a Muslim. His son, Warith Deen Mohammed, who is widely accepted as a "real" Sunni Muslim, believes that his father was indeed a Muslim.[6] In any case, the scholar's mandate—even that of the scholar of religion—does not and should not include delineating the acceptable conceptions of a deity that may or may not exist. That job belongs to prophets, messengers, imams, preachers, theologians, and the like. (2) It may be asking, as a Muslim might, whether Elijah Muhammad will be rewarded with paradise on judgment day. This question is of course unanswerable by the human scholar. (3) Or the question may be taken as an attempt to decide whether Elijah Muhammad's beliefs and practices bear enough of a resemblance to those of other Muslims to merit being labeled "Muslim."

This third framing of the question is the one most likely to be asked by scholars. Interpreted in this manner, the question seems nontheologically motivated, unlike the first two interpretations of the question. However, this way of framing the question is problematic, resting on an underlying notion that the essence of Islam can be reduced to a specific set of beliefs and practices. Either this set has been handed to the scholar by the religious authorities who claim for themselves exclusive rights over the word "Muslim," or the scholar has placed himself or herself in the role of a religious authority who can determine the truth or validity of religious claims. No matter how the question is interpreted, it will not be answered in this book, which seeks to avoid the theological pitfalls outlined above by remaining agnostic on the issue of whether Elijah Muhammad was a Muslim or not. However, the very fact that the question "Was Elijah Muhammad a Muslim?" has been asked is of great import; the question and the enormous lengths to which Elijah Muhammad went to defend his status as a Muslim demonstrates, at the very least, that he is *a figure in Islam*.

Therefore, this book seeks to understand him as such, opting for sociological and psychological approaches rather than theological ones. More specifically, by contextualizing Elijah Muhammad within the larger Islamic tradition, this book seeks to understand him as Muslim (as both he and his opponents defined the word) through a detailed examination of his religious context, his life, his use of the Qur'an, his relationships with other Muslims, his legacy, and his own religious convictions. It argues that to understand him, his movement, and his significance, scholars of religion must abandon the prejudice that he was not a *real* Muslim or that he was merely superficially Muslim. Even his political, economic, and social agendas were inextricable from his religious one. His devotion to promulgating these agendas for forty years despite persecution and ridicule was born in, and sustained by, his fervent beliefs in Allah, in the authority of the Qur'an, and in his having been commissioned by Allah to bring African Americans back to their original religion, Islam. Regardless of how different these beliefs are from those of other Muslims, only by essentializing "Islam" is it possible to consider Elijah Muhammad outside the context of Islam.

A remarkable parallel can be drawn with the relationship of the Church of Jesus Christ of Latter-Day Saints (Mormons) and the rest of Christianity. Mormons disagree with other Christians on such fundamental issues as the nature of God, the prophethood of Joseph Smith, the openness of the Christian canon, the conception of the afterlife, and the hierarchy of authority within the Church. Many mainstream Christian churches and certainly most conservative Christian denominations, such as the Southern Baptist Convention, do not consider Joseph Smith and his followers Christians, whereas Mormons insist that "Mormonism is Christianity; Christianity is Mormonism; they are one and the same. . . ."[7] Be that as it may, the life of Joseph Smith, his religious claims, and the movement that he founded cannot be understood outside the context of Christianity—even if a scholar feels the need to usurp ecclesiastical authority by ruling that Smith and his Mormons are not Christians. Thus, the uniqueness of this book lies in its focus on the primacy and centrality of Islam for Elijah Muhammad and on his "Muslim-ness." Through this focus, it forcefully demonstrates that to consider him otherwise is to misunderstand and distort the man, his teachings, and his movement.

Elijah Muhammad and the Nation of Islam, of course, did not simply emerge in an Islamic contextual vacuum. Therefore, chapter 1 explores Islam among African Americans and within America in general prior to Elijah Muhammad. Although Elijah Muhammad's perseverance, his message of anger and hope, and his unique rhetorical skill convinced thousands of African Americans to accept his version of Islam, many African Americans already offered fertile ground for his ministry. Vestigial memories that many African slaves had been Muslims may have survived. White American islamicism, while quite negative about Islam, contained several characterizations of Islam that would have made it quite appealing to African Americans, such as its perceived hostility to Christianity and Europe and its identification with Africa. And, just prior to the birth of the Nation of Islam, the missionaries of the Ahmadiyya movement and of Drew Ali's Moorish Science Temple of America began to preach their particular formulations of Islam among African Americans. These factors, then, set the stage for Elijah Muhammad's mentor and the enigmatic founder of the Nation of Islam, Fard Muhammad, and the development of the movement Elijah Muhammad would lead for over four decades.

Chapter 2 outlines the life of Elijah Muhammad, including his life before the Nation of Islam, his tutelage under Fard Muhammad, his struggles to keep the movement alive during years of persecution and imprisonment, and his astounding success from the late 1950s through the turbulent years of Malcolm X. The last decade of Elijah Muhammad's life appears superficially as a period of malaise but was actually a time of economic successes and growth for his movement. Divisions within the

Nation of Islam and renewed struggles for power began as the effects of serious illnesses and advancing age made it increasingly obvious that their Messenger would soon need a successor.

To Elijah Muhammad belongs the greatest credit for having introduced the Qur'an to most African American Muslims. The earlier Moorish Science Temple's most Islamic feature was the use of the word "Koran" for the scripture "written" by its founder, Drew Ali. In that regard, the Nation of Islam was clearly much more "Islamic." The status of the Qur'an for Elijah Muhammad, and the use he made of it, are the subjects of chapter 3. A comparison between Drew Ali's Koran and Elijah Muhammad's use of the Bible and predictions of a future scripture highlight Elijah Muhammad's unique understanding of the role of the Qur'an within his formulation of Islam. His understanding of the Qur'an was not monolithic, however. As he became more familiar with the Qur'an and then experienced the negative reaction of other Muslims, his relationship to the Qur'an evolved. Chapter 4 continues this exploration with a more detailed look at Elijah Muhammad's exegetical framework and teachings in light of some major themes in his writings.

Elijah Muhammad and his followers may have honored the Qur'an and insisted on being called Muslims, but many of the beliefs and practices of the Nation of Islam as elucidated by Elijah Muhammad struck other Muslims as heretical and even unislamic, so much so that many Muslims strongly object to the use of "Islam" to describe Elijah Muhammad's movement. The last two chapters address the issues behind these objections.

Chapter 5 focuses specifically on the mutually suspicious, even hostile, relationship between Elijah Muhammad and many other Muslims, and on the various ways scholars have understood the relationship between Islam and Elijah Muhammad. Most scholars recognize that he took the underdeveloped teachings of Fard Muhammad and produced a viable religious movement. However, some scholars maintain that "Islam" is merely a veneer for a militant civil rights movement, or that his was a millenarian sect, whose strong racial and political agenda was garbed in Islamic language. Even those scholars who maintain that Elijah Muhammad must be considered a Muslim ask what is the best way to understand his role in Islam: as a racial exegete? a jihadist? He has even been recast as a "proto-Muslim" or "crypto-Muslim," who guided African Americans through a temporary "unorthodox"—albeit *absolutely necessary*—stage so that they could eventually be brought to Sunni Islam.

Finally, the Muslim legacy of Elijah Muhammad is evaluated in chapter 6 through an examination of his two main successors, Warith Deen Mohammed (originally named Wallace D. Muhammad) and Louis Farrakhan. The tension between orthodoxy and heterodoxy[8] embedded within the Nation of Islam by Elijah Muhammad himself led to the rupture between these two successors. However, regardless of whether Elijah Muhammad is viewed as a "true" Muslim or not, it was his genuine personal attachment and dedication to the religion of Islam that spurred him to engage in the mythmaking that not only led tens of thousands of African Americans directly to Islam and several million more indirectly but also made Islam part of the religious landscape of America.

1

American Islam
before Elijah Muhammad

Many Africans who made the Middle Passage were Muslims. The story of how their religion was all but extinguished in the United States is a remarkable one. Just as intriguing is its seemingly spontaneous reappearance under the charismatic but unlearned and unassuming Elijah Muhammad. Although Elijah Muhammad and his Nation of Islam were almost entirely responsible for bringing African Americans to Islam during the twentieth century, a closer examination reveals that Islam was not unheard of even in the 1930s when he himself converted. Some African Americans were aware that many of their African ancestors had been Muslims when brought as slaves to North America. They were stripped of this religion almost immediately (as they were of their names and other elements of African culture). Nevertheless, the association of Islam with Africa remained. This association was strengthened by white American islamicism. Although the white American view of Islam was quite negative, Islam's presumed antithesis to Christianity and its alleged opposition to slavery would have been intriguing and appealing to many African Americans.

These vestiges of, and imaginations about, Islam made the fertile ground that allowed the seeds of Islam to be sown, first by Ahmadiyya missionaries and then by Noble Drew Ali. These movements and the socioeconomic conditions of African Americans, especially those who lived in northern urban centers but had recently migrated from the rural South (including Elijah Muhammad himself), made them particularly receptive to the radically new formulation of Islam promulgated by Wali Fard Muhammad.

Islam Comes to America

The first Muslim—in fact, the first Muslim African slave—in North America was a Moroccan named Estevan (also known as Estevanico, Esteban,

Estebanico, Black Stephen, or Stephen the Moor). In 1527 he landed in what is now Florida with an ill-fated Spanish fleet, for whom he was a guide. Only four of the 506 men who were part of the fleet survived the first year. They wandered for eight years among Native Americans, but when the three Europeans were finally able to return home, Estevan stayed behind in Mexico. Later, he served as a guide for another expedition, this one north into modern New Mexico, where he was killed by natives in 1539.[1] Given that even historians had long ignored him, it is not surprising that Estevan's origin as a Muslim had no impact on later African Americans.[2] Likewise, the many other early African Muslims within the Spanish and French parts of colonial North America had no discernible religious influence on later African Americans.

American Slaves

Any vestigial influence of Islam on the twentieth-century African Americans of Elijah Muhammad's time came from their slave ancestors, first shipped to the New World in 1501. It is not certain how many of the half a million or so[3] Africans brought to colonial North America and later the United States as part of the transatlantic slave trade were Muslims. The data is scarce because those who recorded it were not generally interested in slaves as Muslims. Moreover, Muslims and their descendents might be reluctant to divulge Muslim practices or ancestry. However, scholars estimate that over half of these slaves were from West Africa, where Islam was prevalent, and perhaps 15 percent[4] of these West African slaves brought to North American were Muslims. These estimates are based not only on the names recorded in the ledgers of slave owners but also on the religious and ethnic milieu of principle regions from which the slaves originated. These figures are supported by other documents such as runaway notices, which contained names, descriptions, and, occasionally, information about geographical or ethnic origins.

The vast majority of these slaves were stripped of their names, their religion, and their culture. However, Sylviane A. Diouf argues that African Muslims resisted.

> That Islam as brought by the African slaves has not survived does not mean that the Muslim faith did not flourish during slavery on a fairly large scale. . . . Muslims were not absorbed into the cultural-religious

Christian world. They chose to remain Muslims, and even enslaved, succeeded in following most of the precepts of their religion.[5]

Historian Michael A. Gomez shares this view and contends that many Muslim slaves

> made genuine and persistent efforts to observe their religion; and even though they perpetuated their faith primarily within their own families, in some cases they may have converted slaves who were not relatives . . . [and some] ostensibly Christian worship practices and artistic expressions . . . probably reflect the influence of these early Muslims.[6]

This claim is supported by evidence from the sparse but important biographical and autobiographical reports of former slaves, such as those of Job Ben Solomon (d. 1773), Ibrahim Abd ar-Rahman (d. 1829), Lamine Kebe (d. after 1837), and Umar ibn Said (d.1864). Several of them were able to obtain their freedom and return to Africa, and some wrote extensively in English and Arabic—a unique characteristic among African slaves, for the arrival of Islam in Africa had encouraged literacy.[7] It is also clear that a few of them adopted a Christian façade in order to secure their return to Africa, suggesting that many slaves may have maintained secret connections to Islam. However, what influence these men might have had on the later Elijah Muhammad is unknown; he did not mention them in his extensive writings. It seems more likely, since he was born and raised in Georgia, that Elijah Muhammad may have heard of Bilali Mohammad and Salih Bilali and their descendents on Georgia's Sapelo Island and the nearby St. Simon's Island, respectively. These two friends and others in Georgia made a concerted effort to preserve within their community and families their Muslim heritage, elements of which survived well into the nineteenth century.[8] Gomez concludes that "the Muslim presence in coastal Georgia . . . was active, healthy, and compelling."[9] Moreover, relatively positive attributes were associated with Muslim slaves; these Muslims were thought by slave owners to be a "more intelligent, more reasonable, more physically attractive, more dignified people" than other Africans.[10] Similarly, these African American Muslim slaves occasionally displayed a sense of superiority over non-Muslim slaves.

There is no evidence, however, that Elijah Muhammad had a direct connection to these Muslims who were geographically so close to him.

He was raised in a Christian household. Both his father and grandfather were Christian preachers. Besides, even the Muslims of the Georgia coast had by the beginning of the twentieth century begun converting to Christianity (though there is evidence of both syncretism and dissimulation).[11] In Brazil and the Caribbean, elements of Islam survived in the syncretic religions of Candomble, Macumba, Umbanda, Voodoo, and Santeria, yet no such continuity is evident with Elijah Muhammad's religious formulation.[12]

American Islamicism

Elijah Muhammad was no doubt influenced by these vestiges of Islam, as well as by the white American perception of Islam. This perception has been described by Timothy Marr as "islamicism," which he defines as an "Islamic orientalism that essentializes Islam, often in distorted and inaccurate ways."[13] Americans' islamicism goes back to the colonial period and certainly did not begin with Elijah Muhammad, nor in 1979 with the Iranian revolution, nor, for a younger generation, on September 11, 2001.

American islamicist cultural rhetoric from the seventeenth through the nineteenth centuries was deployed to universalize national experiences and practices. Marr focuses on two types of islamicism: the *domestic* variety, which "othered" Islam as the idealized antithesis of domestic American situations, and the *comparative* variety, which involved the personal encounters of Americans with actual Muslim cultures. Islam was initially constructed as a cultural enemy, one that was despotic, anti-Christian, and morally corrupt, whereas America was imagined as democratic, Christian, and virtuous. This is demonstrated in the (mostly fictional) literature about Muslim spies and white Christians enslaved by Muslims, and in American interpretation of the events of Barbary captivity, the Tripolitan War, and the Greek war of independence from the Ottoman Empire. Later, American Protestant Christian millennialism and missionary activity to convert Muslims saw the removal of Islam and the consequent return of the Jews to the "Holy Land" as necessary precursors to the return of Jesus. The eastern Muslim (i.e., Turkish) empire was identified with various elements within the Book of Revelation. This eschatology allowed Protestants to understand the persistence of Islam simply as a temporary scourge that was part of a divine plan (to punish errant Christians). Three points are worth noting with regard to Elijah Muhammad. First, Islam is seen as the antithesis of white, Christian America. Second, Islam is largely identified with Africa even by white Americans. Third, the basic eschatological model was also later employed by Elijah Muhammad, except that the protagonist and antagonist religions exchanged roles. Furthermore, the fear and hatred of Islam in Europe (which was almost as old as Islam itself) were inherited by European American descendents and so made it impossible for Muslim slaves to perpetuate their faith.[14] Ironically, Elijah Muhammad capitalized on this fear and hatred of Islam by Whites as he sought to persuade the African American descendents of those slaves to embrace Islam.

Later still, "Islam" was employed within the United States by the antislavery and temperance movements. Though Islam prohibits alcohol consumption and although most Muslims in the United States were slaves, the main strategy of these movements was ironically to associate both alcohol consumption and slavery with Islam, thereby hoping to make them unacceptable to Americans. However, it is more likely that a second strategy employed by these two movements would have had a greater influence on Elijah Muhammad. Islam was also used to shame Americans in that "Turkish" lands prohibited alcohol and began antislavery reforms ahead of the United States. While direct influences of America's Islamic history and perceptions on Elijah Muhammad are difficult to establish, it is clear that the practice of slavery by Muslims was initially unknown to him.

Moorish Science Temple[15]

The first wave of Muslim immigrants came to the United States between 1875 and 1912, mostly from Syria, Lebanon, Jordan, and Palestine. Many were quickly assimilated. Immigration laws passed in 1921 and 1924 put quotas on immigration from particular nations, so the number of Muslims allowed to enter the United States was significantly curtailed. In the 1930s, immigration was only open to relatives of those already in the country. None of these immigrants engaged in any significant or organized missionary activity with African Americans. The first immigrant Muslims to do so were the Ahmadiyyas from India—beginning just a few years prior to the birth of the Nation of Islam.

The first Muslim missionary to the United States was Mohammed Alexander Russell Webb (d. 1916), a white American who converted to Islam while in the Philippines. In 1892 he visited India, where he may have come in contact with Ahmadiyya Muslims. After his return to the United States in 1893, he established the American Moslem Brotherhood in New York

City and a Muslim publishing company. His primary goal was to dispel the negative stereotypes Americans had of Islam, rather than to convert Americans to Islam. Webb made a point of emphasizing that Islam taught equality and universal brotherhood, but this message apparently did not influence Fard Muhammad and Elijah Muhammad.

A more likely source of influence would have been the well-known Caribbean, pan-Africanist Edward Wilmot Blyden (d. 1912). He was an ordained Presbyterian minister who often wrote of Christianity's racism and its demoralizing effect on Blacks while extolling Islam's unifying and elevating qualities. Likewise, Henry McNeal Turner (d. 1915), an African American bishop in the African Methodist Episcopal Church famous for his statement in sermons that "God is a Negro," severely criticized Christianity's racism and was much impressed by the Muslims he encountered in Sierra Leone and Liberia. Certainly, the assumption of Islam's blindness to race extolled by Blyden and Webb was not picked up by Drew Ali, Fard Muhammad, or Elijah Muhammad, though Blyden's and Turner's condemnation of American Christianity's racism was. And, God as a "black man" would become a cornerstone in Elijah Muhammad's formulation of Islam.

Despite the increasing presence of Muslim immigrants in American and the use of Islam in antiracist rhetoric, the first significant number of Americans calling themselves Muslims were the followers of an African American who became known as Noble Drew Ali. Timothy Drew was born in 1886 in North Carolina to ex-slaves living among Cherokee Indians. Beyond these facts, very little is known of his life, for much of the traditional biography is inconsistent hagiography. It is said that his mother foresaw great things in him, but when she died, Drew was raised by an aunt who abused him until he ran away. While living with gypsies, he heard a voice say to him, "If you go, I will follow." So he left, and though there are various versions of this tale, it seems that he became a merchant seaman at the age of sixteen and eventually arrived in Egypt. There he is said to have passed some sort of test in the Pyramid of Cheops and so was renamed Noble Drew Ali. In 1912 or 1913, in response to a dream that told him to found a religion "for the uplifting of fallen mankind," especially the "lost-found nation of American blacks," he created the Canaanite Temple in Newark, New Jersey.[16] Prior to this he had been a Shriner, from which organization he clearly adopted his religious symbols and paraphernalia. The sashes and fezes he adopted, as well as the affixing of "El" and "Bey" after surnames, the prohibition of pork (in fact, all meat) and of intoxicants, the practice of praying (while standing) towards the East, the segregation of women during Friday services, and the use of the word "Koran" for his own scripture were all attempts to imitate what Drew Ali (often mistakenly) believed to be Muslim or Moorish practice.[17]

When an Arab Muslim immigrant came into contact with Drew Ali's followers in Newark in 1918, his more first-hand account of Muslim practice sparked tensions within the movement and led to a split. The Newark group became the Moabite Temple of the World, while Drew Ali relocated to Chicago in 1919.[18] There, he formed the Moorish Divine National Movement, which in 1926 he incorporated as the Moorish Holy Temple of Science and two years later renamed again the Moorish Science Temple of America, Inc. In those years, his teachings also evolved, focusing increasingly on race. For several years Drew Ali enjoyed considerable success, amassing perhaps ten thousand followers. However, rivalries emerged once again within the movement and, when one of those rivals was murdered in 1929, Drew Ali was arrested. He was released on bond but, suspiciously, died shortly thereafter.

Drew Ali's teachings deserve some attention not only because several of them seem to have been picked up by Fard Muhammand and Elijah Muhammad but also because of their significant divergence from the teachings of other forms of Islam. Since this latter issue would also be raised by Muslims regarding Elijah Muhammad's Nation of Islam, the Moorish Science Temple offers an interesting comparison.

According to Drew Ali, African Americans are "Asiatics" and Moors. Their ancestors were the Canaanites who descended from Noah's son Ham. They are also descendants of the biblical Moabites. Their more recent ancestors inhabited West Africa, where they established the Moorish empire that ruled most of Asia and Europe. (Surprisingly, Ireland was considered one of its last strongholds, and so Celts, though white, were considered Asiatics and eligible for membership in the Moorish Science Temple.) The Blacks of America are therefore actually Moors, and their natural religion is Islam, not Christianity. Although Jesus was also a Canaanite, he was merely a prophet. The Romans killed him and then founded Christianity, deliberately distorting the racial background of Jesus so that white Europeans could "claim him as one of their own and establish him as the head of their church."[19]

The American portion of this myth begins in 1682 when, according to Drew Ali, the so-called Black Laws of Virginia exempted Moors (that is, Moroccan nationals) from slavery. In 1774 the Founding Fathers declared only "Negroes" subject to slavery. Legally, therefore, Moors could not be slaves. Unfortunately, the Moors forgot their true identity as Moors and accepted the label of "Negro" and, as a result, the condition of slavery. Had they "honored their mother and father" and not "strayed after the strange gods of Europe," they would not have suffered slavery.[20]

This myth is not particularly complex, but it has some interesting features. First, it is difficult to discern what, if anything, makes this myth Islamic. The religion from which the "Moors" are said to have turned away was Islam, but the Islamic terminology Drew Ali employed is limited, and there was clearly no effort to revise or incorporate Islamic mythology or its individual myths. This tendency is particularly evident in the scripture of the Moorish Science Temple, the *Circle Seven Koran*.[21] Muhammad is mentioned only twice, and very cursorily, once as "the founder of uniting of Islam," and once as the one who "fulfilled the works of Jesus of Nazareth."[22] Christian mythology is also largely ignored. The reference to Ham, though biblical, takes the Moorish Science Temple away from the core of Jewish mythology too. The figure of Ham, who was cursed by his father Noah, had been cited as biblical justification for slavery by some white Christians. Drew Ali seems to have accepted the genealogical claim being made but reinterpreted it to show that Moors had an ancient and noble past.

The purpose of this mythical Moorish empire was also to connect African Americans with a proud heritage, thereby circumventing the then generally accepted picture of Africa, its inhabitants, and their American cousins as savage and uncivilized. The plausibility of both white racists' claims about Africa as savage and those of Drew Ali about the glory of the Moorish empire were no doubt enhanced by the general ignorance of Africa and its history. However, the myth of the Canaanites and the Moorish empire itself was an important strategy that supported the Moorish Science Temple's competition for the hearts and minds of the overwhelmingly Christian African American population. To that end, Drew Ali also stressed that each race had its own religion. Europeans had Christianity; the Moors had Islam. Love would replace hate only when everyone "worship[s] under his own vine and fig tree."[23]

Drew Ali's insistence that Christianity belonged to Europeans was not an endorsement of the equality of Islam and Christianity. He commanded his followers,

Neither serve the gods of their [the Europeans'] religion, because our forefathers are the *true* and divine founders of the *first* religious creed, for the redemption of mankind on earth. Therefore we are returning the Church and Christianity back to the European Nations, as it was prepared by the forefathers for their *earthly salvation*. While we, the Moorish Americans, are returning to Islam, which was founded by our forefathers for our *earthly and divine salvation*.[24]

The chronological and epistemological priority of Islam over Christianity would be a theme upon which Elijah Muhammad would greatly expand. What exactly Drew Ali was implying in the distinction between Christianity's "earthly salvation" and Islam's "earthly and divine salvation" is not clear.

As for the portion of the myth that deals with slavery in America, Drew Ali did not dwell on the evil of slavery or the wrongness of Europeans for enslaving Asiatics but rather emphasized that Moors should never have been enslaved. Doing so was illegal; but "illegal" is not the same thing as "evil"—as slavery would be for Elijah Muhammad. Moreover, the fault is not seen as lying exclusively with white Americans. Moors forgot who they were (though the Founding Fathers and other Whites certainly had a hand in causing them to forget). Had they remembered, such things would never have occurred. For, by taking the Moorish name away and calling them "Negroes," "blacks," "colored," and so forth, "the European stripped the Moor of his power, his authority, his God, and every other worthwhile possession."[25] Thus, the myth serves as both a theodicy and a paradigm for his followers' identity. It explains why slavery occurred and what must be done now. African Americans were being called to a spiritual return to their roots, which guaranteed them "love, truth, peace, freedom, and justice."

Thus, like his contemporary Marcus Garvey, Drew Ali rejected integration.[26] However, unlike Marcus Garvey, who advocated that African Americans physically return to Africa, Drew Ali sought instead a spiritual return. This far more practical approach would be adopted by both Fard Muhammad and Elijah Muhammad—though not Drew Ali's openness to other religions. For example, Drew Ali claimed Confucius among his predecessors, while Elijah Muhammad denounced both Buddhism and Hinduism (along with Christianity, of course) as enemies of Islam.[27] Moreover, while both would also adopt a similar position on the separation of Whites and Blacks, they would not adopt Drew Ali's acceptance of the white race. Instead, they decried it as evil. Despite its indebtedness to him,[28] the Nation of Islam, with its more militant doctrines and more charismatic leaders, would come to eclipse the Moorish Science Temple as the most visible and viable formulation of Islam among African Americans.

Ahmadiyya

The Ahmadiyya movement began with Mirza Ghulam Ahmad (d. 1908) from Qadian in Punjab, in what is now India. He was particularly concerned about the Christian missionaries who came with British rule and the resurgent Hinduism of the Arya Samaj and the Brahmo Samaj (which were also responses to the British hegemony). His goals included not only defending Islam but also emphasizing piety and jihad (which for Ghulam Ahmad meant the propagation of Islam, not fighting the British). As his message developed in the 1880s and 1890s, it came to be more and more at odds with orthodox Sunni and Shi'i Islam. Most problematic were his claims to be the Mahdi (a messianic figure) and a prophet. All of his followers recognized him as a renewer of Islam (a *mujaddid*), but after his death his movement split—the Lahori Ahmadiyyas emphasized that he was merely a *mujaddid* whose statements about prophethood were to be understood metaphorically. The Qadian Ahmadiyyas split even further from other Muslims by emphasizing the prophethood of Ghulam Ahmad and the divine guidance of subsequent leaders of the movement. It is this latter group that in 1920 sent the first Muslim missionary to America— Mufti Muhammad Sadiq.

By the time Muhammad Sadiq arrived in the United States, Drew Ali's Canaanite/Moorish movement(s) had begun to spread along the major urban centers of the east coast of the United States, and immigrant Muslims had begun establishing mosques and organizations, including that of Sāttī Mājid, an outspoken critic of Drew Ali. Sāttī Mājid made contact with Drew Ali, urging him to change the name of his Koran and challenging him to prove his claim to prophethood with miracles. Sāttī Mājid also attempted to enlist the support of the American government and went to court against Drew Ali. He was far more successful in Egypt and the Sudan, where he successfully had several *fatwas* issued against Drew Ali.[29] And, in 1924 Shaykh Daoud Ahmed Faisal founded the first Sunni African American organization in New York City. Faisal was born in Morocco but came to the United States via Grenada. Through his organization, the Islamic Mission of America, he worked to forge connections with the rest of the Islamic world, particularly through Muslim seamen in New York

City.[30] A little later Duse Mohammed Ali, a Sudanese-Egyptian who mentored Marcus Garvey in pan-Africanism while he was in Great Britain and came to America in the early 1920s, established the Universal Islamic Society in Detroit in 1926.

Muhammad Sadiq's message, unlike that of his contemporaries, was not focused on African Americans alone. His first converts included Americans of both African and European ancestry. Sadiq emphasized making connections among Muslims of different racial and ethnic groups, and even among religions. Like the earlier Muslim missionaries in the United States, Sadiq ignored racism amongst Muslims but criticized Christianity for its racism—a theme Elijah Muhammad would develop. However, the subsequent opposition from some white Christian churches led him to focus his missionary activities more on African Americans.

Having converted seven hundred Americans, Sadiq returned to India in 1923. The movement continued to do well for several decades despite competition from the Moorish Science Temple and the Nation of Islam. The Ahmadiyya's internationalist and multiracial concerns set it apart from the latter's American political and racial focus. Perhaps the most important effect of the Ahmadiyya movement was to make available to African Americans (and Elijah Muhammad) their 1917 English translation of the Qur'an—the very Qur'an Fard Muhammad would present to his most ardent disciple, Elijah Muhammad. This Qur'an (and its footnotes provided by its translator, Mawlana Muhammad Ali) would be cited continuously by Elijah Muhammad for forty years, and along with the Ahmadiyya conception of the Mahdi would play a critical role in the development of Elijah Muhammad's formulation of Islam.

The Suitability of Islam

Although no direct connection can be established between African Muslim slaves and their descendents and Elijah Muhammad and his followers, the presence of the Ahmadiyya movement, the Moorish Science Temple, the Islamic Mission of America, and the Universal Islamic Society indicates that Islam was not unheard of among African Americans when Wali Fard Muhammad began to convert followers such as Elijah Muhammad. More significantly, the success of these Islamic movements among African Americans and later that of the Nation of Islam itself suggests that some aspects of Islam must have been very appealing to many African Americans.

These aspects of Islam included the perceived intimate connection of Islam to Africa; Islam's independence from white Europeans and their descendants in the United States, who were almost exclusively Christian; the fact that the civilization and empires of Islam were not centered in Europe; and the fact that Whites seemed both to hate and fear Islam. These four aspects may have resonated with African Americans because of the legacy of African Muslim slaves or American islamicism. Obviously, the Moorish Science Temple and other Islamic movements not only capitalized on these aspects but also gave them greater currency by doing so. There were, however, other characteristics inherent in Islam that made it particularly suitable for African Americans in the early decades of the twentieth century: Islam had a reputation for resistance, especially to Christianity, and the Qur'an's retributive justice would have seemed enticing to those suffering because of anti-Black racism; compared to the trinitarianism of most denominations of Christianity, Islam had a fairly simple unitarian theology; Islam emphasized a conservative social ethic that was remarkably well suited to address some of the social ills that afflicted urban African Americans in the cities of the North; and the lack of an ecclesiastical hierarchy in Sunni Islam permitted (at least at first) a great deal of independence for charismatic leaders such as Drew Ali, Fard Muhammad, and Elijah Muhammad.[31] However, Islam had at least two major drawbacks as well.

First, Islam could not compete with Christianity in "name recognition" and infrastructure. Among African Americans, Jesus, Peter, and Paul were well known; Muhammad, Ali, and Umar were not. Bibles were readily available, even seminaries, but Qur'ans in English were hard to come by and there were no *madrasas*. This disadvantage was mitigated only somewhat by the activities of Ahmadiyya missionaries, the Moorish Science Temple, and other early Muslim organizations. However, as will be shown, the Ahmadiyya translation of the Qur'an into English had an enormous impact on Elijah Muhammad and through him on his followers in the Nation of Islam.

Second, Islam lacked a specifically African American political, social, and economic agenda or a liberation theology. This lacuna is hardly surprising, given Islam's origination in Arabia and its limited practice in the United States prior to the rise of the Nation of Islam. Elijah Muhammad, like Drew Ali before him, overcame this disadvantage, not by seeking some precedent among Muslim societies, but by drawing directly on the secular black nationalism of Marcus Garvey.

Marcus Garvey was born in 1887 in Jamaica but came to the United States in 1916 after sojourns in Latin American and Great Britain. A year later he formed the first American Universal Negro Improvement Association (UNIA) chapter. Its goal, according to the 1929 constitution, was "to work for the general uplift of the people of African ancestry of the world." Garvey urged all Africans and their descendents to unite and, because of racial oppression, put their race first. Although others such as Edward Wilmot Blyden and W. E. B. Du Bois had advocated pan-Africanism, it was Garvey who was able to turn the philosophy into a mass movement that by 1919 had some two million members and was said to have doubled in just two more years. Although Garvey did not express his pan-Africanism in religious terms, preferring a more pluralistic approach, both Elijah Muhammad and Drew Ali made their formulations of Islam explicitly racial. Garvey's influence is obvious too in his economic program, the key feature of which was self-reliance, as demonstrated with the UNIA's restaurants, grocery stores, and shipping line. The program was later adopted wholesale by Elijah Muhammad under the slogan "do for self." The secular nationalism of Garvey, with its emphasis on "back to Africa," also greatly influenced Drew Ali and Elijah Muhammad, though they preferred a religious return to the continent, not a physical one.

Garvey's influence also caught the attention of the Bureau of Investigation (the forerunner of the Federal Bureau of Investigation). It actively sought to have Garvey deported, which occurred in 1927 after he had served a few years in prison in what appears to have been a trumped-up charge of mail fraud. Garvey remained active until his death in 1940, and so his movement and those of Drew Ali and Elijah Muhammad were in competition. Nevertheless, having incorporated or appropriated much Garveyism, both men gave Garvey his due. Drew Ali cast him as John the Baptist to his Jesus: "In these modern days there came a forerunner of Jesus, who was divinely prepared by the great God-Allah and his name is Marcus Garvey, who did teach and warn the nations of the earth to prepare to meet the coming Prophet."[32] Elijah Muhammad was somewhat more circumspect about both men:

I have always had a very high opinion of both the late Noble Drew Ali and Marcus Garvey and admired their courage in helping our people (the so-called Negroes) and appreciated their work. Both of these men were fine Muslims. The followers of Noble Drew Ali and Marcus Garvey should now follow me and co-operate with us and in our work because we are only trying to finish up what those before us started.[33]

It is noteworthy that Elijah Muhammad not only recognized them as Muslims but also saw his work as a continuation of theirs. Elijah Muhammad generally portrayed only one man as having introduced Islam to African Americans and only one man whose work he was continuing: his teacher and god, Wali Fard Muhammad.

Wali Fard Muhammad

The biography of the founder of the Nation of Islam, Wali Fard Muhammad, is problematic and rife with contradiction. His story comes almost solely through his Messenger Elijah Muhammad, who only in the late 1950s began to disseminate it through his speeches, radio addresses, newspaper columns, pamphlets, and books. At about the same time, the Federal Bureau of Investigation took an interest in the movement and began to search for information about this mysterious Fard Muhammad. In both cases, therefore, our main sources for information about Fard Muhammad come after two decades of the movement's development.

Allah in Person

The successor and main architect of the movement, Elijah Muhammad, taught that Fard Muhammad was born to the tribe of Quraysh in Mecca in 1877.[34] "Allah came to us from the Holy City of Mecca, Arabia, in 1930."[35] Prior to Fard's birth, his father had planned for his son to search out his "lost people"—understood to be the "lost" nation of Blacks in America. To that end, though very dark himself, Fard's father married a white woman so that his son would be able to move among the white people in whose midst the lost black people were located. (Even Elijah Muhammad in 1950 is quoted as saying that African Americans in Detroit had "not recognized him as being one of us.")[36] Fard Muhammad's father was a scientist who gathered knowledge from around the world to prepare his son. Fard Muhamamd studied for forty-two years before traveling the world. His native language was Arabic, but he spoke sixteen languages and could write ten fluently. In addition, he had studied in England in preparation for a diplomatic career and had been visiting the United States for about twenty years. He had also enrolled in the University of Southern

California. In 1930 he came to Detroit and gathered twenty-five thousand followers within a year.[37]

One of the earliest extended descriptions of Fard Muhammad's mission portrays him as a savior and martyr:

> He (MR. FARD MUHAMMAD, God in Person) chose to suffer three and one-half years to show his love for his people, who have suffered over 300 years at the hands of a people who by nature are evil, wicked, and have no good in them.
>
> He was persecuted, sent to jail in 1932, and ordered out of Detroit, Mich., May 26, 1933. He came to Chicago in the same year, arrested almost immediately on his arrival and placed behind prison bars.
>
> He submitted himself with all humbleness to his persecutors. Each time he was arrested, he sent for me that I may see and learn the price of TRUTH for us, the so-called American Negroes (members of the Asiatic nation).
>
> He was well able to save himself from such suffering, but how else was the scripture to be fulfilled? We followed in His footsteps suffering the same (persecution).[38]

No doubt the parallels drawn between Fard Muhammad and the Christian account of the persecution of Jesus are intentional. Fard Muhammad's persecution also had salvific and paradigmatic purposes for Elijah Muhammad.[39]

The aforementioned "TRUTH" taught to Detroit's African Americans by Fard Muhammad was that the "so-called Negroes" were members of the lost tribe of Shabazz from Mecca. He had come to resurrect this Lost-Found Nation of Islam in America. The "black man" must return to his original religion, Islam, his original language, Arabic, and the law of Allah. And although Fard Muhammad spoke of himself as the Prophet, he eventually introduced himself as the Son of Man—perhaps due to Elijah Muhammad's prompting. At least some of his contemporary followers, including Elijah Muhammad, thought of him as God in human form.[40]

Elijah Muhammad also describes Fard Muhammad as the "Great Mahdi." While the term may have been adopted from contact with Ahmadiyyas, the conception of "mahdi" is quite different in his use—it implies divinity. Elijah Muhammad attested that Fard Muhammad said, "My name is Mahdi; I am God."[41] He also equated the name "Mahdi" with the angel with great power who descends from heaven according to Revelation

18:1. Elijah Muhammad explained, "This angel can be no other than Master W. F. Muhammad, the Great Mahdi. . . . The Great Mahdi is indeed the most wise and powerful being on earth (God in Person). It is He who with a strong voice announced the immediate doom of America."[42] Elijah Muhammad allowed Fard Muhammad's names to proliferate: "Son of Man, Jesus Christ, Messiah, God, Lord, Jehovah, the Last (Jehovah) and the Christ"—all names employed by "the anti-Christs (the devils)."[43]

After Fard Muhammad placed Elijah Muhammad in charge of the movement, having given him the new surname "Muhammad," the new titles "Supreme Minister of the Nation of Islam" and "Messenger of Allah," an English and an Arabic Qur'an, and a list of 104 books to read,[44] Fard Muhammad disappeared in 1934. The reasons for his departure, as expounded by Elijah Muhammad, were twofold: (1) it was not necessary for him to remain once he had taught and prepared Elijah Muhammad; and (2) "the people are not worthy that God remain among them."[45]

Elijah Muhammad was vague about whether Fard Muhammad would return. There were hints, he said, but as much prophesy suggested that He would not return as suggested that he would. He concluded, "I don't expect Him to return in person, not like that, because there is to [sic] much for us to look forward to that He will not. It is not really necessary if He is going to send His Own people, as they're referred to as angels, to gather the believers of my people, it's not necessary."[46] However, Elijah Muhammad stated that he communicated with him at first via letters and, later, via inspiration.[47] Fard Muhammad also has a significant role to play in the future, according to Elijah Muhammad. In the millennium after the judgment, "the disbelievers will cease to be. And to those who live in that time it shall be binding upon them to serve and obey One God: Fard Muhammad the Great Mahdi, or Allah in Person."[48]

Wallace D. Ford

The Federal Bureau of Investigation collected extensive records on Wallace Dodd Ford—whom they maintain was Fard Muhammad. However, his time and place of origin, according to these records, are still murky. In police records he is described as "white" with a "dark" complexion. His father (Zared Ford) and mother (Beatrice Ford) came from Hawaii, but he was born in Portland, Oregon, in 1891. Other documents state that he was born in New Zealand on February 26, 1891, to a British father and Polynesian mother and only arrived in Portland in 1913. However, he is also recorded as having moved to Los Angeles in 1913 after growing up in Portland. In Los Angeles, he was a restaurant keeper and married a woman name Hazel Barton, with whom he had a son in 1920. Police records indicate that he was arrested on an assault charge in 1918 but was released. At the time, he was called Wallie Ford (which, obviously, sounds suspiciously like "Wali Fard," though the latter term is normally pronounced "Farrad"). In 1926 he was arrested twice, first for possession and sale of alcohol and later for the sale of narcotics. He was sent to San Quentin in June of 1926 and released in May of 1929.[49]

According to the FBI files, he came to Detroit in 1931 after a brief stop in Chicago. There he may have had contact with Ahmadiyyas, Muslims of the Moorish Science Temple, and Garveyites.[50] In Detroit he is said to have been a silk peddler. "His customers were mostly Negro and he himself posed as a Negro. He prided himself as a biblical authority and mathematician."[51]

For the three years Dodd Ford/Fard Muhammad was in Detroit, we need not rely on FBI reports alone. Eyewitness accounts were recorded by sociologist Erdmann Doane Beynon in 1937. According to these accounts, he was variously known as Mr. Wali Farrad (which more accurately reflects how the name "Fard" is usually pronounced), Professor Ford, Mr. Farrad Mohammed, and Mr. F. Mohammed Ali. He sold raincoats and silks. He encouraged African Americans to dress and eat as they did in their "home country" (that is, to avoid pork). His customers were interested in his information about their original homeland to the east, especially its people and culture. This interest often led to invitations to dinner or lunch, which in turn led Fard Muhammad to hold informal meetings in their homes. Soon he had enough followers and contributions to rent a hall for his meetings. His claims included that he came from royalty in Mecca but had abandoned his position to teach freedom, justice, and equality "in the wilderness of North America, surrounded and robbed completely by the Cave Man."[52]

The main message of Fard Muhammad, as reconstructed by Beynon, was somewhat simpler than that given by Elijah Muhammad outlined above:

The black men in North America are not Negroes, but members of the lost tribe of Shebazz, stolen by traders from the Holy City of Mecca 379 years ago. The prophet came to America to find and to bring back to life his long lost brethren, from whom the Caucasians had taken away their language, their nation and their religion. Here in America they were living other than themselves. They must learn that they are the original people, noblest of the nations of the earth. The Caucasians are the colored people, since they have lost their original color. The original people must regain their religion, which is Islam, their language, which is Arabic, and their culture, which is astronomy and higher mathematics, especially calculus. They must live according to the law of Allah, avoiding all meat of "poisonous animals," hogs, ducks, geese, 'possums and catfish. They must give up completely the use of stimulants, especially liquor. They must clean themselves up—both their bodies and their houses. If in this way they obeyed Allah, he would take them back to the Paradise from which they had been stolen—the Holy City of Mecca.[53]

Noteworthy is the absence of any claim to divinity. Fard Muhammad also issued new Islamic names to followers, seemingly following the practice of the Moorish Science Temple. Similarly, members of the Nation of Islam were not considered Americans, but citizens of Mecca.[54]

During his ministry from 1930 to 1934 five to eight thousand African Americans joined the Nation of Islam in Detroit and Chicago. Not surprisingly, all but a handful were recent migrants from the rural South.[55] This success led to more formal organizational structures, including a school (the University of Islam), security forces (the Fruit of Islam), domestic training for women (the Girl's Training and General Civilization Class), and a second in command (the Supreme Minister of Islam, Elijah Muhammad). Towards the end of his ministry, Fard Muhammad was seen less and less by his followers. Success had also led to difficulties. One of his ministers, Abdul Mohammed, who had served as the Supreme Minister prior to Elijah Muhammad, rebelled in hopes of gaining control of the movement from Fard Muhammad. Also, when the police attempted to force the children in the University of Islam to return to public schools, there was a riot. And, in 1932 a member of the Nation of Islam was alleged to have performed a human sacrifice.[56] Perhaps in response to these growing troubles, Fard Muhammad receded into a more administrative role late in 1932. He rarely attended the temple, choosing to instruct and lead his followers through his ministers.[57]

Fard Muhammad was arrested by Detroit police in May 1933. In the police report his ancestry was given as "Arabian" and his profession as "minister." Furthermore, the "official report said Dodd admitted that his teachings were 'strictly a racket' and he was 'getting all the money out of it he could.'

He was ordered out of Detroit."[58] His departure caused his gathered followers to weep. He comforted them, saying, "Don't worry. I am with you; I will be back to you in the near future to lead you out of this hell."[59] For the next year Fard Muhammad lived in Chicago, where Elijah Muhammad saw him for the last time. After that, Fard Muhammad disappeared, despite concerted efforts by the FBI to ascertain his whereabouts. In an article written in 1963, it was asserted that Ford's estranged wife, Hazel, claimed that he had returned to Los Angeles in 1934. Ford stayed for two weeks, visited his son, and then left by ship for New Zealand to visit relatives.[60] Elijah Muhammad, on the other hand, stated in the early 1950s that he received his last letter from Fard Muhammad in March 1934 from Mexico.[61]

While the Nation of Islam may dispute the police and FBI records, these records claim that the fingerprints from the Los Angeles police, San Quentin, and the Michigan state police are all identical. They all also listed Fard Muhammad as Caucasian or White.[62] Responding to the 1963 article, Elijah Muhammad offered one hundred thousand dollars to anyone who could prove that Wallace Dodd Ford was, in fact, Wali Fard Muhammad. For him, Dodd Ford was a "phony" and the accusations were part of the devils' tricks.[63]

Resurrecting the Lost-Found Nation of Islam

It is difficult to distinguish between the teaching of Fard Muhammad and those of Elijah Muhammad. First, the former's teachings survive almost exclusively within the writings of the latter. Fard Muhammad's writings are limited to three pamphlets. "Teaching for the Lost Found Nation of Islam in a Mathematical Way" is a seven-page pamphlet that, consists of a set of thirty-four mostly mathematical problems presented as having a deeper symbolic meaning. The other two pamphlets are known as "Lesson 1" and "Lesson 2," and they consist of a series of fourteen and forty questions and answers, respectively.[64] Most of the major teachings of Elijah Muhammad appear in these two documents, at least in nascent form. This is hardly surprising, however; the questions come from Fard Muhammad as he examined his new minister; the answers came from that new minister: Elijah Muhammad.[65] The origin of these lessons is explicitly ascribed to Fard Muhammad and Elijah Muhammad: "This lesson #2 was given by our Prophet, W. D. Fard, which contains 40 questions answered by Elijah Mohammed, one for the lost found in the Wilderness of North America, February 20th, 1934."[66]

Second, Elijah Muhammad claimed that almost all of his teachings came directly from Fard Muhammad, even decades later. The teachings of Fard Muhammad as summarized by Elijah Muhammad included knowledge of "ourselves, of Himself (God) and the devil, the Measurement of the Earth, other Planets and the Civilizations of some of the Planets other than Earth . . . the history of the Moon, and the history of the two nations that dominate the earth, black and white."[67]

Some of the teachings focused on recognizable Islamic practices. Fard Muhammad told his listeners that "[y]our own people there in the East do not eat pork because it is unclean meat. They do not gamble, they do not drink, they are people of the highest civilization."[68] The more prominent teachings, those about the origin of the white race, who made them, how they enslaved Blacks, and their coming judgment (particularly the doom of America), were new to Islam.

According to Elijah Muhammad's version of Fard Muhammad's teaching, the black race is as old as the planet. Just over sixty-six hundred years ago, however, the evil genius Yakub was born. Though he was a member of the Black Nation himself, Yakub began converting people by promising luxuries. He had discovered the secrets of selective breeding and needed people for his eugenics program. His success eventually caused enough concern in Mecca that Yakub and his 59,999 followers parted company with the remainder of the Black Nation. On an island in the Aegean Sea, the embittered Yakub set up a 600-year program to breed an increasingly whiter and more evil people. After the six hundred years the newly created Whites returned to Mecca and soon managed to turn the Black Nation against itself. As a result, the Whites were driven at gunpoint to Europe. Moses was sent by Allah two thousand years later to try to civilize these hairy, naked, cave-dwelling, tree-climbing savages. Jesus and Muhammad also tried to convert these white devils. They failed, for it had been prophesied that the white race would rule the world for six thousand years and enslave black people in the Americas until the coming of Fard Muhammad to mentally resurrect the Lost-Found Nation of Islam.[69]

The preceding race myth is the backdrop for the history of African Americans within the worldview of the Nation of Islam. Elijah Muhammad marked the 400-year period from 1555 to 1955 as particularly significant. He stated that Allah taught that the ancestors of African Americans were deceived and brought to America in 1555 by a slave trader named John Hawkins in a slave ship, tellingly called "Jesus."[70] Elijah Muhammad wrote,

In 300 years of slavery, we were lashed, beaten and killed; given no education; and reared and cared for like the slave-master's stock (horses, cows and other domestic animals). Our children were separated to different plantation owners. For the last approximately 100 years of so-called freedom, the so-called Negroes have been subjected to the worst inhuman treatment for any people who have ever lived on earth. They (the devils) have lynched and burned the so-called Negroes during the past century as sport for their wives and children to enjoy![71]

However, Fard Muhammad, Allah himself, came to "cut loose every link of the slave chain that holds us in bondage to our slave-masters by giving us a true knowledge of self, God and the devil and wipe away the 400 years of tears, weeping, mourning and groaning under the yoke of bondage to the merciless murderers."[72]

For the "white devils" the future was rather more bleak. Fard Muhammad promised to burn all of them—not one would survive.[73] The United States would burn for 390 years and it would take 610 years until the land was habitable again (for a total of one thousand years). Its destruction would come from a bomb dropped from a "Mother Plane" that would take some twenty-two years to build. Elijah Muhammad claimed that this Mother Plane was the size of a small planet and could carry fifteen hundred bombers whose bombs could each churn up mountains from the earth. Moreover, Fard Muhammad taught that those of his followers who killed four devils "at the proper time" would be given free transportation to Mecca. This last teaching, not surprisingly, piqued the interest of the police.[74]

The mention of Mecca, Moses, Jesus, and Muhammad[75] may seem to be mere superficial references to traditional Islam. Yet it is important that Islam, if not its traditional Arabian mythology, still plays a central role in this race myth. It is the natural religion of the "black man," it is the religion of the prophets, and it is as old as Allah and the universe.[76] More importantly, it stands in opposition to Christianity, which "is one of the most perfect black-slave-making religions on our planet. It has completely killed the so-called Negroes mentally."[77] By that, Elijah Muhammad meant that it teaches Blacks to worship a false white, blonde, blue-eyed god. In effect, it teaches them to worship Whites. It also tells them to turn the other cheek when they are abused and to wait until the next life for justice. Just as the devil roamed on this earth, so heaven and hell were in the here and now—not in the hereafter. For him, Christianity was created by the white devils in their wickedness, while Islam comes from Allah. The two religions have battled in the past: Christianity was "bottled up" in Europe for nearly a thousand years by the coming of Muhammad and the subsequent spread of Islam, though from 1555 to 1955 Whites were free to roam the world and deceive its inhabitants.[78] And they will battle again: with Allah's return, the war of Armageddon will be a religious war between Islam and Christianity.

Although it is not clear whether all of the details of these racial and eschatological myths can be traced to Fard Muhammad, it seems fairly certain that most of the main points can. Elijah Muhammad, it would turn out, was adept at elaborating these myths and at seeing in biblical and quranic passages and in contemporary events evidence to support this framework that had been supplied by Fard Muhammad.

2

The Life of Elijah Muhammad

Elijah Muhammad lived through some of the most racially turbulent times in American history. He was born in 1897—a time of Jim Crow segregation and lynchings. As a young man, he experienced the worst of southern racism and eyewitnessed two separate lynchings. Later, he would be part of the Great Migration of over a million African Americans to the northern United States to escape the racism and poverty of the rural South. He discovered, along with the other migrants, that the North was also rife with racism. And, with the onset of the Great Depression, the North experienced poverty as well, which hit African Americans disproportionately hard. However, a new religion, Islam, would transform him and his understanding of the world. After several years of struggle with obscurity and imprisonment, his movement, the Nation of Islam, would achieve phenomenal success and transform the lives of thousands of African Americans, including Malcolm X. Yet, despite devoting himself to Islam and the "uplifting" of African Americans, he would find himself reviled by other Muslims and even some leaders of the Civil Rights movement. Only after his death in 1975 was his remarkable influence on both American Islam and the African American struggle for equality truly recognized.

The sources for reconstructing the life of Elijah Muhammad must be used with caution. Given that Elijah Muhammad is a religious figure who arose so recently, the need for caution may seem surprising. For the most part, however, our early biographical information comes from only two main sources. The first is the Nation of Islam and consists mostly of materials penned or dictated by Elijah Muhammad himself. These materials, not surprisingly, are informed by what the man had become, not necessarily by what he had been. The second source is the extensive FBI files on Elijah Muhammad. These, however, were produced by an organization that actively sought to discredit him. Neither set of sources, therefore, provides an unbiased account: the former set is often hagiographic, while the latter is often hostile.

Elijah Poole: From Georgia to Michigan

Elijah Poole was born in 1897 in Sandersville, Georgia.[1] His father, William Poole, was a sharecropper and a Baptist preacher. Some sources claim that he was known as Wali Poole, suggesting some vestige of Islam.[2] For his mother, Marie, who worked as a domestic servant, Elijah was the sixth of thirteen children.[3] But Elijah Poole was special in the eyes of his mother: she spoke of a vision that she had as a child in which she would give birth to a great man. And, even as a youngster, he was thought by her to display a pronounced race consciousness and leadership abilities.[4] In the eyes of his father, however, his son could be frustrating: at an early age Elijah Poole showed a disposition to Bible study, preaching, and, to his father's annoyance, theological questioning and debate. However, he would not follow his father's footsteps, despite feeling an early call to preach; he could not bring himself to preach Christianity.

In 1900 the family moved to Cordele, Georgia. In the fourth grade Elijah Poole dropped out of school to help support his family. He and his sister chopped firewood on their farm and went to town to sell it. On one such trip, he witnessed the lynching of an African American accused of insulting a white woman. At eighteen he worked for a white farmer who paid him only eight dollars a month to work from dawn till dusk. This farmer regularly whipped the wives of his African American workers at gunpoint. Later, Elijah Poole worked as a manual laborer in Georgia and served as a foreman. At the age of twenty-three, he saw his second lynching, after which the body was dragged behind a truck.[5] In 1923, at the age of twenty-five, after a white employer insulted him, he moved with his wife, Clara, and their two children to Detroit in search of a better life. Thus, he took part in the early phase of the Great Migration of African Americans from the South to the North between 1914 and 1950. Unskilled labor such as his was needed in Detroit's factories, at least until the Great Depression. In 1929, Elijah Muhammad lost his job and was forced to go on relief. His wife, Clara, had to work to help support the family when her husband could not find work. The distress of long-term unemployment led him to drink: "one day, his wife had to come get him off the railroad tracks where he had fallen in a drunken state."[6]

Elijah Karriem: Three and a Half Years with Wali Fard Muhammad

One of the eight thousand African Americans in Detroit who were swept into Fard Muhammad's movement between 1930 and 1933 was Elijah Poole. He first heard of Fard Muhammad from his father, who knew Abdul Mohammed, formerly associated with the Moorish Science Temple of America and once named Brown El but by then a follower of Fard Muhammad. Elijah Poole and his brother visited Abdul Mohammed several times, learning Fard Muhammad's teachings second-hand. After attending several meetings in 1931, Elijah Poole finally managed to meet Fard Muhammad. According to the later Elijah Muhammad, when they met for the first time after Fard Muhammad had finished preaching, he said to Fard Muhammad, "I know who you are, you're God himself." Fard Muhammad whispered back, "That's right, but don't tell it now. It is not yet time for me to be known."[7] There are several versions of this first encounter, each with a different emphasis:

> When I first heard of Islam it was in Detroit Michigan, back in the early fall of 1931, and I heard that there was a man teaching Islam by the name of Mr. Wallace Fard. At that time He used the initials W.D. Fard, that was in Detroit Michigan. When I heard what was said, I wanted to meet Him and I finally did. When I met Him, I looked at Him and it just came to me, that this is the Son of Man that the Bible prophesied would come in the last days of the world, and I couldn't get that out of me. I shook hands with Him and I said to Him, "You are the One that the Bible prophesied would come at the end of the world under the name Son of Man and under the name The Second Coming of Jesus."
>
> And so, He looked at me a little stern, and then He smiled, put His head down beside my head then whispered in my ear and said these words, "Yes I am the One, but who knows that but yourself," and to "be quiet."[8]

Initially, Elijah Poole referred to Fard Muhammad as "Master" or "Prophet," the latter title being one that he claims to have been the first to use.[9]

Elijah Poole's conversion was quite quick and dramatic. Perhaps his race consciousness and past experiences with Whites both in the South and in the North prepared him for the message of Fard Muhammad: Allah is God; white people are the devil; "so-called Negroes" are Asiatics and the original people; and freedom, justice, and equality would come only when the "so-called Negroes" return to their original religion (Islam), their language (Arabic), and the law of Allah (which includes the avoidance of pork and liquor). Christianity, the religion of Whites, is innately inimical to Islam, and the Battle of Armageddon will be a war between Islam and Christianity in which the former will vanquish the latter.

Elijah Poole did not see Fard Muhammad for another month, but was informed via his wife that he had been given permission to preach. However, he was cautioned by Fard Muhammad not to speak too much of the "Son of Man": "You can do that after I am gone; don't talk to [sic] much about Me." He was to give babies "milk"; they were not ready for "meat."[10] Elijah Poole described himself as studying the Bible intensely, looking for references to Fard Muhammad. He prayed fervently to Allah for the truth while alone in his closet. Consequently, he became a "hundred percent convert." Having come to this certainty, he finally answered his earlier call to preach; he began telling African Americans how to reform themselves, and about future events. Soon he was training to become one of Fard Muhammad's several ministers and was renamed Elijah Karriem.

Elijah Karriem and Fard Muhammad had a special bond and were constantly together for almost two years, with teaching sessions about Islam often going through the night.[11] Elijah Karriem was given special teachings. For instance, Elijah Muhammad later recounted.

> I asked him, "Who are you, and what is your real name?" He said, "I am the one that the world has been expecting for the past 2,000 years." I said to Him again, "What is your name?" he said, "My name is Mahdi; I am God, I came to guide you into the right path that you may be successful and see the hereafter." He described the destruction of the world with bombs, poison gas, and finally with fire that would consume and destroy everything of the present world.[12]

Elijah Muhammad recorded several other unique interactions with Fard Muhammad. His teacher also gave him several Qur'ans, an Arabic one and two English ones, the promise of a future book, and a list of 104 books to read.[13] And, Elijah Muhammad was called to visit Fard Muhammad in jail each time he was arrested to witness his suffering.

The most pivotal event during this three and half years was Fard Muhammad's designation of Elijah Karriem as his "successor." According to later Nation of Islam teaching,

Prior to His leaving in 1934, W. D. Fard had a process of allowing his student ministers to select their own ministers from among themselves. They would always select the most articulate and charismatic person. For whatever reason, they never chose Elijah Karriem. One reason may have been his lack of command of the English language.

After the students made their choices for awhile, W. D. Fard said, "I've let you select yours for awhile, Now I'll select Mine," He said. [sic] "Hey you over there Karriem!"

"Who me," said a humble, soft-spoken Elijah Karriem? [sic]

"Yes, you Elijah Karriem. Come up here with Me," He said. Elijah walked to the front of the class to stand beside W. D. Fard. "From now on this is My Minister," Mr. Fard said to everyone with His right arm around Elijah's shoulder.

He chose Elijah Karriem as Supreme Minister of the Nation of Islam.[14]

Despite having this title conferred upon him by Fard in August 1934, Elijah Muhammad still used the less superlative title of "Minister of Islam in North America" in his own publication, *The Final Call to Islam*, published slightly after Fard Muhammad's departure. However, this same publication confirms that towards the end of their time together Elijah Karriem had been renamed again. He and his whole family were to share Fard Muhammad's own last name.[15] If this anecdote is historical, it stands to reason that the troubles Elijah Muhammad would soon experience were born then, for other ministers would not have been pleased that this less educated and less articulate man was now their superior.

It would be hard to overstate the importance these three and a half years had for Elijah Muhammad and his sense of mission. He stated,

I am not ashamed to say how little learning I have had. . . . My going to school no further than the fourth grade proves that I can know nothing except the truth I have been taught by Allah. Allah taught me mathematics. He found me with a sluggish tongue and taught me how to pronounce words.[16]

Elijah Muhammad may have been understating his own role in developing the teachings of Fard Muhammad. Elsewhere Elijah Muhammad explained,

He did not teach us that he was a prophet. We used to call him prophet. I made the followers calling [sic] him prophet because I do not know exactly what great name to give him. No one called him prophet before me. First I thought that we should call him Master; later I thought that we should call him prophet, and later I told them that he neither of either one; [sic] I said that we should call him the "Almighty God" himself in person because, according to what he has taught us, that must be the work of God and not of a human being.

Thus, both the initial claim of prophethood and later claim of divinity for Fard Muhammad originated with Elijah Muhammad. Only after Elijah Muhammad made these claims on his behalf did Fard Muhammad eventually come to embrace them.[17] However, even the assumption that they collaborated may be overstating Fard Muhammad's role in his elevation to divinity. Elijah Muhammad's August 18, 1934, edition of *The Final Call to Islam* (published shortly after Fard Muhammad's disappearance) still employed only the less lofty expressions "Prophet W. D. Fard" and "Prophet Fard Mohammed." It also made the argument that Fard Muhammad was the prophet foretold by Moses in Deuteronomy 18.[18] Fard Muhammad's elevation to Allah in Person may well have occurred some time after his departure from the scene. Thus, how much of Fard Muhammad's purported teachings are his own creation and how much are the creation of Elijah Muhammad's obviously genuine devotion is very difficult to judge.

Muhammad Rassoull, Gulam Bogans, etc.: Persecution and Prison

The struggle for control of Fard Muhammad's movement in the vacuum created by his final departure in June of 1934 seems to belie Elijah Muhammad's claim that he had been explicitly designated by the founder to be his successor. It is certainly possible that the disregard with which some ministers held Elijah Muhammad continued despite his recent elevation to Supreme Minister. His new teaching that Fard Muhammad was not merely a prophet but the Son of Man and God himself clearly triggered opposition also—which again suggests that the elevation came more (or exclusively) from Elijah Muhammad. Given the numerous and varied versions of the conversation(s) in which Elijah Muhammad recognized the divinity of Fard Muhammad, it seems as though they are apocryphal. Even if they are not, Elijah Muhammad's motivation for elevating Fard Muhammad is obvious. Rarely does a prophet succeed another prophet. With Fard Muhammad elevated to godhood, the position of prophet to this new god was open. As Clegg points out, "the legitimacy of his leadership would be dependent upon convincing others that he alone had been favored by God in person and was uniquely privy to his will."[19]

Soon the police were harassing him too under the pretense that children in the University of Islam were being kept out of school. So, when a contract was placed on his life by a rival, Elijah Muhammad moved to the relative safety of Chicago. Then Theodore Rozier, whom he had left in charge of Detroit Temple No. 1, formed his own independent group. In Chicago, meanwhile, police harassment and renewed rivalry from "hypocrites" (led by his Supreme Captain and own younger brother, Kalot Muhammad, and by his assistant minister, Augustus Muhammad) forced Elijah Muhammad to leave his wife and family behind and flee once more. Elijah Muhammad described this period in these terms:

> In the fall of 1934 most of the followers turned out to be hypocrites and they began to teach against the movement, and to join the enemies of the movement. The situation got so bad that in 1935 it was impossible to go among them because it seemed to me that over 75 per cent of them were hypocrites. And therefore I had to leave them to save my own life. Hypocrisy was arising even within my house; my younger brother, who was living in my house with another assistant minister, aligned against me because he wanted the teachings for himself. They joined my enemy here and in Detroit and they began to seek my life. So Allah warned me to leave again and showed me in a vision nine people; among them was my brother. Therefore I left to Madison, where they followed me; and Allah warned me again to leave Madison.[20]

Clearly, Elijah Muhammad felt persecuted, but this feeling only increased his faith in his sense of mission and guidance from Fard Muhammad. Over three decades later Elijah Muhammad still saw these tribulations as a proof and vindication of his unique, divinely ordained mission. He wrote, "my brother, Karlot's [sic] fall served as a warning to the wistful and proud leaders who want to take upon themselves the honor of the Messenger of Allah, without being chosen by Allah."[21] Whether his brother's rebellion was based on mere ambition or doctrinal differences (presumably over the divine status of Fard Muhammad or lack thereof) is not known. In any event, most of the former membership of Fard Muhammad's Nation of Islam did not share Elijah Muhammad's perspective. In Chicago only thirteen gave their allegiance to him and in Detroit, only 180.[22]

After a brief stay in Milwaukee, the location of Temple No. 3, Elijah Muhammad moved to Washington, D.C. There he lived under the name Mr. Evans and read his list of 104 books in the Library of Congress. Using various aliases, he also traveled to cities on the east coast with large African American populations to proselytize. In 1939 he opened Temple No. 4 in Washington and led it personally, using the name Muhammad Rassoull. His success there brought him to the notice of the FBI and other law enforcement agencies. In 1941, his objection to black participation in a "white war" only increased the attention they gave him. Elijah Muhammad, with his fourth grade education and still one year shy of the 45-year-old maximum, was still eligible for the draft. After months of surveillance, Elijah Muhammad, then living under the alias of Gulam Bogans, was arrested in May 1942 for failing to register for selective service. The FBI interrogated him and also arrested the ministers of other temples. After a few months, the bond money was raised and, fearing that he would never get to trial, he secretly made his way to Chicago. In September the FBI struck the Nation of Islam again, arresting Elijah Muhammad, his eldest son, and over thirty others. Most of them were convicted of draft dodging. Elijah Muhammad and a few subordinates were charged with, and convicted of, sedition and avoiding the draft. From 1943 to 1946, Elijah Muhammad found himself in prison—with his wife, Clara, serving as his connection to the remnant of his community. Denied a Qur'an by prison officials, Elijah Muhammad received pages copied by hand by Clara.

Almost two decades after Fard Muhammad disappeared, Elijah Muhammad recounted these early years:

> I have not stopped one day for the past twenty-one years. I have been standing, preaching to you through out those past twenty-one years, while I was free, and while I was in bondage. I spent three and one-half years in the federal penitentiary, and also over a year in the city jail for teaching this truth. I was also deprived of a father's love for his family for seven long years while I was running from hypocrites and other enemies of this world and revelation of God.[23]

Thus, Elijah Muhammad came to see this period as a time of persecution. These tribulations merely strengthened his sense of mission and destiny. And, when he was released from prison in 1946, the other would-be successors to Fard Muhammad were long gone, and he could return to his family and remaining followers in Chicago.

Nevertheless, there was little left of the Nation of Islam when he finally emerged as the sole leader of Fard Muhammad's movement. Although Elijah Muhammad had managed to maintain the temples in Chicago and Detroit, and to add one in Milwaukee and another in Washington, D.C., the Nation of Islam was collapsing. Whereas Fard Muhammad had had perhaps eight thousand followers in Detroit alone, in 1945 Elijah Muhammad had fewer than four thousand in all four temples combined.[24]

The time spent in persecution and prison was not wasted, however. Not only did it strengthen his lifelong sense of mission and his followers' faith in his authenticity, but this time in jail also marked an important turning point. Two of his greatest innovations were born in prison. First, Elijah Muhammad conceived of his economic program there, perhaps as a result of seeing the agricultural practices of the prison itself. Even before his release he had his followers pool their resources to purchase a farm. Soon there would be a small restaurant, grocery store, and bakery. From these humble beginnings, Elijah Muhammad began one of his greatest achievements in the forty years he led the Nation of Islam: the establishment of an independent African American economy—the most tangible expression of his "do for self" precept. Second, before being released from prison in 1946, Elijah Muhammad realized that no religious or political organizations were trying to help or rehabilitate this segment of the black lower class: criminals, pimps, prostitutes, and drug addicts. His decision to focus his efforts on this group was momentous. Through Elijah Muhammad's efforts the lives of many African American criminals, who had perhaps experienced the worst of white racism and who had the least hope, were transformed into the most loyal and ardent followers. One of those recidivists would become Elijah Muhammad's greatest missionary and spokesman, Malcolm X.

The Honorable Elijah Muhammad: The Rise and Fall of Malcolm X

Malcolm X was born Malcolm Little in 1925 in Omaha, Nebraska. His youth made it inevitable that race consciousness would be a major focus in his life. His father was a reverend and active member in Garvey's Universal Negro Improvement Association (UNIA); even at a young age he took his son to meetings. His father was harassed by white supremacists in Omaha and later also in Lansing, Michigan, where he had moved his family. The Little's house was burned down, and when Malcolm Little was six years old, his father was murdered, probably by white supremacists.

The young Malcolm Little experienced the frustration of a racist school system, the extreme poverty of a family with eight children and no father during the Great Depression, and the separation of his family when his mother became mentally ill.

At the age of fifteen he moved to Boston, then later New York, where he gradually became involved in various illegal activities that included gambling, selling and doing drugs, burglary, pimping, and carrying weapons. However, in 1946 he fled back to Boston after having gotten on the wrong side of another criminal. There he was quite a successful burglar for a while. When he was eventually caught, he received a ten-year prison sentence. Malcolm X later attributed the harshness of the sentence for a first conviction to his sexual involvement with a white woman.

Malcolm Little only served part of his ten-year sentence, but by the time he was released in 1952, he was transformed. Early in his sentence, he earned the nickname "Satan" for his foul language, especially with respect to God and the Bible. Meanwhile, most of his family converted to the Nation of Islam and began to try to convert their brother. As he began to learn more about, and to correspond with, Elijah Muhammad, he continued a self-education program he had begun some years earlier, but now much more intensively. His readings in history seemed to confirm everything Elijah Muhammad had taught him about the evils of the "white man." Soon he was proselytizing in prison and decided to devote the rest of his life "to telling the white man about himself—or die."[25]

In the summer of 1952, Malcolm Little was paroled. He came to Detroit, met Elijah Muhammad, and quickly began vigorously recruiting new Muslims in Detroit. Within a year, he became Temple No. 1's assistant minister. And, for several months Elijah Muhammad personally mentored him. He soon recognized the value of his new protégé. Malcolm X was assigned to be the minister for Boston's Temple No. 11, then Philadelphia's Temple No. 12, and finally New York City's prestigious Temple No. 7. From 1955 to 1959, Elijah Muhammad sent Malcolm X to various cities to hold rallies and help establish new temples. Malcolm X helped found numerous new temples and increase membership dramatically. That is not to suggest that Malcolm X was single-handedly responsible for all of these temples and converts. However, the growth of the Nation of Islam coincided with his ministry: in 1945 there were but four temples, a decade later there were fifteen, and by 1960 there were fifty.[26]

The year 1959 would be a dramatic one for Malcolm X, Elijah Muhammad, and the Nation of Islam. In that year the white American public became aware of their existence. In New York City an innocent Black Muslim bystander to a scuffle was hit by a white police officer with a night stick. Instead of being taken to the hospital, he was taken to jail. In less than half an hour Malcolm X had fifty men of the Fruit of Islam standing in ranks outside the precinct. Not only was he successful in getting the man medical treatment, but Malcolm X and the "Muslims" made the news.[27]

Media attention increased with a five-part television documentary entitled *The Hate That Hate Produced* and a book about the Nation of Islam, *Black Muslims in America*, by C. Eric Lincoln. Furthermore, *Time, U.S. News & World Report, Newsweek, Life,* and *Reader's Digest* all covered the Nation of Islam. Most of this attention was negative and, like the documentary, fixated on the word "hate."[28] To counteract this propaganda Malcolm X began the Nation of Islam's own newspaper, *Muhammad Speaks*, in 1959. But the attacks came from all sides. Harsh African American criticism came from officials of the National Association for the Advancement of Colored People (NAACP), Dr. Martin Luther King Jr., and Thurgood Marshall, who called the Nation of Islam a hate group and referred to them as thugs.[29] Sunni Muslims active with African Americans but not in the Nation of Islam, particularly Talib Ahmad Dawud and Jamil Diab,[30] also denounced the Nation of Islam as unislamic.

The dramatic growth and financial success of the Nation of Islam allowed Elijah Muhammad to visit Muslim countries at the end of 1959. He visited Turkey, Egypt, Sudan, and Ethiopia, leaving Malcolm X in charge of the Nation of Islam in his absence. Then he traveled to Saudi Arabia for the *'umra* (that is, the lesser pilgrimage). He had arrived at the wrong time to perform the greater pilgrimage, the *hajj*. Afterwards, at the beginning of the new year, he left for Pakistan. This intimate contact with "orthodox" Muslims and their culture changed Elijah Muhammad's understanding of Islam and his view of the place of his Muslims within the larger Muslim community.[31]

Invigorated by his travels and the relative silence of his opponents, Elijah Muhammad resumed his speaking tours, in which he emphasized segregation. Malcolm X and others from the Nation of Islam even had a secret meeting with the Ku Klux Klan in Atlanta to discuss their mutual opposition to integration as espoused by the Civil Rights movement. The leader of the American Nazi Party and several of his men in Nazi garb even attended a Nation of Islam rally at which Malcolm X spoke. While they shared the agenda of separation of the races, it is likely that

Elijah Muhammad used the presence of these white supremacists to his own ends. A few years earlier in 1957, for example, J. B. Stoner, archleader and imperial wizard of the Christian Knights of the Ku Klux Klan, and Elijah Muhammad traded hostile and public letters.[32] Stoner sent another letter to Elijah Muhammad in August of 1959, which was published in *The Amsterdam News*. In his rambling two-page letter, he wrote, "I have you black Muslims on the run and I will soon put you out of business. That being the case, why don't you dissolve your Muslim nigger organization of Islam and tell your darkies to go home and be good niggers and stay in their place?"[33] The more hostile Stoner became, the more he played into the hands of Elijah Muhammad. These letters could only enhance Elijah Muhammad's stature among African Americans, who would see such attention as a sign that the Nation of Islam challenged, perhaps even worried, the KKK.[34] And yet, the presence of white supremacists at the Nation of Islam's events highlights that Elijah Muhammad was in some ways not offering a new and radical solution to the race problems of the United States but instead a recapitulation of an older solution, albeit one that radically reversed the roles of Blacks and Whites.[35]

Later, in 1961, Elijah Muhammad became ill and moved to Phoenix to convalesce. He gave Malcolm X autonomy over speaking engagements on the college circuit, but accompanied this license with a prophetic warning: "Brother Malcolm, I want you to become well known. . . . Because if you are well known, it will make me better known. But, Brother Malcolm, there is something you need to know. You will grow hated when you become well known. Because usually people get jealous of public figures."[36] This prophesied jealousy did not take long to manifest itself. Ironically, the man who made the prophecy was one of the first to succumb to it. Although Malcolm X worshiped Elijah Muhammad, the latter's very limited education made him jealous of his protégé's ability to speak at various prestigious colleges and universities. Initially, however, it was other high-ranking members of the Nation of Islam who, perturbed by Malcolm X's fame, began acting against him. By 1962 less and less about Malcolm X appeared in *Muhammad Speaks* (then edited by Elijah Muhammad's son Herbert Muhammad), and the Chicago headquarters began discouraging Malcolm X from holding such large rallies. Also, the two main figures in the Nation of Islam had different visions for the movement: Malcolm X wanted to be more politically active (as in confronting police brutality), whereas Elijah Muhammad preferred a far more conservative, religious separatism.[37] The language of the Nation of Islam was militant, but Elijah

Muhammad made sure his followers obeyed the law and avoided violent responses—regardless of provocation.

Despite these growing tensions, in late 1963 Malcolm X was declared the Nation of Islam's First National Minister by Elijah Muhammad. But then, at this pinnacle of his career, disaster struck. Malcolm X learned that Elijah Muhammad faced two paternity suits from former secretaries—adultery meant expulsion from the Nation of Islam. According to Malcolm X, he confronted Elijah Muhammad, the latter confessed, and they concurred that it was a "fulfillment of prophecy" (citing similar indiscretions by the biblical prophets David, Noah, and Lot). When Malcolm X began preparing other ministers to deal with this situation, however, he was charged instead with spreading the "rumor." Other high-ranking members of the Nation of Islam who were jealous of Malcolm X's rapid rise and influence in the organization saw their opportunity to drive a wedge between him and Elijah Muhammad. Later that year, President Kennedy was assassinated. Elijah Muhammad ordered his followers to make no comment. When Malcolm X did comment, saying that it was an example of "the chickens coming home to roost," he was summoned to Chicago, where Elijah Muhammad ordered him to remain silent for ninety days as punishment. Elijah Muhammad then made a conciliatory gesture to a mourning country by writing some relatively kind words about the president, calling his death a "tragedy" and noting how every president (that is, Abraham Lincoln and John F. Kennedy) who makes positive statements about African Americans "pays for it with his life."[38] He also strongly and publicly distanced himself from Malcolm X's comment:

> [T]he following statement from Mr. Muhammad expresses the views of Muslims on the death of President Kennedy and in correction of a statement made . . . by Minister Malcolm Shabbaz. "When Minister Malcolm addressed the public and mentioned the President's death, he did not speak for Muslims. He was speaking for himself and not Muslims in general. He has been suspended from public speaking for the time being. The Nation still mourns the loss of *our* President."[39]

Malcolm X willingly submitted to his punishment, but in an effort to put him in his place, the report of the punishment was disseminated quickly throughout the Nation of Islam. In January 1964, Elijah Muhammad replaced Malcolm X as the minister of Temple No. 7 in New York City. His intentions seem to have been to gradually remove Malcolm X from the organization. Malcolm X endured these public humiliations and private trials. The final straw, however, came when Malcolm X learned that his death had been ordered—but his remaining friends within the Nation of Islam made sure that it was not acted upon. He left the Nation of Islam in March 1964.[40]

Malcolm X then started his own organization, Muslim Mosque, Inc., based upon orthodox Sunni Islamic principles, and an associated political body, the Organization of Afro-American Unity. His turn to Sunni Islam was in large part due to his experiences during a *hajj* in April 1964. He came to believe that Islam could transcend even the racial divisions of Whites and Blacks in the United States, thus abandoning Elijah Muhammad's racial teachings. After visiting Lebanon, Nigeria, Ghana, Liberia, Seneca, Morocco, and Algeria, Malcolm X gained a more global perspective and began to focus on human rights (as opposed to just civil rights). As a result of these changes, he also accused Elijah Muhammad of being a "religious faker"[41] and immoral, which led to a series of death threats against Malcolm X. Malcolm X was assassinated on February 21, 1965, in front of a large audience by several gunmen, some of whom were alleged to be members of the Nation of Islam.[42]

It has been suggested that, although Elijah Muhammad never called for Malcolm X's death, he contributed to the environment that made it likely. However, Elijah Muhammad specifically wrote, about a month before the assassination, "Allah, the Holy Qur-an says, will not permit anyone to kill them, because death would take them out of their chastisement and grief."[43] Nevertheless, after Malcolm X's assassination, Malcolm X's former Temple No. 7 was set ablaze in retaliation, and death threats were made against Elijah Muhammad.[44]

Even if Elijah Muhammad had no part in the assassination, these events affected him and his movement profoundly. For the first time, absolute obedience to the Messenger became a major theme in his columns, along with a renewed and prolonged attack on hypocrites.[45] Malcolm X and his followers became the "chief hypocrites."[46] He launched a propaganda campaign that portrayed Malcolm X as a power- and attention-hungry traitor.[47] However, Elijah Muhammad mostly allowed others to heap vitriol on Malcolm X. For example, John Shabbaz's letter to Malcolm X in *Muhammad Speaks* called him "the number one hypocrite of all time," claimed that to call him an Uncle Tom is "an insult to all other Uncle Toms on earth," and described him as "a dog returning to his own vomit."[48] The harshest and most sustained attack on Malcolm X came from

Louis X (later, Farrakhan), who systematically critiqued all of Malcolm X's activities and went so far as to say, "Such a man as Malcolm is worthy of death, and would have met with death had it not been for [Elijah] Muhammad's confidence in Allah for victory over the enemies."[49] Elijah Muhammad's own criticism of the "chief hypocrite" included statements such as this one: "This chief hypocrite is not with Allah; if he were with Allah, he would be with me." Elijah Muhammad seemed genuinely hurt by what he saw as Malcolm X's betrayal: "If he is the last of the 22 million, I shall remind him of his evil and wicked acts done to me in return for the good that I did for him. He could not have risen against me if I had not given him so much knowledge of Allah and His religion."[50]

A year after Malcolm X's death, *Muhammad Speaks* went silent on the issue of Malcolm X. Writing in the pages usually reserved for Elijah Muhammad in *Muhammad Speaks*, John Ali was provoked to attack Malcolm X in 1969 when a school in Chicago was named after him. He said that Malcolm X was a mere student of Elijah Muhammad, and not a particularly good one given that he later abandoned those teachings and opted for the "continuing rule of the white man." Malcolm X is lumped in with Jesus, Booker T. Washington, and Martin Luther King Jr. as dead figures whom Whites elevated and glorified in an effort to divide and mislead Blacks.[51] In the late 1960s, the fall of Malcolm X (like the earlier one of his own brother Kalot Muhammad) had become for Elijah Muhammad simply an example of what happens to hypocrites "who wish to scandalize and make mockery of Allah, His messages, and His Messenger."[52] By 1972 Elijah Muhammad seemed to resent Malcolm X's continued fame. In an interview he was asked to make an assessment of Malcolm X's life. Elijah Muhammad refused to answer:

> No, I would not lose any time with a man that has been talked and talked about for years. If the people do not have a knowledge of him after these many years, I am not going to waste my time with going into Malcolm's history. Malcolm, I do not have any time to waste with him, as I think everyone knows Malcolm or did know Malcolm and they know Malcolm's death. He was teaching, according to what I heard, and the people that were there should give a better report than me.[53]

Malcolm X was not Elijah Muhammad's only source of trouble. Also in the summer of 1964, his sons Wallace and Akbar Muhammad broke with the Nation of Islam. Wallace Muhammad had had doubts for a long time and had moved to Sunni Islam while imprisoned for draft dodging a few years earlier. His decision to publicly disagree with his father's teachings and to object to the decadence he saw in the officials of the Nation of Islam was difficult, given that he had just witnessed first-hand the harassment of Malcolm X. After joining the "hypocrites," Wallace Muhammad was similarly excommunicated, harassed, and financially cut off. In response, Wallace Muhammad then publicly revealed the Nation of Islam's darkest secrets: adultery, alcohol consumption, and corruption. Akbar Muhammad, studying at al-Azhar in Cairo—Sunni Islam's most prestigious religious university—also abandoned his father, though in a much less dramatic fashion. He too was labeled a hypocrite, though formally and publicly in the Nation of Islam's newspaper:

> On Sunday, November 26, 1964, at Muhammad's Temple No. 7 in New York City, a speech was made by Akbar Muhammad containing statements and views which were not in keeping with the teachings and principles of the Honorable Elijah Muhammad, the Messenger of Allah. It has therefore been decreed by the Messenger that Akbar Muhammad is no longer to be regarded as a follower of his father in what Allah has revealed to his father in the person of Master W. F. Muhammad. Akbar is now classified as a hypocrite by his father and by all those who follow him.
>
> The Honorable Elijah Muhammad, in the tradition of all great spiritual leaders of modern and ancient times, will forever defend the truths entrusted to him by Almighty God, Allah, and neither kith nor kin nor defectors of Any Kind will be allowed to alter the obligation or the divine mission the Messenger is destined to accomplish for his people.[54]

The stress of this turmoil forced Elijah Muhammad to take ninety days off and hand power over to his inner circle. Perhaps the only good news was his son Wallace Muhammad's return to the Nation of Islam in 1965. With the death of Malcolm X, he had come to realize the cost of open rebellion. He publicly humbled himself before his father and the crowd gathered for the Saviour's Day rally (the Nation of Islam's annual holiday and convention to celebrate Fard Muhammad's birth date on February 26). These victories over the rebels, one now dead and the others humbled, brought a brief respite to Elijah Muhammad. However, these same issues would reemerge in the next decade to threaten the Nation of Islam once again.

The Honorable Elijah Muhammad: His Final Decade

The Nation of Islam had weathered the storms of 1963 to 1965 reasonably well. Elijah Muhammad had not. Earlier he had had to convalesce in Phoenix for bronchial asthma, later he had to deal with stress and high blood pressure, and then in 1965 he was diagnosed with diabetes. By mid-1965 these continuing health problems forced him to once again hand the daily running of the Nation of Islam to his inner circle. His leadership remained active, however. He urged his followers not to retaliate against the police in Los Angeles when they stormed the city's mosque looking for weapons. He also made a half-hearted rapprochement with Martin Luther King Jr.—despite continuing to criticize his goal of integration. And later, perhaps because of the negative reaction to his response to Malcolm X's assassination, Elijah Muhammad learned not to attack a foe once he was dead. When Martin Luther King Jr. died, he issued a simple condolence in *Muhammad Speaks*: "I extend my deepest sympathy and condolences on the loss of Dr. Martin Luther King. A great and courageous black man who died in the effort to get for his people that which belonged to them—FREEDOM."[55]

Financially, Elijah Muhammad and his Nation of Islam seemed to be doing extremely well. He acquired more farmland in various states and a bank in Chicago. In the early 1970s he purchased a $4.4 million former Greek Orthodox church to house Temple No. 2 in Chicago.[56] With this wealth, generated from businesses, donations, and sales of *Muhammad Speaks*, extravagance and corruption continued to plague the Nation of Islam. Yet the grandiose financial projects, such as the new Temple No. 2, required even more money than Elijah Muhammad could muster. This required him to make overtures to oil-rich Muslim countries in the Middle East. His goal was now to seek not legitimacy, but currency. However, he reciprocated with token gestures: his Muslims would now fast during Ramadan as the rest of the Muslim world did and not in December, as had been the established practice in the Nation of Islam.[57] He also criticized the State of Israel in *Muhammad Speaks*. His efforts were rewarded: Muammar Qaddafi, the president of Libya, gave Elijah Muhammad a three-year interest-free loan for $3 million, which funded the purchase of the church. By the time Elijah Muhammad died in 1975 he had some seventy-six temples throughout the United States, most of them associated with a University of Islam. Membership was perhaps as high as one hundred thousand. His business empire was worth $45 million and included fifteen thousand acres of farmland, several aircraft, a fish-importing business, restaurants, bakeries, and supermarkets.[58]

From 1965 to 1970 the Nation of Islam continued to grow in membership—erasing the defections that the tribulations of Malcolm X had prompted. For years, his own position was unassailable. In 1969, Muhammad Ali (formerly Cassius Clay), who had converted to the Nation of Islam in 1964 and whose boxing fame had served Elijah Muhammad so well in the immediate aftermath of Malcolm X's departure, could be suspended for a year. Almost every issue of *Muhammad Speaks* during 1965 had devoted a page to stories and pictures of Muhammad Ali under the heading, "News from the Camp of the Champ." However, in April 1969 Elijah Muhammad claimed that Muhammad Ali's main interest was money and his preference was for "sport and play" rather than Islam. Allah condemned sport as foolish, according to Elijah Muhammad. Consequently, he was removed from "the circle of the Brotherhood of the followers of Islam under the Leadership and the Teachings of Elijah Muhammad, for one (1) year in Class 'F'" and was to be addressed not by his Muslim name but by the name Cassius Clay.[59] A year later, Elijah Muhammad issued a general condemnation of "sport and play." He cited Qur'an 44:38: "And We did not create the heavens and the earth and what is between them in sport." The devil therefore attempts to get people to do the opposite. The danger in sports and playing, which for Elijah Muhammd include bowling, gambling, and games of chance, is their ability to distract black people from the approaching doom and to part them from their money, which could be better spent buying land to grow crops.[60] For several years, however, Elijah Muhammad still recognized Muhammad Ali as a "good Believer," but one who had to repent before he could resume his official ministerial duties within the Nation of Islam. Only in late 1974 was Muhammad Ali once again in good standing and once again extolled within *Muhammad Speaks*.[61]

In 1970 Elijah Muhammad could also afford to replace John Ali, one of his closest advisors who, as the national secretary, controlled the Nation of Islam's financial resources. This period also marked the rise of new figures in the Nation of Islam, the most noteworthy being Louis X of Boston. Louis X had proved his worth during the Malcolm X controversy, abandoning Malcolm X (whose protégé he had been) and becoming his harshest critic. Just prior to his erstwhile mentor's assassination, he even stated that he was worthy of death. Later, Elijah Muhammad gave him his seal of approval, replacing his 'X' with 'Farrakhan' and elevating him to the position of his National Representative.

Yet, tensions and rivalries within the various temples began to grow again, and between 1971 and 1973 open hostilities broke out even within Elijah Muhammad's home territory, Temple No. 2 in Chicago. The various causes of the animosity were not unlike those that led to the break with Malcolm X. The activist younger generation was being stifled by the far more conservative older generation, and everyone was jockeying for position in preparation for the battle over succession.[62] At Temple No. 2 the focus was on the powerful Raymond Sharrieff, the long-time Supreme Captain of the Fruit of Islam. After an attempt on his life in 1971, there was a series of reprisal killings that lasted until 1973. This intra-Muslim violence included the killing of the head of the Malcolm X Foundation, but culminated with the massacre at the house of Hamaas Abdul Khaalis, a former member of the Nation of Islam who had left the Nation long before Malcolm X. He was also a harsh Sunni Islam critic of Elijah Muhammad. On January 18, 1973, men burst into his home and brutally killed seven members of his family, including four infants, the youngest of which was nine days old. Elijah Muhammad, however, was not implicated in the murders.

When another report of intra-Muslim warfare was made after killings at the Orthodox Muslim Mosque in Brooklyn in early 1974, Louis Farrakhan felt obliged to dismiss the media reports of a Muslim "feud" as a hoax. This incident, along with the 1973 murder of Khaalis's family and a 1972 murder in Baton Rouge, were dismissed by Farrakhan as part of a pre–Saviour's Day rally propaganda campaign against Elijah Muhammad orchestrated annually by the American government.[63] Elijah Muhammad's role in all this violence was probably indirect—he may only have helped to create the atmosphere, as he had done before Malcolm X's assassination. In the early 1970s, for instance, he lashed out at the "hypocrites," even those within the headquarters in Chicago. Elijah Muhammad declared that the hypocrites must be removed and charged that Temple No. 2 was full of disbelievers:

The HYPOCRITES who . . . are not set in THE NATION OF ISLAM, must be removed out of our way.

No people nor organization, regardless to [sic] what it is, religious or political, can be successful with HYPOCRITES on its panel.

HERE IN CHICAGO, the die has been set. And, the material has been made according to the die. I hope Allah will Cause [sic] you to see, for I most certainly hope to get you removed out of our Temple No. 2, which is full of DISBELIEVERS as well as in other Temples where they go from one to the other carry[ing] venomous poison of hatred against Brother and against Sister and those who are trying to live the righteous life with the Truth that will bring them into a HEAVEN AT ONCE.

He then warned his followers not to befriend hypocrites:

Being FRIENDS with the HYPOCRITES is dangerous. The Holy Qur-an warns you against taking them for friends, and the Holy Qur-an teaches you and me their disbelieving actions so that you may recognize them, if they be in your family or home, you cannot be successful trying to befriend one who is against your God and Truth, for he is against you for believing it.

He becomes your enemy, regardless; if it is your husband, wife, sons, or daughters. So, remember how the Holy Qur-an teaches us that the Messenger must be hard against such people; and I am. I just hope the day will come that I can weed them out, by the help of Allah, BECAUSE YOU (HYPOCRITES) ARE A GREAT HINDRANCE TO YOUR OWN SALVATION AND THE SALVATION OF OTHERS.[64]

This might be a reference to Elijah Muhammad's struggle with his own son Wallace Muhammad. "Hypocrites" would remain a common motif in Elijah Muhammad's writing well into the 1970s, though the identities of the hypocrites varied.[65]

Just as this destructive internecine fighting was subsiding, Elijah Muhammad's health was failing. Control of the Nation of Islam was already in the hands of others—at least for the day-to-day operations. The success of the organization and the earlier deterioration of his health had made that a necessity. He wrote less and less for *Muhammad Speaks*, and when he did it was often in the form of short and sometimes odd commands. During the first decade of his columns in *Muhammad Speaks*, Elijah Muhammad had contributed about one or two pages of material. In those days, he would occasionally have an earlier column reprinted, or substitute his column with an excerpt from *Message to the Blackman in America* or the transcript of his Saviour's Day speech. From 1970 onwards, however, more reprinted columns appeared. In the last two years of his life, less than one in ten issues of *Muhammad Speaks* had any new material from Elijah Muhammad.

The weakening of the hitherto strong central leadership may also explain the development of new heretical teachings (noted above in chapter

1) and the need for the National Secretary, Abass Rassoull, to issue warnings against exploiting the Nation of Islam by selling unauthorized pictures of Elijah Muhammad and against members of the Nation of Islam issuing "holy names" to themselves.[66]

Elijah Muhammad, nevertheless, had steadfastly avoided anointing an heir apparent, making a point in early 1972 of saying he would not do so:

> I do not do that. I cannot do that. I did not choose myself. God chose me and if He Wants a successor, He Will Choose that one. . . . I do not believe there is one coming up. . . . I don't think God needs one, because when man and God have come face to face, as the old saying goes, then that is the end of it. . . . [S]o what would another one do? There is nothing for him to do.[67]

Perhaps somewhat naively, Elijah Muhammad believed that the Nation of Islam would continue to administer its resources without a successor and would function as a "Divine government." By 1974, when it was clear that the end was near, others at the top of the Nation of Islam hierarchy disagreed and felt there would be much for a successor to do.

The various possible successors began once again to jockey for position. Within the family, Wallace Muhammad, despite his occasional expulsions and decade-long absence from prominence, was the leading candidate. Elijah Muhammad put up no resistance to Wallace Muhammad's growing prominence. Louis Farrakhan was the strongest contender outside of the family (with the possible exception of Raymond Sharrieff, who was also Elijah Muhammad's son-in-law). It seems clear that the Muhammad family—from the very top down—had no intention of allowing an outsider to wrest away control of the Nation of Islam.[68] Nevertheless, the struggle raged on the pages of *Muhammad Speaks*. In the month prior to Elijah Muhammad's death, his son Wallace Muhammad made his first significant appearance in *Muhammad Speaks* in over a decade. His picture was among those attending a Nation of Islam fundraiser alongside other prominent leaders in the Nation of Islam, including Louis Farrakhan (the National Representative), Jam Muhammad (Elijah Muhammad's brother), Abdul Karriem (the Western National Representative). At the fundraiser Wallace Muhammad was said to have been the first to speak, having been introduced by his uncle Jam (the host of the event), but Louis Farrakhan was named the main speaker.[69] However, when the mayor of Chicago declared February 26, 1975, Nation of Islam Day, it was Wallace Muhammad who accepted the proclamation on behalf of his father. However, the same issue of *Muhammad Speaks* devoted seven pages to the double marriage that linked Louis Farrakhan's family with Elijah Muhammad's.[70]

Although ill for decades, Elijah Muhammad had always managed to recover from his various ailments. However, in 1973 the ill effects of his age were far more noticeable; at the Saviour's Day rally he even forgot the year of Fard Muhammad's birth. Another recovery seemed likely, for a year later he was still the keynote speaker at the Saviour's Day rally and at the end of the year he was able to travel to Mexico. Shortly thereafter, however, on January 29, 1975, he was checked into the hospital in Chicago. A few days later he suffered congestive heart failure. Hitherto almost completely silent on this matter, *Muhammad Speaks* was forced to acknowledge his illness as the rumors spread. Other newspapers, such as the *Chicago Defender*, were the first to report Elijah Muhammad's hospitalization and the grave status of his health. In fact, it was three days after his death when the first report of his illness was published in *Muhammad Speaks*. Moreover, this report merely discussed the numerous "get well" cards, telephone calls, and telegrams that were already arriving.[71]

On February 25, 1975, a day before the annual Saviour's Day rally was to begin, Elijah Muhammad died. By the time of his funeral three days later, his son Wallace Muhammad had been triumphantly proclaimed the new Supreme Minister. The Nation of Islam, which for forty years Elijah Muhammad had struggled first to preserve, then to build, and then to protect from various outside forces, was about to be dismantled from within.

3

Elijah Muhammad and the Qur'an

The question of whether the religious movement Elijah Muhammad led for so long is "Islamic" is a challenging one. Were one to focus on doctrines such as the incarnation of Allah in the form of Fard Muhammad, Elijah Muhammad's own status as the Messenger of Allah, the denial of the resurrection and contemporary nature of heaven and hell, the racial framing of Islam, and the focus on the racial conflict in the United States, it would certainly seem that Elijah Muhammad led a movement that was fairly unislamic.[1] A comparison with the five principles of Islam—belief in Allah (including that he does not take material form), in angels, in prophets (the last of which is Muhammad), in scriptures, and in the Last Day (which involves the resurrection of the dead, judgment, and being assigned to heaven or hell)—seems to confirm that appearance. Yet were one to observe instead members of the Nation of Islam identifying themselves as Muslims, worshipping a deity called Allah, praying five times a day, abstaining from pork and alcohol, and, most importantly, using the same scripture used by other Muslims, the Qur'an, one might come to the opposite conclusion. Even those problematic doctrines detailed above find support in the Qur'an, according to Elijah Muhammad. This scripture is generally believed by Muslims to be the literal, eternal, incorruptible, and inimitable speech of Allah revealed to Muhammad the Prophet via the angel Gabriel. That Elijah Muhammad claimed the Qur'an to support his formulation of Islam vexed his Muslim opponents, for they asserted proprietary rights over its interpretation, and it puzzled his would-be African American converts, for they had no familiarity with this text.

Some African slaves in the early days of the nation had been well-versed enough to be able to reproduce the Qur'an from memory in writing after many years of enslavement. However, not until Drew Ali introduced his *Circle Seven Koran* and Elijah Muhammad promulgated the Qur'an was the word "Qur'an," much less the text itself, widely known by

African Americans. It will clarify the context within which Elijah Muhammad disseminated knowledge of the Qur'an if we examine Drew Ali's *Circle Seven Koran* and Elijah Muhammad's use of the Bible. This context highlights Elijah Muhammad's unique and evolving relationship with the scripture of Islam.

The Circle Seven Koran

As we have seen, Drew Ali founded the Canaanite Temple in 1913 in Newark, New Jersey, and fifteen years later it evolved into the Moorish Science Temple of America, Inc. He claimed that years earlier, in Egypt or in Mecca, his prophethood became manifest as a book: *The Holy Koran of the Moorish Science Temple of America*. (To avoid confusion, *The Holy Koran* of Noble Drew Ali will be referred to as the *Circle Seven Koran*, the name used by his early followers because of the symbol on the cover.) It has also been asserted that this book was first published in 1916, but scholar Peter Lamborn Wilson suggests that there was no printed edition prior to 1927.[2] Chapters 2 to 19 are very lightly edited material from *The Aquarian Gospel of Jesus the Christ* by Levi H. Dowling, published in 1908.[3] However, more telling are chapters 20 to 44, which come from a Rosicrucian book entitled *Unto Thee I Grant*, by Sri Ramatherio, whose original publication may date back to 1760 but whose 1925 revision seems to be the one employed by Drew Ali.[4] Both of these originals were eighteenth- and nineteenth-century pseudepigrapha; the former claims to recount Jesus' ministry in India and Egypt prior to his ministry in Galilee; and the latter consists of instructions on social and communal relationships, morality, and theology. The final chapters, 45 to 48, with their more numerous spelling and grammatical errors, seem to have been composed by Drew Ali himself. In these final chapters, Drew Ali outlines his view of Moorish history, including the origin of the Asiatic nation, the birth of Christianity in Rome, and the Canaanite origin of Egypt, the capital of the "Empire of the Dominion of Africa." He closes with an assertion of his prophetic mission. Except for the use of the name "Allah" and two minor references to Muhammad (as the "founder of uniting of Islam" and as he who "fulfilled the works of Jesus of Nazareth"),[5] the contents of the *Circle Seven Koran* owe nothing to the Qur'an or even Islam. In fact, elsewhere Muhammad was even listed with Confucius as one of Drew Ali's predecessors.[6] There is only one reference to the Qur'an in the *Circle Seven Koran*: "The fallen sons and daughters of the Asiatic Nation of North America need to learn to love instead of hate; and to know their higher self and lower self. This is the uniting of the Holy Koran of Mecca, for teaching and instructing all Moorish Americans, etc."[7] This passage might actually be speaking of the *Circle Seven Koran* but, since Muhammad had also been mentioned as the founder of the *uniting* of Islam, this "Holy Koran of Mecca" is probably a reference to the Qur'an.

Aminah McCloud, a scholar of African American Islam, contends that "Islamic belief in the Moorish community focused on central quranic concepts such as justice, a purposeful creation of mankind, freedom of will, and humankind as the generator of personal action (both good and bad). Quranic principles concerning the nature of reality as spiritual and the nature of human existence as co-eternal with the existence of time also figured prominently."[8] The assertion that the Qur'an contains all of these concepts and principles is itself problematic. Moreover, even those that can be found in the Qur'an cannot be shown to have been the source of Drew Ali's teaching. McCloud herself concedes that "[t]here is no evidence that the Moorish Science Temple of America had access to even most of the basic Islamic texts, with the possible exception of the Qur'an."[9]

If the contents of the *Circle Seven Koran* clearly bear no obvious relation to those of the Qur'an, what is the point of using the name "Koran"? After all, the people Drew Ali was addressing had little familiarity with the word and probably none with the contents of the text to which it referred. A clue to Drew Ali's motivations is to be found in the packaging of the contents more than in the contents themselves. The cover of the *Circle Seven Koran* states,

The Holy Koran of the Moorish Science Temple of America
Divinely Prepared by the Noble Prophet Drew Ali
   By the guiding of his father God, Allah; the great God of the universe.
To redeem man from his sinful and fallen stage of humanity back to the
highest plane of life with father God, Allah.

The *Circle Seven Koran* was meant to support Drew Ali's claim to prophecy. Prophets were associated with scriptures, which served as manifestations of their connection with God. Drew Ali's claim to have been initiated in Egypt by passing the test of the high priest in the Temple of Cheops was unlikely to convince many. Drew Ali did perform miracles. A flyer announcing a May 16, 1927, meeting states,

Don't Miss the Great Moorish Drama
    Look! Look!
    Come ye everyone and see
    The Seventh Wonder of the World
    . . . The Prophet Noble Drew Ali, will be bound with several yards of
rope, as Jesus was bound in the Temple at Jerusalem
    And escaped before the authorities could t[ake] charge of Him; so will
the Prophet Drew Ali, perform the same act, after being bound by anyone in the audience and will escape in a few seconds.
    He also will heal many in the audience with[out] touching them, free
of charge, as they stand in fr[ont] of their seats manifesting his divine
power.[10]

The point of these "miracles" is bluntly stated: they were meant to be seen
as manifestations of "divine power."

However, to Drew Ali producing a scripture probably seemed a more
expedient means of manifesting such power. He could not simply produce
a new Bible, of course, since the Bible would have been fairly well known
among his audience and Joseph Smith had done that recently enough
with his Book of Mormon. It was precisely the unfamiliarity with the
Qur'an that allowed him to adopt the name, even though in terms of subject matter, the *Circle Seven Koran* is more biblical than quranic. The same
conclusion can be drawn from Drew Ali's claim to have "[a]ll authority
and power"[11] and his assertion that "to be a real Moorish leader you must
study the Koran and the Divine Constitution that is handed down unto
you by I, the Prophet."[12] His *Circle Seven Koran* was the manifestation of
his divine power, or tangible proof of his prophetic claims. His authority
was not self-evident, and apparently he needed to convince his audience.

That the role of the *Circle Seven Koran* was to be emblematic of his prophetic authority, and not authoritative in its own right, is evidenced by several facts. First, other important Moorish Science texts rarely mention the
Circle Seven Koran. Neither *Charter: Moorish Science Temple of America*
nor *Moorish Science Temple of America: The Divine Constitution and By-
Laws* use the word. Even *Koran Questionary* (also known as *Koran Questions for Moorish Americans*), which had to be memorized by followers,
fails to employ the word "Koran," even though its title implies that it derives from the *Circle Seven Koran*. Not only do the questions and answers
lack references to the Qur'an and even the *Circle Seven Koran*, but they also
are at odds with quranic conceptions of prophets, angels, and Satan:

6. What is a Prophet? A Prophet is a Thought of ALLAH manifested in the flesh. . . .

38. What is an Angel? An angel is a thought of ALLAH manifested in human flesh.

39. What are Angels used for? To carry messages to the four corners of the world, to all nations.

40. What is our Prophet to us? He is an angel of ALLAH who was sent to bring us the Everlasting Gospel of ALLAH. . . .

81. What is the first name of the person into whom Jesus was first reincarnated?

Prophet MOHAMMED, the Conqueror.

82. Was Satan to be bound then? Satan was bound in part.

83. When was the head of Satan taken off? 453 (Byzantine).

84. By whom? By Mohammed.[13]

This absence of quranic material in the *Koran Questionary* may also have something to do with the *Circle Seven Koran*'s relatively late publication (in 1927, as opposed to 1916). Second, the *Circle Seven Koran* also had little ritual importance, unlike the Qur'an. A notable exception is found in Drew Ali's tract, the "Prophet Sends Marriage Law to All Temples": "Chapter 22 from our Koran is to be read first to the husband and chapter 21 is to be read secondly to the wife. These are the instructions of marriage from our Holy Koran. Please obey the law as given you by your Prophet through your Governor."[14] Third, religious services after the death of Drew Ali began with a reading from the *Circle Seven Koran*, purportedly following a pattern established by Drew Ali himself. This reading was to be the basis for a sermon. If this claim is accurate, it seems modeled more on Christian use of the Bible at churches than on Muslim use of the Qur'an at mosques.

One might also wonder if Drew Ali was familiar with the Qur'an and simply chose to ignore it. He makes at least one veiled reference to the original Qur'an. In a tract entitled *What Is Islam?* Drew Ali states, "The Koran, the Holy Book of Islam, tells us that the final abode of man is the 'House of Peace,' 'where' no vain word or sinful discourse will be heard."[15] "House of Peace," which presumably derives from "*dar al-salaam*," does not occur in the *Circle Seven Koran*, but comes from Qur'an 10:25. The second phrase appears in Qur'an 78:35. Since the English translation in this case is unique, Drew Ali seems to have had access to a translation of the Qur'an.[16]

Later, it became clear that members of the Moorish Science Temple did see a close connection between their *Circle Seven Koran* and the Qur'an. According to an FBI report in 1944, at least some members of the Moorish Science Temple of America were aware that their *Circle Seven Koran* "was not identical with that of the true Mohammedan but rather a modified concept called a Koran, which had been designed by the Prophet NOBLE DREW ALI."[17] Furthermore, when a Grand Sheik was asked if his organization employed the same Qur'an as all other Muslims did, he replied, "We have a revised Koran—at least, from the Arabic translation into English. . . . [W]e also have the most simple form translated into English."[18] The claims that the *Circle Seven Koran* is a "modified" or "revised" Qur'an are dubious at best. If indeed the claims go back to Drew Ali, and he had access to an actual Qur'an, then the *Circle Seven Koran* seems a much more manipulative and conscious effort to invoke or lay claim to the older scripture's authority.

On the other hand, it seems that Drew Ali had at least passing familiarity with traditional Islam. He describes Muhammad and the origination of Islam in the Arabian Peninsula and the later contributions of Muslims to the world's culture. He also wrote, "The Koran should be of interest to all readers. It is the Bible[19] of the Mohammedans, ruling over the customs and actions of over 200 millions of people. It is a work of importance whether considered from a religious, philosophical, or literary viewpoint."[20] His actual level of familiarity with the Qur'an's contents remains uncertain, though it seems negligible. While aware of the Qur'an's existence and role in Islam, Drew Ali seems largely to have ignored the Qur'an, for he had little need of it. Like the titles "Noble" and "Prophet," like the sashes and the fezes, and like the Moorish historical claims, the Qur'an validated his authority. What was important, therefore, was only the name itself: "Koran" and what it implied.

The Bible and the Qur'an

In sharp contrast, despite his frequent claims to be relaying the teachings of Allah in the person of Fard Muhammad, Elijah Muhammad never claimed to have brought a scripture of his own from Allah—as Drew Ali had.[21] And he used the same Qur'an that other Muslims used. However, he too relied on a nonquranic text: the Bible. For him both the Bible and the Qur'an contained messages from Allah, and he urged his followers to study them, but these messages had hitherto not been properly understood. Elijah Muhammad stated that Fard Muhammad had taught that both of these texts, like all scripture, were written by twenty-three scientists who pen a new book every twenty-five thousand years and then wait an additional ten thousand years before giving it to a prophet.[22] This is said to have occurred with the Bible and the Qur'an, but the significance of this origin and the time span involved are unclear.

For Elijah Muhammad the Bible and the Qur'an are not equals. He declared that "[t]he Bible is now being called the *poison book* by God Himself, and who can deny that it is not poison? It has poisoned the very hearts and minds of the so-called Negroes so much that they can't agree with each other."[23] The poison of the Bible consists, Elijah Muhammad elaborated, in the accusations it levels at many of the prophets: Noah is accused of drunkenness, Lot of incest, and Jesus of having been born in an act of adultery. Such accusations are reminiscent of *tahrīf*—a standard Muslim polemic against Jews and Christians that charges them with altering their scriptures. More unique was his claim that there were "poison addition[s] of the slavery teaching" in the Bible, such as "love your enemies" and "turn the other cheek."[24]

Despite this harsh condemnation, Elijah Muhammad availed himself of the Bible continuously. In two of his main monographs, *The Supreme Wisdom* and *Message to the Blackman in America*, he cited or referred to the Bible almost twice as often as he did the Qur'an. He explained, "I don't mean to say that there is no truth in it. Certainly, plenty of truth, *if understood*."[25] This is where Elijah Muhammad could assume the role of exegete or *mufassir*. "The Bible means good if you can rightly understand it. My interpretation of it is given to me from the Lord of the Worlds."[26] This "understanding" seemed to have consisted of revealing the message for African Americans that had been allegorically and symbolically encoded in the Bible. John Ali, the long-time National Secretary of the Nation of Islam under Elijah Muhammad, stated, "Mr. Elijah Muhammad is bringing a final truth to the people. He is revealing the secret of the symbols, parables, signs and prophecies of the scriptures. The Old Testament is a book of prophecy in parables, symbols and signs. The New Testament is a fulfillment of a prophecy whose time is now."[27] The true value of biblical stories and prophecies, therefore, resided in their explanations for contemporary and relevant past events, and in their paraenetic messages for African Americans. For example, Jonah, when he is swallowed by the fish, is like the "so-called Negroes" swallowed by America, who needed to turn to Allah for deliverance.[28]

Of course, on a more practical level, there were two reasons for Elijah Muhammad's frequent use of the Bible. First, members in the Nation of Islam were predominantly former Christians. Elijah Muhammad was well aware of this situation:

> It is necessary for me to consult or refer to the Bible . . . because my people do not know any Scripture or ever read any Scripture other than the Bible (which they do not understand), I thought it best to make them understand the book which they read and believe in, since the Bible is their graveyard and they must be awakened from it.[29]

Second, not only were his followers more familiar with the Bible, but also Elijah Muhammad himself was more acquainted with its contents than with those of the Qur'an—at least at first.

The Qur'an

Elijah Muhammad's dedication to the Qur'an goes back to Fard Muhammad. According to Beynon's 1938 article, "The Koran itself was soon introduced as the most authoritative of all texts for the study of the new faith. The prophet [Fard Muhammad], however, used only the Arabic text which he translated and explained to the believers."[30] Given his unique doctrines, it is not surprising that Elijah Muhammad also had an odd understanding of what the Qur'an and its message were. It is tempting to think that these doctrines (as with Drew Ali) arose out of ignorance of the Qur'an's content. However, this was not the case. Elijah Muhammad had read significant portions of the Qur'an, probably all of it. Even while he was in prison during World War II, his wife copied out verses from the Qur'an and sent them to him.[31] The translation of the Qur'an favored by Elijah Muhammad was that of the Ahmadiyya Muhammad Ali—the 1917 first edition or possibly the 1920 second edition. He recommended the translation by Abd Allah Yusuf Ali to his followers as well,[32] but when the Qur'an is cited in his columns and books, it is invariably from Muhammad Ali's text. This seems to have been the English Qur'an given to him by Fard Muhammad during their last meeting.

Elijah Muhammad's dependence on this translation is made explicit when he refers his readers to specific footnotes in Muhammad Ali's text and when he uses his subject headings.[33] It is not always clear if Elijah Muhammad was aware that the headings provided by Muhammad

Ali were not part of the Qur'an. For instance, Muhammad Ali has the section heading "Foreign Believers" for Qur'an 72:4–14. Elijah Muhammad performed exegesis on the heading just as he did on the *sūra's* name and its verses. He wrote, "These verses are so plain that they do not need any interpretation, because these things have come to pass. Foreign Believers here mean white believers; not other than white. The chapter is headed under the name 'Jinn.' *Jinn* here means the devil."[34] Elijah Muhammad frequently alters or miscopies words and phrases in the passages that he quotes. In these emendations, he often Americanizes the spelling or modernizes and simplifies the grammar, such as when "O soul that art at rest" is modified to "O soul that is at rest," though he does not always do so correctly. Elijah Muhammad also felt free to substitute synonyms and to capitalize and italicize words that he wanted to emphasize.

This translation, aside from Ahmadiyya tendencies, is not an unusual translation. It has been suggested that it is responsible for Elijah Muhammad's belief that the Qur'an literally identified people with blue eyes as being unacceptable to Allah:

> Mr Muhammad is thought to have drawn scriptural support for his racist theology from a mistranslated Ahmadiyyah Koran. Correctly written, a passage in the Koran states that God does not accept people with "blurred eyes." But the Ahmadiyyah version which Mr Muhammad purportedly consulted says that God does not accept people with "blue eyes."[35]

Qur'an 20:102 reads, "On the day when the trumpet shall be blown, and we will gather the guilty, blue-eyed, on that day." To this verse Muhammad Ali appended the following footnote:

> The word *zurqá* means *blue-eyed*, and thus it serves as an indication of the nations who are spoken of here as being *gathered*. According to [Baydawī], blue being the colour of the eyes of the *Rúm* (i.e. the Greeks or the Romans), who were the most hated by the Arabs, that colour was regarded by the Arabs as the worst colour for the eye. The word may also signify *blind*, in reference to the guilty being raised up blind on the resurrection day, for which see v. 124. (636, n. 1601a)

Clearly, Elijah Muhammad hardly needed a mistranslated Qur'an to find support for his "blue-eyed" devil doctrine. Furthermore, his followers were also permitted to use the translation of the Qur'an by Yusuf Ali, whose footnote on the same verse is not significantly different.

While the Bible needed to be properly understood because of "poison" alterations, symbolism, and prophecy, the Qur'an was "without mistake" and perfectly pure for Elijah Muhammad. It came directly "from the mouth of Allah" (that is, not even mediated by an angel and prophet). Elijah Muhammad described the Qur'an as follows:

> The book that the so-called American Negroes (The Tribe of Shabazz) should own and read, the book that the slavemasters have but have not represented it to their slaves, is a book that will heal their sin-sick souls that were made sick and sorrowful by the slavemasters.
>
> This book will open their blinded eyes and open their deaf ears. It will purify them.
>
> The name of this book, which makes a distinction between the God of righteous and the God of evil, is: Glorious Holy Quran Sharrieff. It is indeed the Book of Guidance, of Light and Truth, and of Wisdom and Judgement.
>
> But the average one should first be taught how to respect such a book, how to understand it, and how to teach it.

Furthermore, "to get a real Holy Qur'an one should know the Arabic language in which it is written."[36] He also taught, "The Holy Qur'an will live forever. Why? Because it has Truth in it. I will not say it has some Truth in it. It has all Truth in it if you understand."[37] While most of this rhetoric seems in accord with what other Muslims might have said, his references to slavery and the Tribe of Shabazz make it clear that the Qur'an's purpose was subsumed under Elijah Muhammad's primary goal: to free African Americans from the religious, social, economic, and political corruption of Whites.[38] The Qur'an may not have suffered from the alterations and slave teachings found in the Bible, but even it still had to be interpreted by Elijah Muhammad—so that it would be understood correctly.

Generally, when Elijah Muhammad cited the Qur'an, his introductions were normally accompanied by simple paraphrastic commentary. For example, "Let us take a look at the opening of the second chapter of the Holy Quran. Here Allah addresses Himself to us as being the Best Knower and that we must not entertain any doubts about the purity of His Book (the Holy Qur'an)."[39] This was followed by Qur'an 2:2. He added, "Allah Himself speaks in the Holy Quran, not like the Bible which mentions 'Thus says the Lord.'"[40] One is tempted to think that Elijah Muhammad simply was not familiar with passages in which Allah is spoken of in the second person or third person. However, in the very next paragraph he cited Qur'an 2:285—a passage that addresses Allah in the third person.

While the Qur'an was invoked as an authority, it was Elijah Muhammad's racial teachings, especially his race myth and his eschatology, that provided the interpretive framework. The supremacy of his racial teachings was evident in the title of his first major publication, *The Supreme Wisdom*. Although he argued for the holiness of the Qur'an and its unique suitability for African Americans, it is his own teachings from Fard Muhammad, not those of the Qur'an, that were being called "supreme."[41] That is not to say that Elijah Muhammad would have seen any conflict between the two, as for him even his most controversial doctrine, the incarnation of Allah in Fard Muhammad, was evidenced in the Qur'an. "I realized his intention why he was asking me insistingly to read the Koran. I was just to know who he was."[42] Moreover, his references to Fard Muhammad often drew on quranic vocabulary, indicating exactly how Elijah Muhammad read Fard Muhammad into the Qur'an. For example, borrowing the language of Qur'an 1:2, he wrote, "*All praise is due* to the Great Mahdi, who was come and has come, *the sole master of the worlds*."[43]

The Future Book and the Qur'an

Elijah Muhammad's Allah never presented his Messenger with his own scripture, nor did Elijah Muhammad ever produce a new Qur'an himself, as Drew Ali had. He was quite content with the contents of the original—properly understood, of course. Yet other Muslims found his statements about the Qur'an's eventual replacement quite problematic. In the *Supreme Wisdom*, under the heading of "The Future Holy Book," Elijah Muhammad wrote,

> The Holy Quran, the Glorious Book, should be read and studied by us (the so-called Negroes). Both the present Bible and the Holy Quran must soon give way to that holy book which no man as yet but Allah has seen. The teachings (prophecies) of the present Bible and the Quran take us up to the resurrection and judgement of this world but not into the next life. That which is in that holy book is for the righteous and their future only; not for the mixed world of righteous and evil.[44]

Elsewhere, Elijah Muhammad stated that scripture expires every twenty-five thousand years, at which time Allah, understood as the wise black man of Asia, writes a new one for the new era. There seems to be some inconsistency here in this teaching, for Elijah Muhammad had elsewhere also stated that the Qur'an will expire in some nine thousand years, which seems at odds with the statement above that it will "soon give way" to a new scripture. A more contemporary replacement of the Qur'an was implied in this statement:

> Then He told Me, "I will give you a Holy Qur'an when you learn how to read Arabic. I made it Myself." He showed Me that Holy Qur'an in Arabic on September last but I couldn't read it. I could only recognize one letter in it, so I expect Him within a year to come back with the same Book. A Man given a job as I have been given can't take the material things of this world to bring in as a foundation for another world. The things in books that I have read will not do for us to build a New World out of. We have to have New Teachings.[45]

When asked specifically when this new book would appear and who would author it, Elijah Muhammad responded, "Well what's in the book is not yet revealed. But this same Man, Master Fard Muhammad, is the very same One that this book will come from. And He said that He has already wrote the book, but He's not ready to give it to the world."[46] Elijah Muhammad refused to speak more of it and knew none of its contents, for it was the scripture of the future, "the other side." No claims that this new holy book—this new Qur'an—has been revealed were made by Elijah Muhammad or by his followers even after his death in 1975. Clearly, the current Qur'an's authority was not eternal, despite the claim that it would "live forever."

Elijah Muhammad's Knowledge of the Qur'an

If the Qur'an is to be replaced one day and is referenced in the writings and speeches of Elijah Muhammad so much less than the Bible, why did he use it at all? Obviously, Fard Muhammad taught from the Qur'an, and Fard Muhammad gave Elijah Muhammad several Qur'ans in 1934: "He gave Me a Holy Qur'an in Arabic but I couldn't read it so He got Me one in Arabic and English by Muhammad Ali of Pakistan. Later He found one by Yusuf Ali of Egypt and He brought Me that one."[47] Even in his earliest publications in 1934, Elijah Muhammad quoted the Qur'an.[48] To remain true to his belief that Fard Muhammad was Allah, Elijah Muhammad needed to give a central role to the Qur'an. Furthermore, Elijah Muhammad considered himself a genuine and devout Muslim,[49] and the scripture of Islam was the Qur'an. Once, when asked what credentials he had from Allah, Elijah Muhammad simply replied, the "Holy Quran."[50]

Just as it is inaccurate to assume that the Qur'an was somehow peripheral to Elijah Muhammad, it is similarly incorrect to assume that his understanding of the scripture was static. If one examines his use of the Qur'an over time, it is obvious that his familiarity with the text and his willingness to invoke it as an authority changed with time. Three things, however, did not change. First, Elijah Muhammad relied entirely on English translations when reading the Qur'an. Second, the Qur'an was interpreted through the mythology provided by Fard Muhammad. Third, Elijah Muhammad's authority to interpret the Qur'an in whatever way he saw fit came from his status as the Messenger of Allah.

The core of Elijah Muhammad's teachings can be found in his *Supreme Wisdom: Solution to the So-called Negroes' Problem*; *The Supreme Wisdom: Volume Two*; and *Message to the Blackman in America*. *The Supreme Wisdom* is a 56-page booklet containing the essence of Elijah Muhammad's earliest teachings. It was published in 1957 but consists in large part of material drawn from the "Mr. Muhammad Speaks" columns of 1956 in *The Pittsburgh Courier*. As the movement expanded rapidly in the 1960s, a less "poorly written and poorly organized"[51] summary of Elijah Muhammad's message was required. *The Supreme Wisdom: Volume Two* and *Message to the Blackman in America* seem to have met that need.[52] These works do not represent the complete written works of Elijah Muhammad. There were weekly columns in a series of different African American newspapers: for several years (1956–summer 1959) Elijah Muhammad had a weekly column in the *Pittsburgh Courier*, then in the *Los Angeles Herald-Dispatch* (1959–May 1960), and finally in the Nation of Islam's own paper, *Muhammad Speaks*. There were also several earlier short-lived newspapers published by the Nation of Islam, such as the 1934 *Final Call to Islam*. Elijah Muhammad also compiled or "wrote" several other books, including *How to Eat to Live* (1968), for which see chapter 4; *How to Eat to Live, Book No. 2* (1973); *The Fall of America* (1973), for which see chapter 4; and *Our Saviour Has Arrived* (1974). Other texts were posthumously compiled from columns and speeches. Many, however, were published relatively late and were composed of speeches, columns, and articles from as far back as 1959 and from recycled parts of *Message to the Blackman in America*. While none of these three books examined here focused exclusively on the Qur'an, together they supply chronological "snapshots" that highlight major developments in Elijah Muhammad's approach to, and the growing familiarity of himself and his followers with, the Qur'an.

The Supreme Wisdom

The Supreme Wisdom: Solution to the So-called Negroes' Problem was Elijah Muhammad's first major publication. Its fifty-six pages consist of a series of 150 independent pericopes, ranging in length from a few sentences to several short paragraphs. Many may represent the teachings of Fard Muhammad as Elijah Muhammad remembered them. Passages on similar topics such as Allah, Christianity, eating pork, the hereafter, and prayer are grouped together, but not consistently.

Many of the quranic references in this book do not involve citations, but simply the use of quranic phraseology. For example, statements such as "I have the truth from the All-wise One, Allah, to Whom praise is due" and "Anyone who desires to accept Islam . . . must pledge to serve and obey Allah and his Apostle"[53] ensured that when his followers read the Qur'an for themselves, they would read the ubiquitous phrase "obey Allah and his Messenger" as a reference to Fard Muhammad and Elijah Muhammad.

Sometimes quranic passages were cited verbatim and appeared with little or no explanation. For example, in the passage entitled "Holy Quran on the Hereafter," Elijah Muhammad wrote,

> The Holy Quran Sharrieff and the Bible are filled with readings on the Hereafter. Here I shall quote only these beautiful verses from the Holy Quran (89:27-30): "O soul that is at rest, return to your Lord, well-pleased with Him, well-pleasing; So enter among My servants and enter into My Paradise."[54]

Similarly, in the passage "ISLAM—The Perfect Religion," he wrote, "Allah says of Islam in the Holy Qur'an, 'This day I have perfected for you a religion; completed my favor on you and chose for you Islam as a religion' (Chapter 5:3)."[55] Both seem innocuous. However, the former appears after several pericopes in which Elijah Muhammad argued that the hereafter is in the here and now, on earth and not a future spiritual existence.[56] The latter appears after a description of Islam as the original religion of all black humankind and as the religion of the tribe of Shabazz. Thus, the Qur'an is not speaking for itself but is instead speaking out of a particular context constructed by Elijah Muhammad. This technique makes the Qur'an appear to support his teachings.[57]

A few explicit explanations are also provided for some of the quranic verses adduced by Elijah Muhammad. For example, he wrote,

> "He it is who sent His Apostle with the guidance and the True religion that he make it overcome the religions, all of them, though the polytheists may be averse." (The Holy Quran, 61:9)
>
>   In the above verse Allah (God) in the last days of this present world (of wicked infidels) states that He must destroy false religions with the True Religion Islam. It (Islam) must overcome all other religions.[58]

Thus, according to Elijah Muhammad, the Qur'an, like the Bible, is a book of prophecy; its pages are full of allusions to the modern world. The Qur'an's words are not so much addressed to seventh-century Arabs or even to the whole of humankind, but to African Americans. The Allah of the above verse is Fard Muhammad, and His Apostle is Elijah Muhammad. The latter is stated directly when "His Last Apostle" is given the parenthetical gloss "an Apostle whom Allah would raise from the lost and found people of the seed of Abraham in the Days of Judgement."[59] By also interpreting passages mentioning the Day of Judgment and Satan in the Qur'an as references to the present and to the white race, respectively, Elijah Muhammad was able to bring much of the Qur'an into his mythological framework.[60] And, since his followers would have virtually no familiarity with a more traditional interpretation of the Qur'an, they too would have read the Qur'an through this framework. The observations that only a few quranic passages are cited, that they are treated in isolation, and that relevant verses from other parts of the Qur'an are not presented suggest that Elijah Muhammad was not very familiar with the text. His use of quranic language, his citation of isolated quranic passages in the midst of other passages, and his proclivity to read quranic passages as prophecy suggest that his purpose was not so much to explain the Qur'an as to lend legitimacy through reference to it in his mythology of the origin of the races and the coming eschaton.

The Supreme Wisdom: Volume Two

The Supreme Wisdom: Volume Two is also composed of short passages varying in length from a few sentences to a few short paragraphs, but is organized into twenty-two chapters. Virtually every pericope in the first *Supreme Wisdom* appears in some form in this revised edition.[61] Even a cursory examination of the new material indicates that the Qur'an continued to play only a small role in the teachings of Elijah Muhammad. Noteworthy, however, is the increased use of "I say" instead of "Allah says." Although the second volume is roughly twice the size of volume 1, only twelve new citations from the Qur'an are adduced. The Qur'an may be directly "from the mouth of Allah" for Elijah Muhammad, but he had another source for divine words. He stated in his foreword,

> You perhaps wonder why we call this little book "The Supreme Wisdom." It is because most every word of it is from the Lord of the worlds, "THE SUPREME BEING," especially where you read of the History of the Caucasian Race; the History of the Black Nation and Prophets; the Doom of America—how she will be destroyed; the Hereafter; the Future of the so-called Negroes—"Tribe of Shabazz;" what happened 66 trillion years ago, 50,000 years ago and 6,000 years ago. All of the answers are directly from the mouth of Allah (God) in the Person of Master W. F. Muhammad, to Whom all praise is due, the Great Mahdi or Messiah, as the Christians say, and He is also the Son of Man.[62]

Even though Fard Muhammad had "disappeared" over two decades earlier, Elijah Muhammad stated that Allah continued to reveal His truth to him.

In *The Supreme Wisdom: Volume Two*, quranic verses are cited with little or no explanation less frequently than in volume 1. Only in the passage entitled "The Holy Quran on Prayer" are quranic verses cited without comment.[63] That is to say, the use of tacit explanation provided by the context of surrounding pericopes was dropped in this publication. More commonly, when a quranic verse was cited, Elijah Muhammad expressly demonstrated its relevance to his followers. For example, he explained,

> The Holy Quran warns us against mixing the Truth with Falsehood. "*And mix not up the Truth with Falsehood, nor hide the Truth while you know.*" (Chapter 2:42) But mixing up the Truth with falsehood is the policy of the devils, and nearly all the religious leaders of Christianity are guilty of

it—because they don't know which is truth and which is falsehood. The devils are really confused, thinking and planning against the truth and trying to hide falsehood.[64]

The following example shows that Elijah Muhammad continued to read the Qur'an as a book of prophecy:

> We are today being brought face to face with Allah (God) for a show-down between Him and that which we have served as God beside Him. The lost and found members of the Asiatic nation are especially warned in the 112th Chapter of the Holy Quran against the worship of any God other than Allah, for it is Allah, in person who has found them among the worshippers of gods other than himself.[65]

Obviously, he simply equated the quranic reference to "Allah" with Fard Muhammad.[66] These two passages illustrate well the development in Elijah Muhammad's basic approach to explicating the Qur'an. Normally, he reproduced the quranic passage and then paraphrased it. In so doing he identified key words in such a manner as to link the passage with his mythology or his perception of contemporary events.

Message to the Blackman in America

Message to the Blackman in America, first published in 1965, is quite different from the previous two publications. The passages are more organized and the thirteen chapters more coherent. Each chapter is still composed of a number of passages, most of which are now several pages long and commonly begin with a quranic or biblical quotation offset under the title. However, for the most part, scriptural citations continue to be subsumed under the mythology and/or applied directly to current events. For example, under "Islam, the True Religion of God, Part I" Elijah Muhammad writes,

> "*He it is Who sent His Apostle with guidance and the true religion, that he make it overcome the religions—all of them, though the polytheists may be averse.*" According to the Holy Qur-an 6:19 [sic] (the right Scripture for the Time).
>
> In the above verse Allah (God) in the last days of this present world (wicked and infidel) states that he must destroy false religions with the

true religion (Islam). . . . Search the Scriptures of the Bible and the Holy
Qur-an and be convinced. There are two other religions today that oppose the religion of peace (Islam) namely, Buddhism and Christianity.
These two opposing forces will be removed from the people completely
by the light of Islam, Truth, guided by Allah in the person of the Great
Mahdi, Fard Muhammad. I am His Apostle. It will come to pass that you
will not even find a trace of them.[67]

Obviously, this passage is an expanded version of the one cited earlier
from *The Supreme Wisdom*.[68] Although Elijah Muhammad provided more
detailed explanations, he did not alter his main exegetical techniques or
framework. They still dominate in *Message to the Blackman in America*.
Some of this was due to habit, and some no doubt to the fact that this
book was also in part a compilation of earlier materials.[69] However, some
new developments in Elijah Muhammad's approach to the Qur'an are
evident.

A greater familiarity with and dependence on the Qur'an is attested to
by the over two hundred quranic references in *Message to the Blackman
in America*. The chapters on "Islam," "The Devil," "Prayer Service," "Hypocrites, Disbelievers, and Obedience," and "The Judgement" received the
lion's share. This is not surprising because the Qur'an contains much on
these themes, even if most Muslims understand them somewhat differently than Elijah Muhammad did. The chapters on "Allah Is God," "Original Man," and "The Bible and the Holy Qur-an" also quote a number of
quranic passages. Not surprisingly, chapters on "Program and Position,"
"Economic Program," "Persecution of the Righteous," "Land of Our Own,"
and "Answer to Critics" have very few, if any.

Elijah Muhammad's knowledge of the Qur'an developed over the
forty-five years that he led the Nation of Islam. He began his career as
the Messenger without a significant knowledge of its contents—though
he was already citing it in articles as early as 1934. The 1956 newspaper report that his "knowledge of the Koran is of staggering propor-
tions"[70] seems somewhat hyperbolic. Over the years, his familiarity
with the Qur'an increased—though he may never have memorized very
much of it. This assertion is based on the published transcriptions of his
speeches. His columns are replete with quranic quotations and so seem
to have been written with a Qur'an in front of him; his speeches, in contrast, are often devoid of quranic references.[71] As we have seen, in his

writings he began by simply citing quranic passages to support his positions, allowing context to convey meaning. Later, he became increasingly explicit with his explanations, relying primarily on paraphrase and gloss. Despite an increased familiarity with the Qur'an and a slight shift in exegetical methods, there was virtually no development in the framework within which the Qur'an was interpreted. His reading of the Qur'an was always subsumed under his race and eschatological myths. Elijah Muhammad did not cite or deal with quranic passages that might seem to contradict him. For example, Qur'an 5:82, which contains the phrase "You will surely find those closest in friendship to those who believe to be those who say 'We are Christians,'" was never discussed by Elijah Muhammad. Comparison with his exegesis of the Bible reveals that Elijah Muhammad probably only knew how to read scripture in one way. For him scripture either recorded in symbolic form the events of the past or contained prophecies about the most critical event in human history—the immanent destruction of the white world. It was the task of the interpreter, the Messenger of Allah, to discover and tease out these "historical" references to, or the relevant messages for, contemporary African Americans.

The Authority of the Qur'an

But was the Qur'an necessary for Elijah Muhammad? It had not been for Drew Ali; only the name was. Even apart from his personal convictions about the Qur'an because of Fard Muhammad's commitment to it, Elijah Muhammad had good reason to invoke the Qur'an. It was a non-Christian scripture that his Christian religious competition could not invoke, and so it left him with a remarkably independent and unique message. It was also the source of unique and non-Christian rituals. And, its moral teachings were remarkably appropriate for addressing the social ills affecting his followers. However, just as important, the Qur'an already came with a presumed religious "authority," and Elijah Muhammad could make that authority his.

That the Qur'an was not an absolute authority for Elijah Muhammad, however, was made clear by the mid-1960s, when the teachings of Elijah Muhammad became far more well-known outside the Nation of Islam. Not surprisingly, "orthodox" Muslims had begun to criticize those teachings. Of these "orthodox Muslims" Elijah Muhammad stated, "Though they do have the Holy Quran, many of them do not understand the meaning of it, and some of them believe everything that is prophesied in the Bible and the Holy Quran about a last Messenger or Prophet being or referring to Muhammad of 1,400 years ago."[72] Then he turned the Qur'an against these Muslims, arguing that each community's Messenger must speak the language of that community. In fact "I give thee an Arabic Holy Qur'an that I may warn the Mother city" meant for Elijah Muhammad that Muhammad the Prophet had "received two books. One in a foreign language to Arabs and another in the original language [Arabic, presumably]. Both called Holy Qur-an."[73] Such arguments were unlikely to persuade his Muslim critics. Elijah Muhammad could not compete against these Muslims, whose knowledge of the Qur'an and its traditional exegesis far exceeded his.

This fact may have spurred him to revive the doctrine of the future book despite its failure to appear. Elijah Muhammad claimed that "[t]hough the Holy Qur'an is without doubt a true book, but it only takes us up to the resurrection of the dead not beyond. It does not give you real knowledge of Allah and the Devil because it refers to the coming of Allah as the Bible refers to the coming of Allah."[74] In this obvious reference to the future holy book, Elijah Muhammad made a slightly different claim than he had in earlier discussions of this book. The future book was now being invoked to undercut the authority of the Qur'an, since it no longer contained "all Truth." Also, those who would have appeared to have a greater claim to understanding the Qur'an's Arabic content were being told they had misunderstood it. In essence, Elijah Muhammad was proclaiming that he, and not the Qur'an, had the final word. After all, he received his authority and knowledge directly from Allah. As early as 1957 he stated, "I do not make mistakes in what I write pertaining to these two races . . . I have the truth from the All-wise One (Allah), to Whom all praise is due."[75]

Concurrent with increasing opposition from other Muslims to his formulation of Islam and understanding of the Qur'an was Elijah Muhammad's waning interest in other Muslims' interpretations. Acceptance of members of the Nation of Islam as legitimate Muslims may have been necessary from white Americans because he required the freedom from harassment that being a legitimate religious movement would guarantee. The goal, therefore, was to be Islamic, but never "orthodox." By the early 1970s Elijah Muhammad felt no need to be accepted by other Muslims— he could simply dismiss them as deceived.[76]

Although he could abandon other, non–Nation of Islam Muslims, he never abandoned the Qur'an. Drew Ali, having produced his own scripture, needed merely the name to claim prophetic authority. Elijah Muhammad needed much more. His attachment to the Qur'an was rooted in his devotion to his Allah and his Islam. Moreover, for Elijah Muhammad the Qur'an was essential for the claim to "Islamic" legitimacy and authority, and for its independence from Christianity, which was seen as the religion of the "devil white race." Yet none of these requirements dictated that Elijah Muhammad be bound by the traditional interpretations of the Qur'an.

4

The Major "Islamic" Themes in Elijah Muhammad's Quranic Commentary

Since the Qur'an is thought by most Muslims to be the speech of Allah in the form of a book (a belief that closely parallels Christian theology based on John 1:1-14, which sees Jesus as the Word of God in the form of a person), the Qur'an is the primary source of all Islamic beliefs, practices, and laws. So, were one to question the validity of any of Elijah Muhammad's teachings as Islamic, one would probably do so by contrasting them with the teachings of the Qur'an. This, however, would be surprisingly difficult to do, because the Qur'an was his scripture too, and he found support for many of his teachings within it. For over forty years Elijah Muhammad interpreted the Qur'an for his followers. He could be viewed, therefore, as the first and only major African American *mufassir*—quranic exegete.[1]

Elijah Muhammad produced no systematic *tafsīr*, or commentary on the Qur'an, and none of Elijah Muhammad's writings even takes the form of traditional commentaries. Obviously, Elijah Muhammad with his odd doctrines felt no need to rely on traditional *tafsīr bi-l-ma'thūr* (transmitted exegesis) to understand the Qur'an. He was completely unfamiliar with the vast *tafsīr* literature produced over the fourteen centuries of Islam. Elijah Muhammad was well aware of the critiques by other Muslims of his teachings, but still felt no compulsion to defer to their interpretations; his interpretations came from Allah himself, and because he was Allah's Messenger, those interpretations were beyond question. So, he was not a *mufassir* in the traditional sense despite the aforementioned forty years of reading and interpreting the Qur'an.

The way Elijah Muhammad adapted the Qur'an to the twentieth-century African American milieu is evident in some of his most important

"Islamic" teachings. Oddly, for some of his teachings that seem to lend themselves to drawing on material from the Qur'an, such as his teachings about Allah, creation, other prophets, the protection of women, and fasting, Elijah Muhammad felt no need to avail himself of the scripture. However, for discussions of his race myth about Yakub, his eschatology about the Fall of America, his regulations on diet, his polemics against hypocrites, and his description of prayer, he often does. These ten major themes within his formulation of Islam provide a good overview of the concerns of Elijah Muhammad and his exegetical techniques, that is, when he chooses to use any.[2] With this background the question of whether Elijah Muhammad can be considered a real *mufassir* can be addressed.

The Theology of Allah(s)

There are two major ways in which Elijah Muhammad's conception of Allah differs from a more "orthodox" Muslim interpretation. First, he identifies Fard Muhammad with Allah. Since the Qur'an identifies a *mushrik* (one "who associates" things or persons with Allah) as the antithesis of a Muslim, it is not surprising that Elijah Muhammad does not use the Qur'an to justify his conception. This does not prevent him from assuming, however, that most quranic references to Allah are to Fard Muhammad. Second, he seems to ignore the doctrine that Allah is one. That is to say, Elijah Muhammad is not a strict monotheist:

> There were more Gods than One god. We are just now coming into the One God. The One God is Present to Change the world into a new world . . . a world of His Choice and of His Making. But, between This God there were many other gods, from the Creation until today. Each God had a limited time to rule. The time of rule of Yakub's made man (white man) was limited to 6,000 years. But, before this one[,] God had 25,000–35,000 years to rule. Then, His Wisdom was replaced by another God. All of these Gods who rule from 25,000–35,000 years, were Black People. Do not get the idea that they were gods of different colors, as we never had any colored gods until the Black god Yakub made a colored god.[3]

His willingness to admit that even Yakub was a god, who made a "colored god," indicates that Elijah Muhammad does not conceive of gods as necessarily omnipotent, omniscient, omnibenevolent, and eternal.

One of the functions of these gods is to create scripture. In the *Lost-Found Lesson 2*, which is ascribed to Fard Muhammad but the bulk of which consists of Elijah Muhammad's answers to Fard Muhammad's questions, the origin of scriptures is addressed:

1. Who made the Holy Koran or Bible? How long ago? Will you tell us why does Islam re-new her history every twenty-five thousand years?

Ans.—The Holy Koran or Bible is made by the original people, who is Allah, the supreme being, or (black man) of Asia; the Koran will expire in the year twenty-five thousand. Nine thousand and eight years from the date of this writing [sic] the Nation of Islam is all wise and does everything right and exact. The planet Earth, which is the home of Islam and is approximately twenty-five thousand miles in circumference, so the wise man of the East (black man) makes history or [the] Koran, to equal his home['s] circumference, [that is,] a year to every mile and thus every time his history lasts twenty-five thousand years, he re-news it for another twenty-five thousand years.[4]

Elijah Muhammad's belief in a future book provided by Fard Muhammad may be linked to this belief—though it does not fit the 25,000-year framework (even if one accepts his belief that the Qur'an is some fifteen thousand years old, that is, written eighty-four hundred years before Yakub began his eugenics program).[5]

The god in the person of Fard Muhammad had a unique function. He was to serve as a savior of his people. "Before we ever suffered ourselves, Master W. Fard Muhammad, our God and Savior, the Great Mahdi, Almighty God Allah in Person, Himself suffered persecution and rejection. All for you and for me!"[6] The notion of "suffering" and "persecution" is reminiscent of Christianity's god in the person of Jesus. However, Elijah Muhammad added that the Savior was not sent for the Jews, nor was he sent to save African Americans from sin in the Christian sense: "A Savior has come to save you from sin, not because you are by nature a sinner but because you have followed a sinner. You have been taught by a sinner."[7] His desire to make this distinction from Christianity was made easier through his adoption of the Islamic term "mahdi," which refers to a messianic figure in Shi'i Islam and in Sunni Islam (though the Mahdi is less accepted and less important in the latter).

Despite this more Islamic term, finding quranic support is problematic. Elijah Muhammad wrote with regard to the many titles of Fard

Muhammad, "These meanings are good and befitting as titles, but the meaning of his name 'Mahdi,' as mentioned in the Holy Qur-an Sharrieff 22:54, is better. All of these names refer to Him. His name, Fard Muhammad, is beautiful in its meaning. He must bring an end to war, and the only way to end war between man and man is to destroy the war-maker (the trouble-maker)."[8] Oddly, neither Yusuf Ali nor Muhammad Ali, the translators of the Qur'ans employed by Elijah Muhammad, identify Qur'an 22:54 with the Mahdi. The verse contains the expression, "Allah is the Guide" ("*hādi*"), which is etymologically related to "*mahdi*," but not identical to it. Therefore, it is unclear how Elijah Muhammad came to associate this verse with the Mahdi. However, because of the identification of Mirza Ghulam Ahmad as the Mahdi, an Ahmadiyya connection seems likely.

The Heavens and the Earth

Another role assigned to Allah in the Qur'an is that of creator. Elijah Muhammad does not have a creation story, but states that the earth as we know it is sixty-six trillion years old and was formed when God, failing to unite the people in one language as he wanted, decided to destroy the planet by blasting it in two. The Asiatic black tribe of Shabazz survived the division of the planet into earth and moon and settled in the Nile Valley and Mecca. Africa is, for Elijah Muhammad, East Asia.[9] He explained,

> His idea was to force his rule upon the people of our planet and force all to speak the same dialect, which He was not able to do. Then he decided to destroy all, including the earth and Himself. He went to work by attempting to drill a tube into the earth's surface. It must have reached approximately the center of the earth. Then He filled it with high explosives which we call dynamite. However, it was 30 per cent more powerful than the present dynamite. Then He set it off. This explosion blasted away a piece of our then-earth, which according to the moon's diameter is approximately 2,160 miles, or about 1/3 the size of our planet earth.[10]

This moon turned and emptied its water onto the remaining earth and as a result, was unable to sustain life. Elijah Muhammad found this lack of water significant and claimed that dry riverbeds would be found on the moon. Furthermore, the moon's separation from the earth and its current lifelessness symbolized the history of African Americans, and its age of sixty-six trillion years symbolized the 6,600-year existence of the white race.[11]

This revived interest in the moon in Elijah Muhammad's writings of the late 1960s and early 1970s was sparked by man's (i.e., "the white man's") landing on the moon. This ability reflected not their power, but Allah's, who gave them the power.[12] Prior to the moon landing, however, Elijah Muhammad had suggested, following Qur'an 72:8, that the heavens are protected by guards and flames (meaning, for him, meteors). The lack of water and oxygen, and particularly the moon's magnetic power, would kill the unshielded astronauts.[13]

Fard Muhammad seems to have had a significant interest in astronomy, or at least the solar system (or perhaps just the "heavens"). While this is not a particularly prominent feature in the teachings of either man, Fard Muhammad taught Elijah Muhammad that, though the moon is lifeless, Mars is not.

> Allah (God) Could Prevent the white man from seeing a creature of Mars. Allah (God) Talks with the Martians, for He Knows their language. I would like to see one of those people myself as Allah (God) Taught me what they look like. But that is up to Allah (God) whether or not he will let me see one. Allah (God) May Let me see one.

These people on Mars live to the age of twelve hundred years.[14] Elsewhere he warned,

> Allah (God) taught me that the Original Black Man has pictures of the people on Mars and even has extracted their language and now understands how to communicate with them in their own language. This, the white man would like to learn: if this is true or not, by his exploration of space and the planets. I am sorry, Mr. White Man, these are secrets that you are not permitted to learn. You may be able to send a camera over the planets, but I advise you to stay away from them.[15]

Once again, given the Qur'an's focus on the heavens as signs of Allah's power and goodness, Elijah Muhammad's failure to cite the Qur'an in this context seems odd.

Prophets and Prophethood

The same is true for Islamic prophets, who are mentioned ubiquitously in the Qur'an. This neglect is particularly evident in Elijah Muhammad's elaborate reinterpretation of the life of Jesus. Mary became pregnant by Joseph out of wedlock—though they were engaged. Joseph was only willing to claim the child after he was told that his son would turn out be a prophet one day. After the birth of the child, Mary fled on a camel to Egypt to protect herself (as an unwed mother) and Jesus from Jews. Among the "black people" of Egypt, he was safe. There, he was told by an old prophet that he would be the last of the prophets to the Jews. After completing his schooling with the old prophet, Jesus returned to the land of the Jews—making no attempt to teach the Arabs and Blacks of Egypt or Africa, for he was never meant to be their prophet. After twenty-two years, Jesus learned that these "infidels" could not be reformed, and opted to sacrifice his life for Islam. After an altercation with a Jew in front of his store, Jesus was arrested. The reward for Jesus was fifteen hundred dollars if brought in alive and twenty-five hundred dollars in gold if brought in dead. So, the officer suggested to Jesus that, since he was planning to give himself up to be killed anyway, Jesus allow him to kill him painlessly with a knife. Jesus agreed. So the officer took Jesus to a deserted store (boarded up to protect the glass windows from stone-throwing boys). There, with his arms stretched out against the wall, and therefore in the shape of a cross, he was stabbed in the back through the heart. Jesus died instantly and pinned in that position until the authorities came. Jesus was embalmed and buried in Jerusalem.

> No Christian is allowed to see the body, unless they pay a price of $6,000 and must get a certificate from the Pope of Rome. The tomb is guarded by Muslims. When Christians are allowed to see Jesus' body, they are stripped of their weapons, handcuffed behind their backs, and well-armed Muslim guards take them into the tomb. But, Muslims can go to see his body at any time without charge.

The source of this myth and its fairly elaborate details is unknown, but it clearly does not draw from material on Jesus in the Qur'an. Elijah Muhammad was aware of the Ahmadiyya claim that Jesus died in Kashmir, but he dismissed it.[16]

Elijah Muhammad wrote that Fard Muhammad had taught him that it was Nimrod who was born on December 25, not Jesus, who had been born during the first or second week of September. Nimrod was born as an opponent to Moses' teachings. Thus the teachings of Moses lasted not two thousand years but only seventeen hundred, for they were cut short by the three hundred years of Nimrod's teachings. Nimrod was an "evil, devil man."[17]

Very little is said about Muhammad and Moses. Moses attempted to civilize the white devils in Europe two thousand years after their creation. The prophet Jesus came to the Jews (i.e., those who had earlier followed Moses) only to have his message misinterpreted by the white race for its own purposes. He was followed by the prophet Muhammad, who helped keep the white Christians in check for a thousand years.

The only other messenger to receive attention is Elijah Muhammad. Not only had he been instructed face-to-face by Allah but Elijah Muhammad also continued to receive instructions from Fard Muhammad. In 1972 he described these communications:

> I do not say really visions, but I do have voices at times. . . . That comes when I am not, say, really confining myself to expect something like that or seeking something like that. That just comes—just so. . . . I know God. I was with Him about three years and about four or five months. I know His voice. And when He Speaks, I know it. . . . It is the Same Voice. In the past and at the present, I have not had to go into such things as fasting and praying that I hear Him or see Him. Whenever I hear him, it is just so. Just like something happens all of a sudden out of a blue sky, like thunder. . . . Whenever the time is necessary that He Speak to me. How often that takes place? I do not keep a record of it. . . . I have had Him Speaking to me in my ears now, in Person yes. There does not pass a year, that I do not Hear His Voice some time in that year.[18]

That Elijah Muhammad was not merely claiming divine inspiration for his own ideas is made clear by his occasional willingness to admit that he had not received some knowledge from Allah. For example, with respect to the dietary habits of Martians, he said, "I do not know what they eat of their planet life, as Allah (God) did not Teach me what they eat. And I did not ask Him in the first place."[19] Likewise, he did not know exactly when the Fall of America would take place or when the future book would be revealed. Thus, not only did he distinguish between his ideas and those he believed to come from Allah, but he also did not always get the information he wished to receive from Allah.

Elijah Muhammad also did not comment on the founders of other major religions. He did, however, occasionally comment on other religions:

> The true religion of Allah and His Prophets Noah, Abraham, Moses and Jesus was Islam, and it is to overcome all religions. *"He (Allah) it is, who sent His Apostle with the guidance and the true religion, that he may make it overcome all other religions, though the Polytheists may be averse"*—THE HOLY QURAN 61:9. That is why the white race and the Indian Hindus have always been and are now enemies of Islam and Muslims.[20]

In *The Supreme Wisdom*, Elijah Muhammad also comments on Buddhism. In the pericope entitled "Christianity, Budhism [sic], and Islam," he stated, "What a difference there is between the three religions! The first teaches that there are three Gods, not one. It also requires worship of Mary, the mother of Jesus, and of the desciples [sic] of Jesus. The second, Buddhism, requires belief in 're-carnation,' [sic] and contains many ignorant practices."[21]

Women

Generally, when Elijah Muhammad addressed issues related to women, he did so by telling men how they should protect and control their wives and daughters. Men were told, "The woman is the man's field to produce his nation. If he does not keep the enemy out of his field, he won't produce a good nation." This may be a reference to Qur'an 2:223 ("Your wives are a tilth for you"). It is one of the very few allusions Elijah Muhammad makes to scripture on the subject.

His views on the nature and role of women were explicitly patriarchal, with a strong emphasis on men controlling women. He generally addressed men, not women:

> Our women are allowed to walk or ride the streets all night long, with any strange men they desire. They are allowed to frequent any tavern or dance hall that they like, whenever they like. They are allowed to fill our homes with children other than our own. Children that are often fathered by the very devil himself. . . . Islam will not only elevate your women

but will also give you the power to control and protect them. . . . Stop our women from trying to look like them [that is, the white race]. By bleaching, powdering, ironing and coloring their hair; painting their lips, cheeks and eyebrows; wearing shorts; going half-nude in public places; going swimming with them and lying on beaches with men. Have private pools for your women and guard them from all men. Stop them from going into bars and taverns and sitting and drinking with men and strangers. Stop them from sitting in those places with anyone. Stop them from using unclean language in public (and at home), from smoking and drug addiction habits.[22]

When he did address women directly, it was on a limited number of subjects. These included prohibiting the marriage of his female followers to "foreigners"—defined in such a way as to include Muslims who were not part of the Nation of Islam. He also mandated the robes and head gear that he had designed; African tribal styles were forbidden. Failure to follow these instructions meant a woman was no longer his follower.[23]

The most oft-repeated directive for women was the practice of modesty. For several years, *Muhammad Speaks* included a short column with two drawings: the first was a white woman standing beside her daughter and the second a black woman and her daughter. All four are in miniskirts whose hemline is just above the knee. Although the captions changed, most commonly "The Shyless" and "The Disgrace" appeared over each, respectively. In between was Qur'an 7:27, which warns the "children of Adam" not to let the "arch deceiver" seduce them as he had seduced their parents (presumably, Adam and Eve) and then pulled off their clothes. Elijah Muhammad explained that Yakub did this to the black people who followed him from Arabia.[24] For him, miniskirts were Yakub's white race's efforts to strip black people naked once again. Elsewhere, he accused black women of being "half-nude" and "like wild game in the jungle" when they wore dresses that came above the knee. Elijah Muhammad urged women to wear dresses that came below the knee, and better yet, halfway down the calf of the leg, for "the woman who is modestly dressed, always looks better to a man."[25] Qur'an 24:31—"And say to the believing women that they lower their gaze and restrain their sexual passions and do not display their adornment except what appears thereof. And let them wear their head-coverings over their bosoms"—the most obvious of several quranic verses for Elijah Muhammad to cite on this subject, is not cited.

Fasting

Members of the Nation of Islam did not fast during the month of Ramadan, as most other Muslims do. Elijah Muhammad earlier explained the reasoning and the practice of the December fast:

> We fast the 12th month of the Christian year to relieve ourselves of the once worshipping of that month as the month in which Jesus was born. . . .
>
> In this month of fasting, we shall keep our minds and hearts clean, and we shall not indulge in the eating of meats (land meats). You may eat fish and such fat products which come from land animals such as butter and cheese.
>
> In this month, we should keep our minds on Allah, Who came in the Person of Master Frad [sic] Muhammad; my God and your God and my Saviour and Deliverer and your Saviour and Deliverer to Whom be praised forever for giving us life after our mental death for the past 400 years.
>
> During this month, eat before day and after the sun goes down (if you wish) but not during the daylight hours. This also goes for drinking; drink whatever you are going to drink either before dawn or after dark. The eating before dawn is for those of us who love to eat breakfast in the mornings. But if you eat one meal a day, you may eat that meal either before dawn or after dark. It is best for your health's sake, however, to eat one meal after dark.
>
> Keep up prayer, and let us all be grateful to Allah for His coming in the Person of Master Fard Muhammad throughout the month of December and every month. And during this month, let there be no quarrelling or disputing in our homes or abroad.[26]

Elsewhere, Elijah Muhammad adds that "fasting takes away evil desires. Fasting takes from us filthy desires. Fasting takes from us the desire to do evil against self and our brothers and sisters."[27]

In the early 1970s, he declared that what Muslims, both his Muslims and "orthodox Muslims," do is not fasting. Abstaining from food for part of the day is not a fast. Only going two days, preferably three days, without food can be considered a fast. He also challenged other Muslims' fast during Ramadan in several ways. (1) Muslims fast to celebrate the revelation of the Qur'an, but Elijah Muhammad pointed out that the Qur'an was revealed over a 23-year period. (2) Even so, the coming of the Qur'an should be rejoiced, whereas fasting aids in forestalling evil desires. Elijah Muhammad's December fast, by contrast, was designed to "drive out . . . the old white slave-master's worship of a false birthday (December 25th) of Jesus." (3) Fasting, according to Elijah Muhammad, is something one does in hopes of receiving something. So, he asked, why fast when the Qur'an was first revealed without any fasting having taken place?[28] Therefore, the switch to the fast of Ramadan a year later was a significant concession on the part of Elijah Muhammad. Again, entirely absent from all of his discussions on fasting is any reference to the many passages in the Qur'an enjoining fasting and extolling its virtues.

Yakub and the White Devils

Given the limited use of the Qur'an by Elijah Muhammad for the aforementioned "Islamic" themes, it is surprising that one of the main uses to which Elijah Muhammad put both the Qur'an and the Bible was that of proving the part of his myth of origins that deals with the white race. He finds support for even its least "Islamic" features: the creation of the devils by Yakub, their exile to Europe, and the six thousand years during which the white race was permitted by Allah to rule the world. This period has been a time of war and destruction in which they used their "tricknology"[29] and spread their wickedness over the whole earth. The greatest crimes of the white race were manifest in the invasion of America, the stealing of the land of the Native Indians, and the capture and enslavement of Africans. For three hundred years these slaves were forced to work and shed their blood for a nation that repaid them with hatred.

Elijah Muhammad supported many parts of this race myth with scriptural references. According to him, that Whites were created by the original black people is demonstrated by the use of the first person plural pronouns "we" and "us," in both the Qur'an's and the Bible's accounts of the creation.[30] Thus, in the phrase, "Let us make man in our image" of Genesis 1:26, the "us" refers to the 59,999 "black men and women making or grafting them into the likeness or image of the original man."[31] The Qur'an is specifically said to support this claim in 15:28: "Surely I am going to create a mortal of the essence of black mud fashioned in shape." The black mud is, for Elijah Muhammad, "the black nation."[32] Thus, the creation story in Genesis and its parallels in the Qur'an are seen as the record not of the creation of humankind but of the creation of the white race. Adam represents the white race; the tree of knowledge of good and evil is the creator of the white race, Yakub; the tree of life is the Nation of Islam (that is, the black Muslim people); and the expulsion from the Garden of Eden is the exile to Europe.[33] Elijah Muhammad asserted that their time in the caves of Europe has a whole chapter devoted to it in the Qur'an—presumably Qur'an 18 (The Cave).[34] Even the respite given to the devil white race to make mischief in the world is "foretold" in the Qur'an. Elijah Muhammad explained,

> The Holy Qur-an says: "But the devil made them both fall from it, and caused them to depart from that (state) in which they were; and we said: "Get forth, some of you being the enemies of others, and there is for you in the earth an abode and a provision for a time!" (The time here refers to the limited time of the Adamic race. The time is 6,000 years.)[35]

The next verse speaks of Adam learning words from his Lord—"the Oft-returning and the merciful." These terms describe Allah, not Yakub. But this interaction of Allah with Adam is incongruent with Elijah Muhammad's interpretations. The apparent contradiction is not noticed, suggesting that Elijah Muhammad tended to read the verses of the Qur'an as discrete, unconnected entities.

A similar apparent inconsistent reading is evident in Elijah Muhammad's discussion of Adam's (that is, the white race's) evil fondness for nudity. He wrote,

> Chapter 7, 26th Verse: O children of Adam we have sent down to you clothing to cover your shame, and clothing for beauty, and clothing that guards against evil. That is the best. This is the message of Allah that they may be mindful.
>
> This is referring to the white race, after they stripped off their clothes and were naked in the caves and hillsides of Europe to remind them today that they were given clothes to cover their body and shame, and then He clothed them with beauty, the clothing that guards against evil.

In his paraphrase, Elijah Muhammad makes clear that the expression "children of Adam" means the white race. Regarding the very next verse and just two paragraphs later, he wrote,

Chapter 7, 27th Verse: O children of Adam let not the devil seduce you as he expelled your parents from the garden, pulling off from them their clothing that he might show them their shame. He surely sees you. He as well as his host from which you see them not. Surely He made the Devil's [sic] to be the friends of those who believe not.

Those who believe not is referring to the American so-called Negro (Black Man). The devil becomes their friends and guardians and they adopt indecency and the devil's way of civilization, and thus become the enemy of God and their Nation of righteousness (Black Nation). And therefore, their doom is that of the devil's (white man).[36]

Here the devil is the white race and "those who believe not" are African Americans not of the Nation of Islam. Either Elijah Muhammad also permits "children of Adam" to refer to the latter, or the former must rather awkwardly refer to both those who seduce and those who are seduced. This is only an issue when the two adjacent verses are read as connected to each other—which is not Elijah Muhammad's wont.

By examining a longer, representative passage by Elijah Muhammad on this subject, one can see even more clearly his handling of scriptural materials:

The Bible and the Holy Qur-an Sharrieff are full of teachings of this bloody race of devils. They shed the life blood of all life, even their own, and are scientists at deceiving the black people.

They deceived the very people of Paradise (Bible, Gen. 2:13). They killed their own brother (Gen. 4:8). The innocent earth's blood (Gen. 4:10) revealed it to its Maker (thy brother's blood cryeth unto me from the ground). The very earth, the soil of America, soaked with the innocent blood of the so-called Negroes shed by this race of devils, now crieth out to its maker for her burden of carrying the innocent blood of the righteous slain upon her. Let us take a look at the devil's creation from the teaching of the Holy Qur-an.

"And when your Lord said to the angels, I am going to place in the earth one who shall rule, the angels said: "What will Thou place in it such as shall make mischief in it and shed blood, we celebrate Thy praise and extol Thy holiness"["] (Holy Qur-an Sharrieff 2:30).

This devil race has and still is doing just that—making mischief and shedding blood of the black nation whom they were grafted from. Your

Lord said to the angels, "Surely I am going to create a mortal of the essence of black mud fashioned in shape" (Holy Qur-an Sharrieff, 15:28).

The essence of black mud (the black nation) mentioned is only symbolic, which actually means the sperm of the black nation, and they refused to recognize the black nation as their equal though they were made from and by a black scientist (named Yakub).[37]

Several observations can be made from this passage. First, Elijah Muhammad had no difficulty moving between the Bible and the Qur'an—though he hardly did so seamlessly. Second, individual verses are again treated as discrete entities and adduced as needed with little regard to their original context. Third, the verses are made to fit his narrative. That is to say, the race myth is the framework into which both quranic and biblical verses were placed.

The Fall of America

Along with the events of the creation of the white race, the eschatological events that culminate around the "so-called Negroes" in America are among the most frequently and thoroughly discussed by Elijah Muhammad, who devoted numerous columns to the subject (that were later collected into *The Fall of America*). For him, the events of the last day have been foretold in the Qur'an and the Bible. Allah in the person of Master Fard Muhammad, the Mahdi, the Messiah, came from Mecca in 1930 in fulfillment of the prophecies to resurrect the "mentally dead so-called Negroes" and to initiate the end of the rule of the devil. The first of these tasks involved teaching Blacks the true history of the world and their true religion of Islam so that they could escape hell, which is the world of the Whites, and enter heaven, which is now, here on earth; there is no life beyond the grave in which one can hope for justice, freedom, and equality, just as there is no "spook" god. The second task involved the coming war of Armageddon. As we have seen, Allah will first punish America with the weapons of nature: floods, drought, hailstorms, fire, earthquakes, and so forth. Only territorial separation (achieved by dividing up the continental United States) will protect the (144,000)[38] Muslims from this punishment of white America. Later, Allah will destroy England and the United States using a spaceship known as the Mother Plane.

According to Elijah Muhammad, "The Mother Plane was made to destroy this world of evil and to show the Wisdom and Mighty Power of the God Who Came to Destroy an old world and set up a new world." It is the wheel that appeared in Ezekiel's vision. This Mother Plane, "a little human-made planet," can travel forty miles above the earth's surface, but returns to the earth every six to twelve months for oxygen and hydrogen. According to Elijah Muhammad, the "devil scientists" are aware of its existence and have unsuccessfully sought to destroy it. It can hide behind stars and make itself invisible. "There are scientists on the Mother Plane who know what you are thinking about before the thought materializes (Holy Quran Ch. 50:16). Therefore, it is impossible to try to attack the Mother Plane. She can attack you, but you cannot attack her." When it attacks, it will do so with bombs that will fall upon cities only, burrow into the ground for one mile, and then explode. These are the same types of bombs that were once used to create the mountains on earth.[39]

According to his early writings, the Fall of America should have begun in 1965 or 1966.[40] "[I]t is the end of the time of the white race. This race of people was not created to live on our planet forever; only for six thousand years."[41] This dating is a bit confusing, for the prophesied four hundred years of being lost in the wilderness of North America came to an end in 1955,[42] yet the end of the 6,000-year rule of Whites was said to have occurred in 1914. The significance of this earlier year is also unclear, though it may be connected to C. T. Russell's predictions of a 1914 Armageddon and, later, Jehovah's Witnesses' assertions that 1914 was the beginning of the last days. Elijah Muhammad probably came in contact with Judge Rutherford's teachings through the radio broadcasts. According to one scholar, it was some time just prior to the year 1914 that the "brothers in the East" became aware of the "lost Nation in the wilderness of North America."[43] The date of judgment of the white world was therefore delayed approximately sixty years to allow African Americans time to reconvert to Islam.[44] On the other hand, Elijah Muhammad wrote of an extension being granted by Allah, depending on how the "righteous" were treated. He then echoed the claim that there can be no judgment until the "so-called Negroes hear Islam."[45] Whenever it is, "Hell" will then come to an end and the eternal period of "Heaven" will be ushered in.

Just as the first book of the Christian Bible, Genesis, figured very prominently in Elijah Muhammad's account of creation, so its last book, the Book of Revelation, was the main source for the prophecies of "the Judgement," as he called it. It is Yakub, the father of the white race, who is said to have written the Book of Revelation. Sixty-six hundred years ago, while exiled to the Island of Pelan, he foresaw the future of the people he had created. The Qur'an, with its vivid descriptions of the Last Day, also seems to have lent itself to Elijah Muhammad's eschatological narrative. His methods were the same as those used for his race myth: the biblical and quranic materials are subservient to his larger narrative, with verses usually treated as discrete entities and cited as appropriate with simple glosses of ambiguous or symbolic terms.

Thus, the devil that Allah will destroy, according to Qur'an 7:14, is the white race.[46] Whites are also the "beast" of the Book of Revelation and the "man of sin" in II Thessalonians 2:2–9.[47] And, the Babylon of the Book of Revelation and of Jeremiah is America. Elijah Muhammad explained,

> The description it [Rev. 18:2] gives is as follows: "And he *(angel)* cried might[i]ly with a strong voice *(with authority)* saying, Babylon the great is fallen, is fallen and is become the habitation of devils *(Allah has declared the people to be a race of devils)*, and the hole of every foul spirit and a cage of every unclean and hateful bird." *The description here given to the* [sic] *Babylon by the Prophets compares with the present history and people of America and their fall.*[48]

Elijah Muhammad then identified the "unclean and hateful bird" as the "low-based, evil-minded" immigrants to America whose uncleanliness consisted of sexual promiscuity and homosexuality. The so-called American Negroes were addressed by the subsequent verse: "Come out of her that ye be not partakers of her sins and that you receive not of her plagues."[49] For Elijah Muhammad there was a sense of urgency, for America's prophesied end, for which Qur'an 56:57–59 provides evidence, was imminent.[50]

With regard to the battle between Islam and other religions, Elijah Muhammad taught,

> "He is it who sent His Apostle with the guidance and the True religion that he make it overcome the religions, all of them, though the polytheists may be averse." (The Holy Quran, 61:9)
>
> In the above verse Allah (God) in the last days of this present world (of wicked infidels) states that He must destroy false religions with the True Religion Islam. It (Islam) must overcome all other religions.[51]

Through paraphrase and gloss, Elijah Muhammad interpreted this verse, traditionally thought to refer to the Prophet Muhammad's mission to the pagans of the pre-Islamic Arabia, as referring to his own mission. The scriptural support for Elijah Muhammad's description of the matériel to be used in this battle, the forces of nature, was drawn primarily from the Bible, such as Ezekiel 14:13, though Qur'an 44:10 was presented to support Allah's promise to use drought. Other references that proved Allah's penchant for the use of natural disasters to punish evildoers, such as the use of water against the people of Noah, fire against Sodom and Gomorrah, and plagues against Pharaoh and his people, could have come from either scripture.[52]

After this war and the Fall of America, there will be a time of joy and peace in the presence of Allah. There will be no war, sickness, gambling, cursing, and so forth. Hell will be at an end. The hereafter is, however, eternal and everyone will live much longer. Of course, there will be no bodily resurrection of the dead, nor will the living remain alive forever—that is slavery teaching, according to Elijah Muhammad. The resurrection is a psychological, social, economic, and political one. None of the numerous verses in the Qur'an that speak of physical resurrection was included in this discussion—though elsewhere he made it clear that such verses are to be interpreted metaphorically. He adduced only the invitation of Qur'an 89:27–30: "O soul that is at rest, return to your Lord, well pleased with Him, well pleasing. So, enter among my servants, and enter into my Paradise."[53]

Again, a longer passage illustrates Elijah Muhammad's handling of scriptural texts:

The day of decision between the dark races or nations was begun by God Himself in the person of Master Fard Muhammad, to Whom be praised forever, as is prophesied in the Bible: "Multitudes in the valley of decision, for the day *(before or by 1970)* of the Lord is near in the valley of decision" (Joel 3:14).

It is clear that the armies of the nations of the earth have geared themselves for a showdown between their forces and Allah and the Nation of Islam. We, the so-called American Negroes, the lost and found members of our Nation, are in this decision. The second and third verses of this same chapter (Chapter 3) read like this: "I will also gather all nations and will bring them down into the valley of Jehoshaphat *(Europe and Asia— between black and white)* and will plead with them there for my people and my heritage *(the lost and found, so-called Negroes),* Israel whom they have scattered among the nations and parted my land *(between the*

European white race) and they have casted lots for my people and have given a boy for a harlot and sold a girl for wine that they might drink" (Joel 3:2,3).

America has fulfilled this to the very letter and spirit with her slaves (the so-called Negroes) under the type of Israel. The Egyptians did nothing of the kind to Israel when they were in bondage to them. In fact, and as God has taught me, the Bible is not referring to those people as His People, it is referring to the so-called Negro and his enemy (the white race). The seventh verse also gives us a hint in this way:

"Behold, I will raise them out of the place where you have sold them and will return your recompence upon your own head" (Joel 3:7).

The slave-masters of our fathers must reap what they have sown. Allah calls them to war in the ninth verse of the same chapter.

"Proclaim you among the Gentiles, prepare war, wake up the mighty men, let all of the men of war draw near, let them come up" (Joel 3:9).

All the mighty men of science and modern warfare have been called in an effort to devise instruments and weapons against God and the armies of heaven.[54]

Once again, there are several features of note. First, Elijah Muhammad felt no obligation to include any quranic material. Second, he employed intralinear comments that identify (what were for him) ambiguous or symbolic words or phrases. Third, the scriptural passages, both these from the Book of Joel and those previously cited from the Qur'an, appeared within the framework of Elijah Muhammad's narrative of the Fall of America.

Towards the end of his life, Elijah Muhammad reiterated that all Whites are devils, but then in response to a white reporter's question "Is there any hope for me?" replied in a manner atypical of, inconsistent with, and far more generous than, earlier statements on the issue:

Now, I must tell you the truth. There will be no such thing as elimination of all white people from the earth, at the present time or at the break out of the Holy War. No, because there are some white people today who have faith in Allah and Islam though they are white, and their faith is given credit. They are not born or created Muslims, but they have faith in what the Muslims are and [how they are] trying to live. It is only through Islam that white people can be saved. But you see there would be a Holy War (they call it a Holy War which means right is against wrong and wrong against right).[55]

Dietary Laws

Elijah Muhammad often wrote on the dangers of pork, which he had learned from Fard Muhammad. From 1965 onward, he published numerous articles in *Muhammad Speaks* on what he considered a proper Muslim diet. Many of these articles reappeared in his *How to Eat to Live*, first published in 1968, and in his *How to Eat to Live, Book No. 2*, first published in 1973. Elijah Muhammad's purpose in writing *How to Eat to Live* was to teach his followers how to attain good health and prolong their lives by controlling the food and drink they consume. Although this subject involves no significant narrative, similar patterns emerge with respect to Elijah Muhammad's use of the Bible, the Qur'an, and his own authority.

The most prominent feature of Elijah Muhammad's dietary regulations was his prohibition of the consumption of pork. This prohibition, along with the requirement that his Muslims eat only one meal a day, was treated at length and mentioned continuously throughout *How to Eat to Live*. His main argument against pork rested on his own authority and his access to unique knowledge, divine or scientific. Elijah Muhammad argued,

> Beyond a shadow of a doubt the swine is the filthiest and foulest animal human beings have resorted to for food. . . . Worms and insects take to its flesh while in the farmer's curing stage faster than to any other animal's flesh. And in a few days, it is full of worms. . . . It is divinely pro[h]ibited flesh, and God (Allah) has prohibited you and me, my brothers and sisters of the Black Nation, from eating it or even touching its dead carcass. Please, for our health's sake, stop eating it; for our beauty's sake, stop eating it; for our obedience to God and His laws against this flesh, stop eating it; for a longer life, stop eating it[;] and for the sake of modesty, stop eating it.[56]

The Qur'an could have provided ample support for Elijah Muhammad's prohibition. Qur'an 2:173, 5:3, 6:145, and 16:115 all forbid pork. However, these four verses were never explicitly cited. And although Elijah Muhammad stated three times that the food of (orthodox) Jews is acceptable according to the Qur'an, the passage that verifies this claim, Qur'an 5:5, was not invoked.[57] This oversight once again suggests the lack of a comprehensive familiarity with the contents of the Qur'an on the part of Elijah Muhammad. On the other hand, the Bible played a relatively greater role in his arguments. The prohibition against swine in Leviticus 11:7–8, the warning to those who do eat it in Isaiah 66:17, and the casting of demons into swine by Jesus were all discussed at length.[58]

Elijah Muhammad frequently employed the phrases "Allah taught me" and "Allah has said." But he clearly was not making references to the Qur'an when he did so: he meant Fard Muhammad. This is particularly evident when he discussed animals not mentioned in the Bible or the Qur'an. For instance, chickens are dirty animals, but permissible to eat; beef, lamb, and camel are also permissible, but should be avoided if possible; rabbit, deer, raccoons, possums, turtles, turtle eggs, and frog legs are not permissible.[59] The distinction between Allah's direct words and those mediated by the Qur'an was made explicit when Elijah Muhammad stated, "The main thing Allah, as well as the Qur-an, reminds us of is that when it comes to meat and fish, Allah forbids us to eat the flesh of swine or of fish weighing 50 pounds or more."[60] At times, Elijah Muhammad seemed very defensive, such as when he stated, "The hog is a grafted animal, so says Allah to me—grafted from rat, cat and dog. Don't question me. This is what Allah has said, believe it or leave it alone."[61]

Hence, it is not surprising that for many of his dietary regulations Elijah Muhammad saw no need to provide scriptural evidence. Among the foods whose consumption was prohibited were collard greens, turnip leaves, white potatoes, sweet potatoes, peas, beans (except for the small navy beans, both the "brown pink" ones and the white ones), cornbread, and, of course, pork. On the other hand, spinach, rutabaga, and rice were acceptable, but in moderation. There were no restrictions on garlic, onions, fruits (better raw than cooked), whole wheat bread (as long as it is not fresh), and young pigeons. Elijah Muhammad justified these regulations by saying that the prohibited foods were cheap foods given to slaves by their slave masters, unfit for human consumption, suitable only for hogs, or not digestible for those with office jobs.[62] The only scriptural allusion was to Adam being told in the book of Genesis to eat whatever he wishes. Adam, of course, represents the white race for Elijah Muhammad, and so this passage from Genesis indicated, for him, that the white race eats much that is poisonous.[63]

One of the only extended passages of scripture cited by Elijah Muhammad to justify his dietary regulations is Isaiah 65:1–5:

I am sought of them that asked not for [me] *(The lost-found members of the Black Nation are the ones who never sought after Allah, because they did not know how. The enemy did not teach them how to seek Allah, since they did not obey Allah, themselves)*; I am found to them *(lost-found Black people—so-called Negro)* that sought me not: I said, Behold me, behold me, unto a nation that was not called by my name. I have spread out my hands all the day unto a rebellious people, which walketh in a way that was not good *(This is referring to Israel, to whom God sent prophet after prophet, to guide them into the right way, who rebelled against the right guidance and then made a religion called Christianity, after their way of thinking, and put the name of Jesus on that religion to make us drink down the falsity they added to Jesus' teachings)*, after their own thoughts; A people that provoketh me to anger continually to my face; that sacrificeth in gardens, and burneth incense upon altars of brick *(they barbeque the hog upon bricks and call it their barbeque stand)*; which remain among the graves *(the graves mean their homes)*, . . . which eat swine's flesh, and broth of the abominable things is in their vessels *(this is referring to hog or swine in their vessels)*; which say, stand by thyself *(This is referring to the Muslims, when it says stand by thyself)*, come not [near to me (]mean[s] only Israel or the white race, but the white race has made the so-called Negro follow his religion, say the same and especially those who claim santification [sic] in Christianity)*. These are a smoke *(the offensive smell of the cooking of swine flesh)* . . . a fire that burneth all the day *(the Christian is cooking the flesh of the swine all day long and the Muslims and the obedient servant of Allah (God), smell this flesh, prohibited by God, which is a stink to their nostrils, being cooked. They feel they are guilty of being partakers of the cooking and eating of the swine flesh, by smelling the poisonous odor.)*[64]

From this rather lengthy passage several notable exegetical techniques are evident. Once again the biblical material is more prominent than the quranic. Intralinear notes are common, many of them involving the glossing or specification of vague pronouns or terms—at least vague when taken out of their original context. This specification always transports the adduced text into a pronouncement on life and race relations in present-day America. And in that sense, even Elijah Muhammad's stipulations about dietary practice displayed a tendency to be subsumed under his larger narrative on the rise and fall of the white race.

The Hypocrites

There are two subjects, hypocrites and prayer, for which Elijah Muhammad employed almost exclusively quranic materials. The former was discussed under the heading of "Hypocrites, Disbelievers, and Obedience" in *Message to the Blackman in America*. A discussion of this nature was entirely absent from *The Supreme Wisdom* and almost so from *The Supreme Wisdom, Volume Two*. In the latter, only white Christians were identified as the "hypocrites of the first order."[65] The term "hypocrite" had initially applied to those followers of Fard Muhammad who opposed Elijah Muhammad's succession in Detroit in favor of some of Fard Muhammad's other ministers. Later, Elijah Muhammad used the term for his rivals in Chicago in the mid-1930s. In his weekly columns, it began to appear in the middle of 1959.[66] The term would never disappear for long from Elijah Muhammad's vocabulary, but it returned with a vengeance in the mid-1960s. As Claude Andrew Clegg explains in his biography, Elijah Muhammad,

> perhaps out of paranoia and his decades-old sense of persecution, came to believe that extreme measures were warranted when internecine challenges to his leadership emerged. If it meant . . . eliminating the "hypocrites" (now defined as anyone he believed to be a threat to his supremacy in the Nation) through suspensions, isolations, or even death, he was willing to do what was necessary.[67]

The renewed interest in the issue of hypocrites in 1964 and 1965 was precipitated by several events, including the appearance of complaints by members of the Nation of Islam about Elijah Muhammad and other officials having spent too much money on homes[68] and especially the defections of Malcolm X and Elijah Muhammad's sons Wallace and Akbar Muhammad.[69] He did not pull punches even with family members, calling hypocrites the "the most hated of all people" and the "enemies of Islam."[70] In 1968, in *Muhammad Speaks,* he reprinted over ten times the same column railing against hypocrites. From 1970 to 1972 occasional articles and columns on the theme appeared every few months.[71]

Elijah Muhammad was always vehement on the subject of hypocrites. In *Message to the Blackman in America* he began by arguing that Qur'an 32:3, "Thou mayest warn a people to whom no warner has come before that they may walk aright," referred to him and not to the Prophet

Muhammad. Mecca had had previous warners, Abraham and Ishmael. The prayer of Abraham, which in Qur'an 2:129 asks for a messenger to be sent to his people, refers, therefore, to none other than Elijah Muhammad himself. Likewise, the future prophet of Deuteronomy 18:18, who would be a prophet like Moses, is Elijah Muhammad as well, and the life of Moses' people is paralleled most closely by the "so-called Negroes of America."[72] Elijah Muhammad then launched into his diatribe against hypocrites. They are the most hated people; they are worse than disbelievers; they seek to deceive believers, they only pretend to be believers; and they befriend the enemies of Islam. But, they shall not overcome the Messenger. In support of these declarations Elijah Muhammad cited or referred to a litany of quranic passages: Qur'an 2:9 and 15; 63:1–3; 4:150–52; 5:53; 4:144–45; 47:23 and 25–28; 66:9–10; 104:1–9; 2:6–15; 4:107, 109, 113–15, and 124; 8:46; and 9:73–74.[73] For example, Elijah Muhammad wrote,

> This Verse (4:150) reads like this: "Those who disbelieve in Allah and His Messengers and desire to make a distinction between Allah and His Messengers and say, [']We believe in some and disbelieve in others; and desire to take a course in between['] (4:151). These are truly disbelievers; and We have prepared for the disbelievers an abasing chastisement." . . .
>
> This is going on today among my followers. Many of the hypocrites who go out from me will still say to you that they believe in Allah but do not believe that I am the Messenger of Allah. This is as if they said that they do not believe in either one of us. You cannot get to Allah unless you come through a Messenger, Apostle or Prophet of Allah.

Elijah Muhammad then paraphrased the verse and introduced Qur'an 2:15 by paraphrasing it as well. He then added the following discussion, which again highlights that the Qur'an's message is entirely a contemporary one:

> The Holy Qur-an (63:1) reads: *"When the hypocrites come to thee, they say: We bear witness that thou art indeed Allah's Messenger. And Allah knows thou art indeed His Messenger. And Allah bears witness that the hypocrites are surely liars [63:2]. They take shelter under their oaths, thus turning [men] from Allah's way. Surely evil is that which they do [63:3]. That is because they believed, then disbelieved; thus their hearts are sealed, so they understand not."*
>
> They desire to make the Messenger think that they are true believers by saying they believe he is the Messenger of Allah, while in their

hearts they do not believe that he is the Messenger, and Allah knows what is in their hearts—that they are liars. They come in believing and then disbelieve. After their disbelief, Allah seals their hearts so that they cannot understand or believe. In the 150th verse of the 4th Chapter, they are warned against trying to deceive Allah and His Messenger. They say that they believe in one and disbelieve in the other. But disbelief in God or His Apostle means a disbelief in both.[74]

As his discussion of "Obey Allah and his Messenger" of Qur'an 3:31 makes obvious, hypocrisy and disobedience are almost equivalent for Elijah Muhammad.[75]

The chief hypocrite, Malcolm X, received special attention. Qur'an 68:10–16, traditionally identified with the Muhammad's Meccan opponent Walīd b. Mughīra, is now identified with Malcolm X.[76] "I will never forget this hypocrite's hateful acts against me," declared Elijah Muhammad. He warned the hypocrites,

> According to the Bible and the Holy Qur-an, punishment is sure to overtake hypocrites and those who seek to oppose Allah and his Apostle. I quote here a verse from the Holy Qur-an.
>
> "Do they not know that whoever acts in opposition to Allah and His Apostle, he shall surely have the fire of hell to abide in it, that is the grievous abasement" (Holy Qur-an 9:63).
>
> That is the hell that the hypocrites and disbelievers will suffer, and it begins with their feeling of fear and excitement—fear that someone is going to do harm to them (as they plan to harm those they oppose).[77]

Although it is not explicitly stated here, Elijah Muhammad seemed to be alluding to Malcolm X's prescient statements prior to his assassination.[78]

In general, this attack on the hypocrites may seem atypical, but this was not entirely so. Elijah Muhammad did identify the appearance of opposition as a precursor to the Fall of America.[79] And, in all of these passages, Elijah Muhammad continued to rely on identifying unspecified groups, individuals, or activities mentioned in the Qur'an with his contemporaries and current events. As before, paraphrase was used to apply a quranic passage directly to a person or event, such as the defection of Malcolm X, but his explanations became longer and more detailed. In the citation of Qur'an 63:3 there was a parenthetical gloss that indicated that the hypocrites do not turn away from Allah's way, but that they turn "men" away from Allah's way. Elijah Muhammad used this technique constantly when explaining biblical passages, but generally does not tamper with quranic citations in this manner. More generally, quranic passages were still treated in isolation, without reference to their historical context or even to their context within the Qur'an. More notably, for the first time Elijah Muhammad drew verses from several parts of the Qur'an simultaneously to support his position. This was not quite *naẓīr* (or "textual analogy," in which quranic passages with similar wording or themes are used to explicate each other). In other words, Elijah Muhammad is not using one verse to explain another. Also, on this subject, quranic passages were adduced with greater frequency than biblical passages, which may suggest a greater and growing familiarity with, and dependence on, the Qur'an.

Prayer

Elijah Muhammad's discussion of Muslim prayer was another topic for which he drew more material from the Qur'an than from the Bible. Biblical references were largely restricted to passages that demonstrated the efficacy of prayer, such as Solomon's prayer for forgiveness in II Chronicles 6:36–39 and Jonah's prayer in the fish in Jonah 2:2–4.[80]

In *The Supreme Wisdom* Elijah Muhammad did little more than extol the virtues of prayer and quote the "Muslim's oft-repeated prayer," Qur'an 1 (i.e., the *Sūrat al-Fatiha*).[81] Prayer was also described as beautiful and recommended in *The Supreme Wisdom: Volume Two*, and to further encourage prayer, Elijah Muhammad simply cited passages in the Qur'an such as 20:30, 17:78, 17:116, and 29:45.[82] However, in *Message to the Blackman in America* he cited numerous quranic verses. "Surely prayer keeps (one) away from indecency and evil; and certainly the remembrance of Allah is the greatest (force) and Allah knows what you do" (Qur'an 29:45) led off his discussion of "Prayer in Islam." And "O you who believe, remember Allah, remembering Him frequently and glorifying Him morning and evening. He it is Who sends His blessings on you, and so do His angels, that He may bring you forth out of utter darkness into the light and He is merciful to the believers (Prayer is better than sleep)" (Qur'an 33:41–43) prefaced his "Significance of Prayer."[83] The former verse he then paraphrased and the latter he elucidated by stating, "This alone is salvation, just to be brought out of the darkness of ignorance into the light of truth. Who is in more need of the truth than the American so-called Negroes who do not have the knowledge of self. . . ?"[84]

Despite the relatively abundant citations from the Qur'an, much of Elijah Muhammad's discussion of prayer was still connected to his race myth, eschatology, and belief that Fard Muhammad was Allah. In a description of the morning prayer, Elijah Muhammad explained that part of the prayer is known as "Fard." The significance of that, he elaborated, was as follows: "And Allah's using Fard as His name here on His coming teaches us that if we expect to be successful, we must bow in submission to the will of Master Fard Muhammad; the All Wise God in Person who is worthy to be praised and praised much."[85] Elijah Muhammad also included a description of the prayer rituals with some discussion of their meaning in light of what he perceived to be the needs of the so-called Negroes and a critique of Christian prayer with some discussion of what it implied about white Christians.

In addition, Elijah Muhammad provided some suggested prayers, which he cited verbatim from an orthodox manual of prayer.[86] Perhaps it was this manual that was the source of the following curious passage:

"Observe prayers in the early morning, at the close of the day, and at the approach of the night. Prayers are good deeds which drive away the evil doing" (Holy Qur-an 11:116).

"Glorify Allah (by rendering prayers to Him) when it is evening and in the morning—praise to Him in the heavens and the earth—and in the afternoon and at noontide" (Ibid., 30:17).

"Put up then with what they say; and celebrate the praise of your Lord before sunrise, and before sun setting, and during the night do thou praise Him, and in the extreme of the day, so that thou mayest be well pleased" (Ibid., 20:130).

"Observe prayers at sunset until the first darkening of the night and observe reading (the Qur-an) at daybreak. Lo! The recital of the Qur-an (that is, rendering prayer) is ever witnessed. And some part of the night awake for it, a largess for thee. It may be that your Lord will raise thee to a praised state" (Ibid., 17:78–79).

"Take aid by observing patience and prayer" (Ibid., 2:45).

"When you have fulfilled your prayer, remember Allah, standing and sitting and lying on your sides. And when you are in safety then be steadfast in prayer. Verily prayer is a timed ordinance on the believers" (Ibid., 4:103).

"That which leads man to infidelity is neglect of prayers."

"No one of you must say his prayers in a garment without covering the whole body."

"Allah accepts not the prayers of a woman arrived at puberty unless she covers her head as well as the whole body."

"The five stated prayers erase the sins which have been committed during the intervals between them, if they have not been mortal sins."

"The prayers of a person will not be accepted, who has broken his ablution until he completes another ablution."

["]Order your children to say the state[d] prayers when they are seven years of age, and beat them if they do not do so when they are ten years old."

"[']Tell me if any one of you had a rivulet before his doors and bathed five times a day therein whether any dirt would remain on his body?['] The companions said, 'Nothing would remain.' The Prophet said, 'In this manner will the five daily prayers as ordered by Allah erase all minor sins.'"[87]

This passage is one of the very few in which quranic verses were allowed to speak entirely for themselves. Elijah Muhammad added no comments, interlinear or otherwise, as he normally did. Moreover, the quranic citations in this passage come from a hybrid of Rodwell's and Pickthall's translations of the Qur'an, not from Muhammad Ali's. Furthermore, the presence of *ḥadīth*s (that is, reports of Muhammad the Prophet's words and activities, which collectively comprise the Sunna)—virtually nonexistent in the rest of Elijah Muhammad's writings—suggests that his discussions on prayer were atypical of his other writings and dependent on outside sources. These sources seem generally more orthodox in both their presentation and concerns. For example, the subjects of ablution and modesty were consistent with Elijah Muhammad's teachings elsewhere, but their presence within a discussion of prayer was unusual. Perhaps this passage indicates that Elijah Muhammad was far more willing to defer to other Muslims when the subject was not directly related to his main concern of race relations.[88]

In addition to the Ahmadiyya translation of the Qur'an that he favored, Elijah Muhammad was, of course, dependent on many sources: instruction from Fard Muhammad, personal contact with other Muslims (and the literature of the Islamic Mission Movement of America), and various other Christian writings and preachers, such as his contemporary, Judge Rutherford of the Jehovah's Witnesses. The borrowing of ideas, interpretations, and methods from these diverse sources, even if verbatim as with the preceding passage, should not be adduced as evidence that

Elijah Muhammad was not engaging in an act of interpretation. He was not merely compiling or manipulating the works of others; both the act of selection and the act of presentation in a given context are already acts of interpretation.

A Mufassir?

From this examination of the Qur'an's application to the race myth, eschatology, dietary regulations, diatribes against hypocrites, and prescriptions for prayer, and the scripture's noteworthy absence from his discussion of theology, creation, prophets, women, and fasting, it is quite evident that the question of whether or not Elijah Muhammad can be considered a *mufassir* is not an invalid one. Certainly he was not a typical *mufassir,* nor did he claim to be one. Only on rare occasions did Elijah Muhammad make it clear that he was providing commentary and doing so in a fashion typical of other *mufassir*s. When he did, he would cite a passage of the Qur'an (with the verses in italics). Then, under the subheading "Commentary," he would summarize or contextualize the verses and provide several paragraphs of explanation of the verses (in roman font).[89] At other times, he simply referred the reader to the verses and explained, verse by verse, what particular phrases meant. Occasionally, he invoked an earlier Muslim authority, whom he usually cited by name. Those authorities, however, were Muhammad Ali and, less often, Yusuf Ali, the authors of the footnotes in the translations of the Qur'an that he used.[90]

Significant sections of his *Message to the Blackman in America*, such as his political program of separation, his economic program of self-sufficiency, and his demand for a black homeland within the continental United States, drew on no scriptural support—neither biblical nor quranic.[91] His reliance on biblical material over quranic material for some issues is also problematic, though perhaps the early Muslim *mufassirs'* dependence on biblical material (i.e., the *isrā'īlīyāt*) establishes some precedent for Elijah Muhammad's approach. More significant is the hegemony of his race myth and the situation in America over the traditional interpretations of the Qur'an (or the Bible, for that matter). It is not that the traditional interpretations are necessarily wrong, but for Elijah Muhammad, scripture is more about the present than the past: "Everything mentioned in the Bible and Holy Qur'an such as plagues and judgments taking place in ancient times of the Bible and the Holy Qur'an against the opponents of Allah is to warn you and me that the same thing is coming upon America and Europe but America is No. 1 (first)."[92] This interpretation certainly appears unislamic—not unislamic in the sense of being opposed to Islam, but unislamic in the sense of not sharing many of the readily identifiable characteristics that make any belief, practice, and so forth seem Islamic.

At a more technical level, of the exegetical devices typically used by *mufassirs*—variant readings, early and pre-Islamic poetry, lexical explanations, grammatical explanations, rhetorical explanations, periphrasis, analogy, abrogation, circumstances of revelation, identification, prophetical tradition, and anecdote—only the last four are employed.[93] Elijah Muhammad's use of identification or specification (*ta'yīn* and *tasmiya*) in the form of glosses is quite obvious from the various passages cited above. One can even see the use of anecdote in the narratives that normally provide the framework for passages he cited. However, circumstances of revelation and prophetic tradition can be said to be used by Elijah Muhammad only if one means by "prophetic" things that refer to Fard Muhammad and/or Elijah Muhammad. Given his apparent unfamiliarity with the Islamic exegetical tradition, and even Arabic, it is certainly reasonable to argue that Elijah Muhammad was not a *mufassir*.

On the other hand, historian John Wansbrough makes a useful observation with regard to the different narrative techniques found within the biography of the Prophet Muhammad (i.e., the *sīra*) that may be applicable to Elijah Muhammad's use of the Qur'an. He sees three types of techniques in use in what he terms "haggadic" or "narrative" exegesis: they are the exegetical, parabolic, and paraphrastic. In the exegetical technique, extracts from scripture provide the framework for the narrative. In the parabolic, the narrative is the framework for frequent allusion to scripture. "In the exegetical style scriptural extracts, however discrete and truncated, exhibit the canonical text; in the parabolic style scriptural allusions are implicit only, exhibiting diction and imagery but not the verbatim text of the canon."[94] The third technique, by contrast, involves the "paraphrastic versions of scripture in the form of anecdote."[95] All three of these techniques are evident in some form in Elijah Muhammad's writings, particularly within the extended passages cited above.[96] Insofar as one is willing to see Ibn Isḥāq (d. 768), the author of the *Sīra*, and Muqātil ibn Sulaymān (d. 767), the author of a *tafsīr*, as *mufassirs*, one should recognize Elijah Muhammad as a *mufassir*. The narrative framework provided by the earlier two *mufassirs* is not that of Elijah Muhammad, but the methods, the production, and the purposes are much the same. For all three it is the story that matters: the quranic texts (and in the case of Elijah Muhammad, the biblical texts too) are subordinate conceptually (and often syntactically) to the narrative.[97] Wansbrough argues that the original context for haggadic or narrative exegesis is the popular sermon and that it had a central role in the process of community self-definition and formation.[98] Elijah Muhammad's writings are also rooted in the popular sermon. And the myth of Yakub and the white race of blue-eyed devils, their imminent destruction, the establishment of common practices in diet and prayer, and the attack on the hypocrites are clearly central to establishing and protecting his community of the Nation of Islam. And so, since he works toward these goals using the Qur'an and Islamic terminology, Elijah Muhammad is indeed a *mufassir*.

5

Elijah Muhammad,
Other Muslims, and Islam

Was Elijah Muhammad a Muslim? Can the Nation of Islam be considered part of the larger Islamic tradition? These questions vex scholars and Muslims alike. A broad definition of Islam might begin with the Five Principles of Islam: belief in Allah, angels, prophets, scriptures, and judgment day. Obviously, Elijah Muhammad's teachings are at variance with several of these principles as traditionally defined. Not surprisingly, therefore, many Muslims have objected to some of the more prominent features of Elijah Muhammad's formulation of Islam. They rightly ask, if the assertions that Fard Muhammad was "Allah in person," that Elijah Muhammad was Fard Muhammad's Messenger, that heaven and hell are here on earth, that the white man is the devil, and so forth do not exclude one from the Islamic tradition, what does? Given these beliefs, many Muslims outside the Nation of Islam continue to vehemently object to the use of the words "Islam" and "Muslim" by Elijah Muhammad and his followers.

Several scholars are likewise hesitant to link Elijah Muhammad with traditional Islam. For instance, Sherman A. Jackson claims that "there was only the most perfunctory attempt to integrate even the most basic Islamic doctrines and rituals into the religious life of the community, from the Five Pillars to the finality of prophethood resting with Muhammad of Arabia."[1]

Many scholars, however, have attempted to minimize the differences between the Muslims of the Nation of Islam and "orthodox" Muslims. Aminah McCloud argues that the differences among the various Muslim groups can be traced to the relative importance each places on the concepts of the larger and inclusive *umma* (community of believers) and narrower *'asabiya* (solidarity). This latter concept, which is a key theme of nation building, is in tension with the former, but Islam, according to McCloud, has always incorporated such diversity and multiculturalism.[2]

Most other scholars seek to establish the Nation of Islam as a heretical sect, but one that is still part of Islam. C. Eric Lincoln acknowledges that differences exist, but argues that the Nation of Islam is a legitimate sect of Islam.[3] According to Steven Barboza, for most Muslims, calling members of the Nation of Islam "non-Muslims" might be going too far, but they still consider members of the Nation of Islam to be too politicized, racist, and/or heretical.[4] And recently, Claude Clegg concluded that "[o]verall, the basic outlines of both religious traditions do appear to overlap enough to allow the black organization to reasonably claim membership in the body of Islam, albeit as a heretical limb."[5] As discussed at the outset of this book, these rationalizations seem to place the scholar in the role of arbiter of orthodoxy—largely because scholars, like their Muslim counterparts who have come to the opposite conclusion, still assume that there is something they can identify as "orthodox," "normative," "heretical," or "sectarian" Islam.

An even more vehement polemic suggests that the Nation of Islam does not even constitute a religion. Scholar of African American Islam Edward E. Curtis IV, however, demonstrates clearly that by any standard definition of religion, even one as simple and concise as the system of beliefs and practices relative to supernatural beings,[6] the Nation of Islam is a religion. "Of course, not every activity of NOI members was religious in nature, and it is important to emphasize that their religious activities, like those of all other human beings, were tied inextricably to their politics, social location, and their cultural orientations."[7] Thus, the issue for the scholar is not whether the Nation of Islam is a religion; it clearly is.[8] Curtis also points us in the right direction for the question of whether the Nation of Islam, whose members vocally state that they are Muslims, is a form of Islam:

> [There is no] minimal definition of what it means to be a Muslim. Instead, wherever and whenever a person calls himself or herself Muslim, scholars should include this person's voice in their understanding of what constitutes Islam. The mere fact that one has labeled oneself a Muslim indicates some sort of participation, however slight, in the process of Islamic history.[9]

If one were to attempt such a "minimal definition," however, despite the inherent difficulties of doing so, it might be something akin to "a Muslim is someone who holds the Qur'an revealed to Muhammad to be the central authoritative source of his or her beliefs about Allah and what He has dictated for those who claim Him as their deity." Elijah Muhammad easily meets such a basic definition, even if he deviated from what most other Muslims claim Allah has dictated. One might be tempted to add to the definition the belief in the Sunna (the example of Muhammad the Prophet, which stands next to the Qur'an as the second most important source of Muslim belief and practice). However, not all Muslims have agreed on the role of the Sunna and what exactly comprises the Sunna. Even Sunnis and Shi'is have separate collections. What they do agree on is the Qur'an, though that too is interpreted differently by them.

This point is not meant to minimize the tensions between Elijah Muhammad and other Muslims, be they Sunnis, Shi'is, and even Ahmadiyyas. Even with the latter group, whose translation of the Qur'an he employed, tensions emerged. In 1971 an Ahmadiyya Muslim criticized Elijah Muhammad and the Nation of Islam on the radio. *Muhammad Speaks* responded by claiming that the movement originated in British India and was financed by Christians to help pacify Muslims who were revolting against British rule. It was also (very oddly) claimed that "[t]he movement tailored the Holy Quran to meet the needs and objectives of the foreign occupier."[10] In fact, it is all of these tensions that merit further examination, for the growing animosity during the last decade and a half of Elijah Muhammad's life between himself and other Muslims provides an insight into what he believed Islam to be and the role he saw for himself and his movement within the larger Islamic tradition.

Other Muslims on Elijah Muhammad

There were always a few Muslims from outside the Nation of Islam, such as the Pakistani author and regular columnist in *Muhammad Speaks* Abdul Basit Naeem, who supported the efforts of Elijah Muhammad and had great respect for this Muslim leader. Some accepted—or, better, tolerated—his racialist form of Islam largely because it at least moved its followers closer to their understanding of what constituted "orthodox" Islam. Naeem was unusual in his wholehearted embrace of Elijah Muhammad's teachings.[11] In the mid-1960s he regularly contributed to *Muhammad Speaks*, where he would extol the achievements of Elijah Muhammad, chastise Muslims from the East for criticizing him, and repeatedly and vehemently lash out at Malcolm X.[12] For his introduction to *The Supreme Wisdom*, Naeem stated that he was aware that the teachings of Elijah Muhammad were controversial for some Muslims. However, Naeem stated, "As far as I am concerned, I consider the differences between Islam of the East and teaching of Mr. Elijah Muhammad to be of relatively minor importance *at this time*, because these are not related to the *SPIRIT* of Islam, which I am sure, is completely shared by *all* of us."[13] That is to say, for Naeem the ends justified the means, and he was confident that soon Elijah Muhammad's followers would study the Qur'an and be instructed on the correct performance of prayers and other Islamic duties.[14] In fact, in *The Supreme Wisdom* Elijah Muhammad did encourage his followers (apparently with limited success) to read the Qur'an and to perform the five daily prayers. Later, Naeem again wrote what Elijah Muhammad wanted said: "I do, however, believe that it is neither imperative nor entirely beneficial for my brothers and sisters in Islam in the Western Hemisphere to look to the 'East' for guidance and advice—especially in matters essentially 'local' in nature and character."[15] He argued further that Muslims of the East were a "live" people who were unaware why white people were regarded as "devils." Elijah Muhammad, on the other hand, was addressing a "mentally dead" people who were still under the tyranny of these devils. In fact, it is the Nation of Islam that might provide guidance to their Eastern coreligionists: "I, for one, see no reason why the U.S. Muslims—followers of the Honorable Elijah Muhammad—could not be instrumental in reviving or giving a new meaning to the spirit of Islam."[16] Nevertheless, most Muslims outside the Nation of Islam who were aware of Elijah Muhammad were not so generous.

The first major Muslim critic to very publicly attack Elijah Muhammad was Talib Ahmad Dawud, who led a rival organization called the Muslim Brotherhood USA. The two men exchanged theological and personal barbs in the printed news media. Dawud's attack focused on predictable targets: the incarnation of Allah in Fard Muhammad, the demand for racial segregation, the future book, and the improper prayers used by the Nation of Islam:

> Mr. Muhammad's followers do not make prayer properly; they do not face the East and say their prayers five times a day, as all true Muslim's [sic] do; their houses of worship are called "temples," while the houses of worship of the true Muslim's [sic] are called Mosques. . . . All true muslims believe that the Koran will be here until the day of Judgment, but Mr. Muhammad tells his followers that the Koran will be superseded by a book written for black people. Another basic difference, . . . the Muslim

faith does not teach hatred of any particular group, but on the contrary, welcomes people of all races and colors so long as they abide by and live up to the teachings of Islam. . . . The true Muslims worship Allah, but Mr. Muhammad and his followers claim that Allah is a man named W. Fard Muhammad. . . .[17]

Furthermore, he claimed that Fard Muhammad was a Turkish white man who was once a Nazi agent. He also accused Elijah Muhammad of being a fake, an ex-convict, and a teacher of racial hatred. Having recently completed his own *hajj*, Dawud asserted that Elijah Muhammad would be forbidden entry into Mecca since he was not a "true" Muslim.[18] Both he and his wife, the singer Dakota Staton, on separate occasions reiterated the last claim, trying to distance themselves from Elijah Muhammad. Staton stated that there is "absolutely no connection between Elijah Muhammad [sic] group . . . and the Muslim Brotherhood USA, of which I am a part," and Dawud maintained, "There is no connection whatsoever between the Moslem's [sic] of Elijah Muhammad and the bonafide Muslims who worship Allah."[19] A few years later, Dawud announced plans to file a lawsuit to prevent Elijah Muhammad from using the words "Islam" and "Muslim" when speaking of the Nation of Islam.

Jamil Diab, a Palestinian Arab who came to the United States in 1948, was another outspoken critic of Elijah Muhammad. Although never a member of the Nation of Islam, he had served as the principal of Elijah Muhammad's University of Islam. He was fired for teaching orthodox Islam and then became the director of the Islamic Center of Chicago. Of the Nation of Islam, Diab argued,

> This cult is totally lacking in the requisites which constitutes any Muslim group. They have different religious books, prayers, their fasts, in fact the criteria by which Muslims and non-Muslims judge an organization or group to be an Islamic one—cannot be applied to this group. . . . The very cornerstone of Islam, universal brotherhood of man, black as well as white, has been turned into hatred by them. . . . [The Nation of Islam] is not now, nor has it ever been part of [Islam].[20]

Diab's questionable assertion of a race-blind Islam notwithstanding, the other claims, like Dawud's, were problematic for Elijah Muhammad. Later, others, such as the Ahmadiyya Adib Nurud-din in 1962, also dismissed Elijah Muhammad's teachings as absurd. These Sunni Muslim critics may have had centuries of traditional Islamic doctrine on their side, but Elijah Muhammad's form of Islam had a significant head start within the African American community, and so their effect was limited.[21] However, since Malcolm X was the most visible and well-known spokesperson for the Nation of Islam, it fell to him to answer many of these challenges. Consequently, they may have provided an initial impetus for Malcolm X to reevaluate his mentor's racial teachings.[22]

This flurry of denunciations was in part prompted by the Nation of Islam's sudden media attention from 1959 onwards. When it came to the attention of white America, it also came to the attention of other Muslim groups, many of whom hurried to dissociate their religion from what was being almost universally labeled as a "hate group." The denunciation from Muslims outside of the Nation of Islam continued throughout the 1960s and 1970s, but most of these critics had no significant support within the African American community. Nevertheless, these types of polemics even outlived Elijah Muhammad. For example, in the 1990s an early definition of Islam available on the internet asserted,

> ISLAM, and so-called "Nation of Islam," are two different religions. The only thing common between them is the jargon, the language used by both. "The Nation of Islam" is a misnomer; this religion should be called Farrakhanism, after the name of its propagator. The religion of Elijah Muhammad and W. D. Fard died with their death because their officially and popularly elected successor, W. D. Muhammad, integrated the community with the Muslim community at large. . . .[23]

The author of the definition, Asim Mughal, then juxtaposed standard Islamic teachings with those of the Nation of Islam with regard to Allah, the Prophet Muhammad, the Last Day, the Qur'an, the Bible, the *shahāda* (the confession of faith: "There is no God but Allah; Muhammad is the Messenger of Allah"), prayer, almsgiving, fasting, pilgrimage, things permitted and prohibited, and the role of the Sunna. Mughal concluded that the Nation of Islam is a "pseudo-Islamic cult."[24]

Elijah Muhammad on Other Muslims

In the early years, Elijah Muhammad made no mention of tensions with other Muslims. His only significant critique was that some Arab Muslims continued to believe that they could convert Whites to Islam.[25] He also recognized that his goals and those of other Muslims differed. He asserted that the aim of *Islam in America* is

1. To teach our people the truth
2. Clean them up and make them self-respecting and unite them on to their own kind
3. Bring them face to face with our God, and teach them to know their enemies.[26]

Elijah Muhammad, of course, believed these goals to be compatible—probably even identical—with the Islam of other Muslims.

In *The Supreme Wisdom* he painted a utopian image of Muslims in the East. These Muslims had no slavery, they had peace, they lived in the best and richest part of the world, they were true brothers and sisters to each other, and so on.[27] Elijah Muhammad, perhaps a bit naively, suggested that any black follower of his would be "welcomed with sincere and open arms and recognized by his light-skinned or copper-colored Arab brother."[28] This view was confirmed to him when Malcolm X sent a report from Arabia in the summer of 1959. He described Arabs as "many different shades, ranging from regal black to rich brown, but none are white." He added that Arabs see African Americans as "our brothers of color" and that there "is no color prejudice among the Moslems."[29] However, several events dramatically changed his view of Muslims from the East. First, American Muslims not in the Nation of Islam attacked him as a non-Muslim. Second, he saw first-hand during his travels that the utopia he envisioned in the East did not exist. And third, even Muslims from the East denied that he was a Muslim.

Elijah Muhammad's understanding that black people were (or were supposed to be) Muslims and white people were not (and could not be) Muslims caused problems for the movement. There were several incidents of Arab Muslims being refused entry into the Chicago Temple—presumably because they were not black. Then came the criticisms of Diab and Dawud. These attacks were taken very seriously by Elijah Muhammad. His retort in his weekly column was both vehement and personal:

Talid Ahmad Dawud and his TV blues-singing Miss Dakota Staton (who the paper says is Mrs. Alijah Rabia Dawud in private life) and whom the world can hear her filthy blues and love songs and see her immodestly dressed, were successful last week in getting a chance to breathe their venomous poison against me and my followers in this paper and in the local Chicago paper, The Crusader. Mr. Dawud is from the West Indies (Antigua) and was born a British subject. He was known by the name Rannie (sounds like a devil's name). He is jealous of the progress with which Allah (to whom praises are due) is blessing me and my followers, and this jealousy is about to run Mr. Dawud insane. (The Crusader erroneously called him an Imam.) Mr. Dawud and Miss Staton should have been ashamed to try to make fun of me and my followers while publicly serving the devil in the theatrical world. I do not allow my followers to visit such, nor do I allow my wife and the believing women who follow me to go before the public partly dressed. If they would, never would I claim them to be mine any more.

Mr. Dawud has been trying for some time to do me and my followers harm in the Islamic world through the Muslim Embassy in this country and abroad, but he is only hurting himself. [30]

It seems likely that this rivalry, though apparently one over doctrine, was motivated primarily by a desire of each man's organization to be "the pre-eminent Islamic movement in the United States, and to tap into patronage from Arab leaders."[31] For his part, Elijah Muhammad felt that Muslims from the East now living in the West had been corrupted, turning "them into hypocrites of the worst type." [32]

At this stage in the late 1950s and early 1960s, there were still no harsh words for the Muslims of the East. Even when Elijah Muhammad first challenged the charges that his movement was not really Islamic, he thought the differences between his Muslims and other Muslims were merely a product of the differing contexts:

My brothers in the East were never subjected to conditions of slavery and systematic brainwashing by the slavemasters for as long a period of time as my people here were subjected. I cannot, therefore, blame them if they differ with me in certain interpretations of the Message of Islam. In fact, I do not even *expect* them to understand some of the things I say unto my people here.[33]

At least with regard to the accusation that prayer in the Nation of Islam did not conform to orthodox standards, especially with regard to the use of English instead of Arabic, Elijah Muhammad attempted to explain again the effects of the different context to his Muslim critics:

My followers here in the wilderness of North America do not speak a language of their own. They lost their original tongue when the devil (European) slave-master had made their foreparents his slaves and brought them here from their native homeland (Africa) against their will and consent.

Today we are forced to worship our own God, Allah in an alien language. . . . But the All-Wise and Most Merciful Allah, to Whom all praises are due forever, does not demand of us that we pray to Him in a language we no longer can use or have mastery of. He promises to hear and grant our prayers no matter how we beseech His help and guidance.

Moreover, many of your followers are not yet qualified to learn and recite the daily prayers in their own language. . . . Before they go after that, they have to prepare and prove themselves to be deserving and worthy of it. . . .[34]

With his *'umra* (the "lesser pilgrimage," which can be performed at any time but is normally performed with the *hajj*) and tour of Muslim countries in late 1959 and early 1960, he answered the domestic charges that he was not a Muslim: after all, Dawud had claimed that Elijah Muhammad would not be permitted to enter Mecca. Having completed the *hajj*, he had all the evidence he needed to claim that the rest of the Muslim world recognized him as a Muslim.[35] However, it was during this trip that for the first time he saw his "brothers in the East" in person.

On the one hand the pilgrimage nudged Elijah Muhammad closer to Sunni Islam. For instance, apparently Elijah Muhammad planned to rename his temples "mosques." On the other hand, he was forced to confront some harsh realities about his coreligionists in the East: instead of opulent wealth, he found poverty; instead of a society of brilliant scientists, he found premodern societies.

Muhammad's disappointment with the Middle East caused him to deemphasize the importance of making overtures to Arab and African Muslims and to stress traditional elements of the Nation's doctrines. To a large degree, he lost respect for those he had esteemed as the Tribe of Shabbaz in East Asia. . . . Interestingly, the Afro-Asian tour had afforded him credibility and validation, but it also instilled in him a measure of disillusionment that reinforced the very beliefs and practices for which orthodox Muslims had scorned him.[36]

Fortunately for Elijah Muhammad, acceptance from Muslims of the East was far from the most pressing concern for his followers in the inner cities of the United States.

Nevertheless, Elijah Muhammad continued to confront Muslims who questioned his orthodoxy. In 1963, he still sought to minimize differences, writing, "we are not enemies" and "They, too, are gradually coming over with me in the understanding for the first time in their history; the realization of the devils. It is in the Holy Qur-an that these people are the devils, and the scholars of Islam know it." But he also felt increasingly comfortable emphasizing his independence: "I am sent from Allah and not from the Secretary General of the Muslim League. There is no Muslim in Arabia that has authority to stop me from delivering this message that I have been assigned to by Allah. . . . I am not taking orders from them, I am taking orders from Allah (God) himself."[37] Later, however, he became even less concerned with currying favor with "orthodox" Muslims. Knowing the political, social, and racial problems of eastern Muslims may have made the break with them easier; but having met and spoken with so many learned Muslims during his travels, he was undoubtedly aware of how much more they knew about the Qur'an than he did, and this realization may even have made the break with them necessary.

On doctrinal issues, he began challenging these Muslims in 1965 by claiming that his Islam was supplanting theirs:

> The Orthodox Muslims will have to bow to the choice of Allah. Allah will bring about a new Islam. As for the Principles of Belief, they remain the same. . . . We are seeing this change now and entering into it. The devils oppose this change, and the Orthodox join them in opposing us because of their desire to carry on the old way of Islam.[38]

And, when he was challenged on this reading of the Qur'an, he retorted,

> Many Orthodox Muslims do not want to believe that Allah has appeared in the Person of Master Fard Muhammad or that He has made manifest the truth that has been hidden from their religious scientists—the truth of God and of the devil as revealed to me. Though they do have the Holy Qur-an, many of them do not understand the meaning of it, and some of them believe everything that is prophesied in the Bible and Holy Qur-an about a last Messenger or Prophet being or referring to Muhammad of 1,400 years ago.[39]

Other Muslims whose sensibilities were troubled by Elijah Muhammad's claim to be a Messenger of Allah sent to his people in America were told they had misunderstood the Qur'an, for it teaches that each community must have its own messenger who speaks its language.[40] They were likewise mistaken about the nature of God:

> Some Orthodox Muslims mock us for the sake of being accepted as a friend of their and our enemy. They are spooky minded and believe that Allah (God) is some immaterial something. . . . The ignorant belief of the Orthodox Muslims, that Allah (God) is Some Formless Something and yet He Has An Interest in our affairs, can be condemned in no limit of time. I would not give two cents for that kind of God, in which they believe.[41]

Thus, in the mid-1960s Elijah Muhammad saw his Muslim detractors as simply conservative and confused, or, more ominously, as attempting to curry the favor of Whites.

By 1972, however, Elijah Muhammad's rhetoric had evolved yet again. He charged other Muslims not simply with being allied to the "white devils" and confused but with being "white" and deceived: "We have a New Islam coming up. The Old Islam was led by white people, white Muslims, but this one will not be. This Islam will be established and led by Black Muslims only."[42] The earlier "copper-colored" Muslims were now "white" Muslims, and their forms of Islam were equated with Christianity: "The Christians and most old world Muslims are alike: not having a true knowledge of the Supreme One, referred to as Allah, and God makes most people believe that God is something other than a man."[43]

Elijah Muhammad's claim to be Muslim and his authority to lead his Muslim followers was never predicated on acceptance by "orthodox" Muslims. That authority came directly from Allah himself. Elijah Muhammad claimed, "God, Almighty appointed me" and "The Apostle is considered one in Allah and Allah is one in the Apostle. So, when you look at one, you see both; when you hear one speak, you hear both."[44] To those who claimed to believe in Allah but not his Messenger (a defining characteristic of hypocrites, according to Elijah Muhammad), he said, "they err, because it is impossible for one to believe in either One—God or the Messenger—and not believe in Both, for the Messenger is the only source of communication and guidance for the people. So, rejecting the Messenger is rejecting God, The Sender of the Messenger."[45] In his early writings, he had appealed to his coreligionists to the East, but when push came to shove, his authority overruled that of all other Muslims, and he was willing first to abandon them and then to reject them.

Elijah Muhammad's Islams

Obviously, there is no monolithic Islam, except perhaps in the minds of Muslims with *salafiyyah* inclinations (i.e., so-called fundamentalist Muslims) and in the minds of scholars with orientalist inclinations. Some scholars have a litmus test for Islam, which Elijah Muhammad fails. For instance, Sylviane A. Diouf suggests that

> [a]ccording to Islam, nothing is more unforgivable and heinous than *shirk*, the association of others—such as Waly Fard—with the worship of God. Likewise, to believe that other prophets—such as Noble Drew Ali and Elijah Muhammad—follow Muhammad cannot be reconciled with orthodox Islam. These affirmations are not differences of interpretations; they are contrary to the most fundamental teachings of the religion.[46]

However, there has been no shortage of Muslims who have had beliefs and practices that were considered heretical by their coreligionists and who brought their own background, culture, or agenda to their understanding of Islam in the same way that Elijah Muhammad had done. Many, including Sufis and Shi'is, have been accused of *shirk* by a few. A more fruitful approach is to ask why Islam should be employed at all by Elijah Muhammad, given the sometimes hostile but always ambivalent relationship between him and other Muslims, be they Sunnis, Shi'is, Ahmadiyyas, or Sufis. Because of this ambivalence, some scholars argue that Islam was merely a façade for Elijah Muhammad. Others see Elijah Muhammad as the leader of a Muslim millenarian movement. Still others put Elijah Muhammad much more firmly inside the Islamic tradition, as a *mufassir*, jihadist, or proto-Muslim. Each of these views has some merit, but neither individually nor collectively do they fully explain the critical role Islam played for Elijah Muhammad personally.[47]

The Aegis of Islam

For several scholars Elijah Muhammad's Nation of Islam was not primarily a religious movement. The most significant advocate of this position was C. Eric Lincoln, who argued that the Nation of Islam only required the façade of Islam:

> [T]he aegis of orthodox Islam means little in America's black ghettos. So long as the movement keeps its color identity with the rising black peoples of Africa, it could discard all its Islamic attributes—its name, its prayers to Allah, its citations from the Quran, everything "Muslim," without substantial risk to its appeal to the black masses.[48]

In other words, the appeal to Islamic figures, language, scripture, and so forth by Elijah Muhammad was at best superficial—perhaps merely a vestige of the impetus of Fard Muhammad. Lincoln does not deny the social benefits arising from invoking Islam, but he does deny Islam's centrality: "although the Black Muslims call their movement a religion, religious values have a secondary importance. They are not part of the movement's basic appeal, except to the extent that they foster and strengthen the sense of group solidarity."[49]

A variation of this view comes from sociologist Clifton E. Marsh. For him, the Nation of Islam was primarily a "black separatist movement." Through it, Elijah Muhammad sought to solve the problem of racism and inequality in the United States with an emphasis on black pride and practical economic programs.

> The fact that the organization was not purely Islamic does not tarnish the reality of the Nation of Islam having been an important vehicle for social change. Many black people did not adhere to the organization's beliefs, but the Nation of Islam did raise their consciousness of African heredity and provided jobs for many inner-city residents.[50]

For both Lincoln and Marsh, therefore, Elijah Muhammad constructed a racialist movement, not necessarily (or at least not primarily) a religious one.[51]

Evidence in support of this position could come from within the Nation of Islam as well. Far more important than the Islamic links, or even the original Asiatic links, were the African links. Elijah Muhammad himself said as much: "The Black African, the Aboriginal Black People of the earth, are our real brothers. We are part of, and belong to each other."[52] Support could also be drawn from Warith Deen Muhammad, the son of Elijah Muhammad and one of his successors. In an interview in 1979 he was asked if the Nation of Islam was a social movement or a religion. He replied, "It was a religion and a social movement organization. In fact, the religion as it was introduced to the Nation of Islam was more a social reform philosophy than Orthodox Islam."[53]

There are, however, at least two problems with this view. The first is a serious theoretical failing. As Curtis points out, Lincoln distinguishes between "politics" and "religion" in a way that simply does not reflect the way the Nation of Islam functioned:

> His use of religion and politics as analytical categories ultimately obscured more than they revealed since he underemphasized the legitimately religious aspects of the movement's nationalistic activity. In reality, of course, the line between religion and politics was and is often more blurry than he indicated. Indeed, politics and religion were wedded in fascinating and problematical ways within the movement.[54]

Curtis adds that viewing "Islam" as a religion in this way essentializes it and puts the scholar in the position of judging what constitutes true Islam. Similarly, the line between Elijah Muhammad's economic program and his religion is blurry. Having been called a "black capitalist," he responded by arguing, "whatever I'm doing has nothing whatsoever to do with this 'ism' or that 'ism' or any kind of 'ism.' . . . My work is all in the line of what Allah, the Almighty God, Who Came in the person of Master W. Fard Muhammad, to Whom praises are due forever, specifically assigned me to do. . . ."[55]

A second problem exists, even if one were to permit this artificial and problematic separation of religion and politics: the important role religion played for Elijah Muhammad is oversimplified. Clearly Elijah Muhammad did not feel the need to seek the approval of Muslims outside his movement. And yet, when he came under attack from other Muslims, he did not reject Islam; he rejected them (as "white Muslims"), suggesting that Islam—as he understood it—was integral to him. In fact, Elijah Muhammad merely focused most intensely on those features of Islam that were most relevant to African Americans—that is, those that dealt with "color identity." The perceived connections of Islam with Africa, the centuries of confrontation of the "Muslim world" with Christendom, the glory of earlier Islamic civilizations, the assumed lack of "slave teachings" in Islam, and the antipathy of white Americans towards Islam were critical to the identity that Elijah Muhammad was trying to forge in the members of his movement. Some "religious" aspects of Islam were important too: rituals such as prayer, for instance, fostered the critically important social cohesion and gave tangible expressions to new identities that Elijah Muhammad sought to forge. Thus, even if Elijah Muhammad boldly declared that it is "far more important to teach the separation of Blacks and Whites in America than prayer,"[56] prayer services (along with the rallies) were the most visible expression of that separation. But the aforementioned ideological aspects of Islam were the most crucial. The "color identity" that Lincoln and Marsh take to be the essence of the Nation of Islam is inextricably intertwined with Elijah Muhammad's unique formulation of Islam. Most importantly, for Elijah Muhammad himself, his own authority and everything from his race myth to the new Islamic identities and his economic programs were founded entirely upon his unique prophetic access to "the eternal and transcendent authority" of Fard Muhammad (i.e., Allah incarnate). Therefore, this key feature of his mythmaking required the religious credibility that the aegis of Islam provided for that claim. Islam as a "religion," if not all of its "orthodox" practices and beliefs, was indispensable. As Curtis points out, the intellectuals of the Nation of Islam expended considerable energy and displayed considerable ingenuity defending their leader's Islamic legitimacy. Even though they occasionally doubted some of his more problematic claims, they maintained that Elijah Muhammad was crucial to being a Muslim and practicing Islam.[57] Although it is not for the scholar of Islam to decide whether Elijah Muhammad was a "real Muslim," it is impossible to understand him, his movement, and his teachings apart from Islam.

Sherman A. Jackson suggests a far more nuanced and intriguing variation of the façade-of-Islam argument—one that, unlike Lincoln's and Marsh's, does describe the Nation of Islam as essentially a religious movement. Jackson explains, "Black Religion functioned as the core, with the trappings (namely vocabulary) of Islam serving as the outer shell."[58] "Black Religion" for Jackson is a subset of African American religion that is characterized by a pragmatic, folk-oriented "holy protest" against, and opposition to, white supremacy and anti-Black racism.[59] As such, Black Religion is a uniquely American religion born out of a uniquely American reality. Furthermore, Black Religion can appropriate either Christianity or Islam; that is, it can "[enlist] the aid of a set of nonindigenous ideas or doctrines in [its] own existential or ideological struggle" without deferring to the traditional authorities over those ideas and doctrines. "A black adopts Islam or Christianity, in other words, not in order to become an honorary Arab or white but in order to become a truer, more authentic 'black man!'"[60]

While Jackson's variation does not suffer from the weakness of an artificial distinction between politics and religion, it does still seem to minimize the importance of Islam for Elijah Muhammad. According to Curtis's analysis of the Nation of Islam from 1960 to 1975, the same centrality of Islam for ordinary members of the Nation of Islam is also evident.[61] And, as we saw earlier, Jackson sees numerous characteristics of Islam that made its marriage to Black Religion "felicitous." Some of these characteristics included the perceived connection of Islam with Africa; the independence from white Europeans and their descendants; a reputation for resistance; a non-European-centered civilization; a simple theology, at least compared with trinitarianism; a conservative social ethic; the retributive justice of the Qur'an; the lack of an ecclesiastical hierarchy in Sunni Islam; and the hatred and fear of Islam by Whites.[62] However, the importance of Islam to the ideological claims made by Elijah Muhammad and the tenacity with which he clung to Islam in the face of opposition suggest that one should view these characteristics as *necessary* instead of simply *fortuitous*. Doing so, to use Jackson's terminology, would move Islam from the "outer shell" to the core.[63]

Elijah Muhammad's Roles in Islam

Many other scholars see Elijah Muhammad and his Nation of Islam as fully inside the Islamic fold. Some of them, therefore, focus on describing Elijah Muhammad's role within Islam using terminology drawn from Islam itself or from the study of religion. Thus Elijah Muhammad has been reimagined as the leader of a millenarian movement, a *mufassir*, a jihadist, and even a "crypto-orthodox" Muslim or "proto-Muslim."

Political scientist Martha F. Lee, emphasizing Elijah Muhammad's teachings on the doctrine of the Fall of America, argues that his Nation of Islam was a millenarian movement. She defines millenarianism as "the belief in an imminent, ultimate, collective, this-worldly, and total salvation."[64] Elijah Muhammad's conception of the apocalypse included the imminent demise of the six thousand years of devilish white rule. These devils would be completely destroyed and only the faithful—those Blacks who had separated themselves mentally and physically from Whites—would survive. Only then could they assume their rightful place: with the evil of this world removed, a renewed and perfect (black) world of eternal peace and justice would arise. All the elements of millenarian movements, therefore, are present in Elijah Muhammad's prophecy of the Fall of America: the past and present suffering is explained, the means by which the end will come is provided, the steps that must be taken to avoid the cataclysm are elaborated, the unity against a common foe is engendered, and the punishment of the wicked and the consequent role reversal was envisioned. For Lee, the various moral, social, political, and economic programs of Elijah Muhammad were all preparations for the coming Fall of America.

Not all millenarianism is religious (e.g., Marxism). However, most iterations are, and in examining the Nation of Islam from this perspective, Lee produces excellent insights that might also explain the role of Islam in Elijah Muhammad's thought. There is no doubt that Elijah Muhammad was a millenarian. However, many of his teachings are directed towards improving life for African Americans in the here and now. His economic program was designed to free them from white domination. This program, like his various moral, social, and dietary requirements, could be seen as merely necessary preparations for the Fall of America. However, all these aspects of Elijah Muhammad's teachings were not dependent on millenarianism, for they continued long after the predicted end times had to be postponed indefinitely. Millenarianism is certainly an important characteristic of Elijah Muhammad's Islam, but hardly its defining characteristic.

We have explored how Elijah Muhammad interpreted the Qur'an. He used many techniques that traditionally trained *mufassir*s would have used. Not surprisingly, he ignored—or more likely was unaware of—most of the classical tradition of quranic exegesis. His was an exegesis rooted in the methods by which popular preachers used the Bible. If he became aware of differences, Elijah Muhammad felt that his understanding of the Qur'an was both superior and sufficient, whereas classical exegesis of the Qur'an was either incorrect or unnecessary. In this regard, he displayed a confidence in his formulation of Islam characteristic of many Muslim *mufassir*s.

Since he introduced the Qur'an to tens of thousands of African Americans, both by having them read it and by showing them *how* to read it, he could certainly be classified as the first African American Muslim *mufassir*. However, his intent was not primarily to try to explain the Qur'an to African Americans. Nor did he define himself as a *mufassir*. He defined himself as a prophet. Thus, while he acted as a commentator on the

Qur'an to his African American followers, this activity likewise does not fully explain his role in Islam.

Richard Brent Turner places Fard Muhammad and Elijah Muhammad in a long series of African American Muslims who sought to combat the injustice, inequality, and racism of the United States with jihad—not a jihad of violence against unbelievers, but a jihad of words that attempts to defend and propagate Islam through preaching, education, and self-transformation.[65] Elijah Muhammad certainly fits this description, as long as one defines the word "jihadist" very narrowly. Although the Fruit of Islam were trained for combat, Elijah Muhammad never advocated such measures. Elijah Muhammad did, however, refer to the "Great War of Armageddon" as the "Holy War." The carrying of weapons had always been forbidden by Elijah Muhammad.[66] Only rarely did he even seem to advocate any kind of violence:

Surah 2:100

Fight with those who fight with you, and know that Allah is with the believers.

Surah 9:20

Fighting is prescribed for you, and you dislike it, but it is possible that you dislike a thing which is good for [sic] and that you love a thing which is bad for you.

Surah 2:216

Surely Allah will defend those who believe: Surely Allah loveth not a traitor.

Surah 22:38

Muslims must not trust hypocrites and disbelievers of Islam, even though they be your near of kin.

We Muslims may have to learn it the hard way. You like to be soft and kind to the hypocrites thinking that they are likewise, but you could be deceived.

Fight anyone who fights you. This is the Law of Nature. BE NOT A COWARD.[67]

Naeem, Elijah Muhammad's Pakistani sycophant, however, argued that members of the Nation of Islam, because they are a minority and surrounded by "openly hostile elements," must be considered to be living in a perpetual stated of jihad and be classified as *mujahids*.[68] Presumably, Elijah Muhammad permitted Naeem to make this argument.

Even so, as with the label *"mufassir,"* Elijah Muhammad never described himself as a jihadist. The very absence from his rhetoric of a term that would have lent itself so well to his teachings is odd. Nevertheless, preaching, education, and psychological, sociological, and economic self-transformation are all hallmarks of Elijah Muhammad and his message. He dedicated his life to equating power with blackness.[69] However, this ideology was thoroughly conservative: it did little to physically challenge the status quo in the United States—much to the chagrin of some of his followers, including Malcolm X. In this broader sense, there was no jihad, and Elijah Muhammad was no jihadist—at least not in any normal usage of the term.

The Crypto-/Proto-Orthodox Muslim

Wallace Muhammad (later known as Warith Deen Mohammed) succeeded his father, Elijah Muhammad, when he died in 1975. It was through his efforts that the Nation of Islam was renamed and transformed into a Sunni Muslim organization. All the "heretical" teachings of the Nation of Islam, such as Fard Muhammad being Allah, Elijah Muhammad being his Messenger, the race myth, and the political demands, were abandoned. Fard Muhammad was reduced to being a "very wise man" and Elijah Muhammad to being a "wise leader," not Allah and his prophet, respectively.[70]

More recently, Warith Deen Mohammed portrayed Fard Muhammad as someone whose true but secret purpose was to bring African Americans to "orthodox Islam" (that is, orthodox as understood by Warith Deen Mohammed). "He wanted that we study the Qur'an" but told his follower Elijah Muhammad not to teach the Qur'an. Instead, he told him, "When the time comes, your children will learn the Qur'an, and they will teach you." Thus, Fard Muhammad had "created this thing as a strategy, a temporary strategy, a temporary language environment, to hold uneducated Blacks . . . long enough to come into an independent mind . . . and then later study the Qur'an." In fact, according to Warith Deen Mohammed, Fard Muhammad knew things would get better in America for African Americans. Eventually, as they became more educated, they would question the very racial myth that Fard Muhammad had created. They would discover that even Fard Muhammad himself had ridiculed it.[71]

Moreover, Warith Deen Mohammed reinterprets the meaning of the predicted future book. According to him, Fard Muhammad had told Elijah Muhammad that "there is coming another Islam. You will get another holy Qur'an."[72] When Fard Muhammad gave Elijah Muhammad an Arabic book, it appears that the latter took it to be that new Qur'an. For years he kept it wrapped in its green cover, mounted in a place of honor. Later, when his sons Akbar and Wallace Muhammad had studied Arabic, he had them read it: to everyone's surprise it was the Qur'an. They discovered that it was the same Qur'an used by other Muslims. For Warith Deen Mohammed, this is a clear indication that Fard Muhammad had always intended African Americans to move to Islamic orthodoxy. It had been his secret plan: his followers would "choose the Islam that is in the Qur'an." His purpose was to establish true Islam, but he had to establish independent thinking first. Likewise, the fact that Elijah Muhammad appointed his son Wallace Muhammad, whom he had expelled several times for his orthodox Sunni proclivities, as his successor demonstrated that just prior to his death Elijah Muhammad was in complete agreement with Fard Muhammad's hidden agenda.

This mythic revision by Warith Deen Mohammed is hard to reconcile with history. First, Elijah Muhammad was aware that the books that he had been given by Fard Muhammad were Qur'ans: two in English and one in Arabic.[73] Second, Elijah Muhammad stated that the future book had been written, but he had not yet received it. In 1969, long after Wallace Muhammad and Akbar Muhammad would have read this special Qur'an, Elijah Muhammad still expected his future book to appear: he wrote, "This last Messenger is bringing it out in a book that was written by Allah (God) himself—a book that was Sealed and Kept by Allah (God). This book has not, as yet, been released. But, it is promised to a last Messenger who lives among the beasts (human beasts), (Bible Rev. 6:3)."[74] Third, Warith Deen Mohammed later admitted that he had not been explicitly appointed by his father. In fact, it was so obvious to members of the Nation of Islam that Wallace D. Muhammad had not been appointed the successor that immediately after he assumed the leadership of the Nation of Islam in 1975, he was asked in an interview (by his own brother, Herbert Muhammad), "Why did your Father never teach the Muslims concerning His passing, nor openly tell them that they are to look to His family for spiritual direction, and to you especially?"[75] Nevertheless, Warith Deen Mohammed is not the only one to make the claim about his father. Some Muslims, such as Muhammad Abdullah (the leader of the Lahori Ahmadiyyas in California) in 1989 claimed, "Elijah followed the real Islam, but he thought that if he taught the real Islam, black people would not follow him. Elijah thought that he should push certain things to arouse curiosity so he and Fard Muhammad invented this story."[76]

This later reimagining of Fard Muhammad and Elijah Muhammad into "crypto-orthodox" Muslims whose followers were in fact "proto-Muslims" is also not congruent with the vehemence with which Elijah Muhammad taught his race myth, his hostility to Muslims who disagreed with him, and the expulsion of his own sons in the late 1960s and early 1970s for their "orthodox" beliefs. To see all of this as a ruse or even a pedagogical ploy does not, therefore, explain the role of Islam within Elijah Muhammad's myths and movement.

If one feels the need to engage in such a revisionist strategy, a more plausible tactic would be to argue that Elijah Muhammad was a "proto-Muslim" himself.[77] Curtis suggests that Elijah Muhammad's use of the Qur'an to justify his own teachings "elevated the status of traditional Sunni Islamic discourse, especially its sacred texts, within African-American Islamic thought. . . ."[78] The consequences of this elevation not only gave the upper hand to Elijah Muhammad's Sunni opponents but also eventually affected key players within the Nation of Islam, most notably his own sons Akbar and Wallace Muhammad and his first protégé, Malcolm X. Thus, Elijah Muhammad's exegetical techniques made the eventual move to some form of orthodoxy, while unpremeditated, inevitable. If he is to be considered a proto-Muslim, it cannot be by the ends he hoped to achieve, as Warith Deen Mohammed suggests, but by the means he used to achieve his other ends.

6

The Legacy of Elijah Muhammad

Drew Ali, Fard Muhammad, and especially Elijah Muham-
mad, because they were located so far away from the traditional centers of
Islam, had the unique opportunity to define and redefine Islam for many
years without significant interference from Muslims with more traditional
understandings of Islam. They seized this freedom to experiment with
novel conceptions and formulations of Islam. However, as the historian of
Islam Yvonne Haddad points out, "this freedom is fraught with the danger of innovation and deviance: the great range of options available in the
American context carries the threat of sectarian division and fragmenta-
tion."[1] Nowhere is this experimentation and deviation more apparent than
in Elijah Muhammad's Nation of Islam. But what kind of impact did Elijah Muhammad's redefinition have on American Islam and Muslims? In
other words, what was his legacy?

There are many ways to evaluate the legacy of Elijah Muhammad's particular formulation of Islam. Certainly he achieved great economic success and served as a model for how African Americans could improve
their socioeconomic status. He was also successful in profoundly altering
the lives of many recidivists and criminals. He forcefully equated blackness with power:

> No other historical personality has had the kind of prolonged impact on
> black consciousness that he has had, and no recent group in the African-
> American community has promoted—largely by example—economic
> self-help, cultural regeneration (or redefinition), and moral living more
> vigorously than his Nation of Islam. The Muslims were "black" long be-
> fore it became fashionable to be labeled as such, and the Black Power
> Movement and all subsequent African-American protest styles, from the
> rhymes of the nationalistic rap group Public Enemy to the raison d'être of
> the Million Man March, are undeniably offshoots of the legacy of Elijah
> Muhammad.[2]

But to this legacy must be added some caveats. He was extremely conservative economically, morally, socially, and politically.[3] Economically, he never deviated from the notion of Western capitalism. He simply sought to create an independent, black capitalist society—one whose measures of success were wealth and property. Morally, he enforced modest dress and harsh penalties for sexual infractions. Socially, he created a patriarchal organization in which women often fared poorly. Elijah Muhammad, not unlike some Muslim leaders in some countries, argued that women needed to be protected and controlled by their fathers and husbands and had to dress extremely conservatively.[4] Politically, he was a racial separatist, arguing for segregation[5] and demanding that African Americans be given several states within the continental United States for their own independent and separate territory. Furthermore, though his rhetoric advocated activism, his restrictions enforced quietism. But even on some racial issues, his views were surprisingly stereotypical. For instance, he saw Africa as a mere extension of Asia; Blacks were Asiatics, not Africans. Moreover, he considered Africa uncivilized and, except for the Christians and Muslims, full of naked jungle dwellers.[6] These positive and negative aspects of his legacy, however remarkable, are not central in defining his *Muslim* legacy.

The Muslim Legacy of Elijah Muhammad

Elijah Muhammad was arguably the most influential American Muslim in the twentieth century because he brought so many (African) Americans to Islam and was instrumental in establishing Islam in America.

> Because of him, there was a temple or mosque in a hundred cities where no mosques had existed before. There was a visible presence in the form of a hundred thousand Black Muslims—conspicuous in their frequent rallies and turnouts, and their little groceries and restaurants and bakeries and other small businesses. The clean shaven young Muslims hawking their newspapers on the streets, celebrating their rituals in prisons, debating their beliefs in the media gave to the religion of Islam a projection and a prominence undreamed of in North America.[7]

Most of the other significant African American advocates of Islam who might rival his stature and accomplishments, including Malcolm X, Louis Farrakhan, and his own son Warith Deen Mohammed, were first introduced to Islam through Elijah Muhammad; they are part of his Muslim legacy.

By placing Malcolm X within Elijah Muhammad's legacy, I am not minimizing Malcolm X's influence on African Americans. Especially in the decades after his death, his influence rivals and all but eclipses that of Elijah Muhammad in cultural and political black nationalist philosophy. In that regard, he even easily overshadows Warith Deen Mohammed and Louis Farrakhan. However, in terms of Islam as a religion, Malcolm X did not live long enough to challenge Elijah Muhammad or his two successors. Other members of the Nation of Islam had rejected Elijah Muhammad's formulation of Islam for a more Sunni formulation prior to Malcolm X, but with limited success. How exactly Malcolm X, with his energy, charisma, intellect, and influence, would have formulated his Islam and how successful he would have been cannot be known. It is equally tantalizing to speculate about the relative effectiveness of the transformation of African American Islam by Warith Deen Mohammed and Malcolm X. Although both came to reject Elijah Muhammad's formulation of Islam, they did so in radically different ways. As will be discussed below, the son of Elijah Muhammad chose gradual reform from within. And despite the resistance from Louis Farrakhan and his followers, he was largely successful. Malcolm X, in contrast, opted for immediate revolution from without. Once again, unfortunately, a comparison and analysis of Warith Deen Mohammed's and Malcolm X's methods are just not possible because of the latter's death less than a year after his revolution (in terms of Islam) began.

Both of these men, along with all of Elijah Muhammad's thousands of followers, had to struggle with the dual, ironic aspects of the Islamic legacy: they were brought into the tradition of Islam by a man who was, and still is, largely rejected by that tradition. The latter two men, Warith Deen Muhammad and Louis Farrakhan,[8] who came to vie for the authority of Elijah Muhammad, epitomize the ways in which Elijah Muhammad's followers dealt with his dichotomous Muslim legacy.

Warith Deen Mohammed

Warith Deen Mohammed was Elijah Muhammad's seventh son, born in 1933 in Detroit—the last child to be born before Fard Muhammad disappeared. His father named him Wallace Delaney Muhammad after Fard Muhammad. He had little contact with his father during the first thirteen years of his life since Elijah Muhammad was away preaching or, later, in prison until 1946. Nevertheless, Wallace Muhammad received his entire formal education within the Nation of Islam's University of Islam. He also studied Islam and Arabic for several additional years under orthodox Muslims, including Jamil Diab. Already in the late 1950s and early 1960s, Wallace Muhammad was seen by many of Elijah Muhammad's followers as the logical successor to his father.[9] In many ways he followed his father. In 1959, he accompanied Elijah Muhammad on his 'umra and tour of the Middle East and Pakistan. In 1961, Wallace Muhammad was also convicted of draft evasion. On his twenty-eighth birthday he started serving his three-year sentence in a federal penitentiary, opting for the prison sentence over community service because he felt the latter would still aid the war effort in Vietnam.

In prison, with time on his hands to study the Qur'an, Wallace Muhammad began to see that his father's teachings differed significantly from those of orthodox Islam. Even as a young man, he had doubts about the teachings of his father. Wallace Muhammad had noticed that, in the famous oil painting of Fard Muhammad that Elijah Muhammad kept in his house, the founder of this black Islamic movement looked very much like a white man. Just prior to his incarceration he had even approached his father with concerns. Upon his release, Wallace Muhammad did not confront his father again, but resumed his position as minister within the Nation of Islam.

Wallace Muhammad's first break with Elijah Muhammad was not based solely on religious matters. He was one of the people who confirmed to Malcolm X that Elijah Muhammad had fathered illegitimate children. They conferred to try to find biblical and quranic justifications for these extramarital activities[10]—the very same justifications that Malcolm X later broached with Elijah Muhammad. Malcolm X wrote, "I felt that Wallace was Mr. [Elijah] Muhammad's most strongly spiritual son, the son with the most objective outlook. Always, Wallace and I shared an exceptional closeness and trust."[11] Wallace Muhammad had also tried to convince Malcolm X that "the only possible solution for the Nation of Islam would be its accepting and projecting a better understanding of Orthodox Islam."[12] He remained loyal to Malcolm X after the latter was expelled from the Nation of Islam. For his role in this scandal, he was briefly suspended from the movement in 1964, and then a few months later left the Nation of Islam. As we have seen, after Malcolm X was assassinated, Wallace Muhammad hastily returned to the fold, perhaps out of fear.[13] However, he was later suspended at least two more times—though now solely for matters of belief. He could not accept the belief that Allah had existed in human form in his namesake. He was reinstated in 1969 and again in 1971, but only in 1974 did he regain his position as a minister in the Nation of Islam. Wallace Muhammad claimed that when he was accepted back by his father, Elijah Muhammad gave his consent to move the Nation of Islam to Sunni orthodoxy and abandon its racialist teachings, saying, "My son's got it, my son can go anywhere on earth and preach."[14]

Prior to Elijah Muhammad's death in 1975, Wallace Muhammad secured the support (or at least obedience) of key members of the Nation of Islam, including Louis Farrakhan, Raymond Sharrieff, and two of his brothers. One day after his father's death, at the annual Saviour's Day rally, Wallace Muhammad was acclaimed his father's successor in front of the thousands of Muslims in attendance. The event included having the key members publicly pledge allegiance to him. This seems to have been part of the initial propaganda campaign. Within *Muhammad Speaks* this campaign included showing two pictures of Wallace Muhammad within a picture of Elijah Muhammad on the first page of the issue announcing the latter's death; including the famous picture of a seated Elijah Muhammad with Wallace Muhammad standing beside him with his hand on his father's shoulder (with the oil painting of Fard Muhammad behind them and the Qur'an in front of them); having pictures of the top officials of the Nation of Islam and family members (e.g., Yusuf Shah, Nathaniel Muhammad, Abass Rassoull, Raymond Sharrieff, Muhammad Ali, Abdul Karriem, Abdul Rahman, Jeremiah Shabbaz, and Louis Farrakhan) over the heading "Muslim Ministers Declare Support for New Leadership"; printing Wallace Muhammad's rambling Saviour's Day speech where Elijah Muhammad's column would usually have been; and having the editor and the Middle East columnist both devote their columns to proclaiming the succession of Wallace Muhammad.[15]

As its new Supreme Minister, Wallace Muhammad rapidly reformed the Nation of Islam. Financially, he separated the businesses from the Nation of Islam. Despite being worth $46 million ($30 million less than had been thought), the Nation of Islam had millions of dollars of debt. Financial necessity forced the selling off of businesses to pay creditors, including the Internal Revenue Service. Far more significantly, the racial superiority doctrine, the demonizing of Whites, the demand for a separate state for African Americans, and anti-American and anti-Christian slogans were dropped or reinterpreted. For example, Whites were no longer devils, but the mindset that had dominated them was devilish. This kind of relabeling was a key feature of his reforms. The nationality of his followers was changed from the tribe of Shabazz to Bilalians. (Bilal was an African slave in Mecca who converted to Islam in the time of Muhammad the Prophet. Although Muhammad's opponents could not directly physically persecute him, Bilal, as a slave, was attacked. Later, he became the first muezzin, the one who called people to prayer.) This identification with Bilal would also prove problematic and was later dropped. Most significantly, as we have seen, Fard Muhammad became a "wise man" instead of Allah in person and his father became "Master" as opposed to Allah's Messenger. Finally, even Wallace's own role, title, and name, as well as the name of the Nation of Islam, were changed; he was not a messenger but a "*mujeddid*" (a reviver of Islam);[16] he was not the Supreme Minister of the Nation of Islam, the Honorable Wallace D. Muhammad but Imam Warith Deen Mohammed—with the change in spelling of "Muhammad" indicating an intentional break with any claim to be a messenger; and the Nation of Islam was first renamed the World Community of al-Islam in the West and later changed to the American Muslim Mission. Thus, a year and a half after Elijah Muhammad died, his movement also died.

As Warith Deen Mohammed, Wallace D. Muhammad also found a way incorporate his father's mythology, though at the same time rejecting it. That is, as we have seen, Warith Deen Mohammed claimed that the move to "orthodoxy" was not only acceptable but also always intended and prophesied by Fard Muhammad himself. Fard had consciously, though secretly, sowed the seeds for the Nation of Islam's own demise in favor of the move to Sunni Islam. What Warith Deen Mohammed's motivation was for reimagining Fard Muhammad is not certain. However, several possibilities exist. First, denigrating Fard Muhammad might have undermined Warith Deen Mohammed's own mystique. He was Elijah Muhammad's seventh son, the only one born during the time of Fard Muhammad, predicted by Fard Muhammad, and named after Fard Muhammad. This mystique was at least partially responsible for his acclamation as leader after his father's death, despite his having been excommunicated several times by his father.[17] In fact, initially Warith Deen Mohammed had even capitalized on and played up this mystique; just a month after his ascension in 1975, in answer to the question "Why were you chosen to succeed your Father, rather than one of the elder brothers?" he answered,

> My personal answer would be it was God's intention. It was God's plan. But I have also heard my Father, Himself, say that when I was born or I was conceived in my mother, He had been born as the Servant, the

Messenger of God, who manifested Himself with W. F. Muhammad; and by me being born at the time when He was in contact with His Savior, the God in Person, helped to form me, not only as a child of His loins, but a child for the Mission. . . . [T]here was never any doubt in His mind that I would be the one who would come to this office.[18]

A second reason for his reimagining Fard Muhammad relates to Louis Farrakhan. Warith Deen Mohammed also extended the olive branch to Farrakhan, who so disagreed with Warith Deen Mohammed's reforms that he "resurrected" the Nation of Islam with its original teachings and has led it for over three decades. Warith Deen Mohammed may have simply been showing greater respect for their shared heritage in order to bring the two groups closer, particularly as both leaders approach the end of their lives.

And third, many members of Warith Deen Mohammed's organization came to Islam via the Nation of Islam. For many years Fard Muhammad was their Allah and Elijah Muhammad was his Messenger. The myth of Fard Muhammad's secret plan to bring African Americans to Sunni Islam as constructed by Warith Deen Mohammed made it possible to understand their earlier "unislamic" beliefs as a prerequisite stage. It reflected their own journey, validating who they *were* and who they *are*.

In a final irony, Warith Deen Mohammed managed even to separate his own father, Elijah Muhammad, from the Nation of Islam: he believed that Elijah Muhammad wrestled with Fard Muhammad's words and was convinced that his father lived to reject privately the heretical notions of Fard Muhammad as God and himself and as his prophet.[19] In other words, Elijah Muhammad died an "orthodox" Sunni Muslim.

Louis Farrakhan

Scholar of African American religion Lawrence Mamiya has argued that the changes in ideology and practice wrought by Warith Deen Mohammed were largely successful because Elijah Muhammad's "do for self" economic program had been remarkably effective. By the mid-1970s the socioeconomic status of many members of the Nation of Islam had changed as a result of that progress. The "black particularism" ideology that had drawn lower-class members to the movement was not appropriate for their new middle-class lives. For them, Warith Deen Mohammed's transformation to "universalist" Islam came at the right time for many members of the Nation of Islam: middle-class African Americans did not need or want the strict discipline, the racial barriers, and the alienation from mainstream American political, social, and economic life.[20]

However, many African Americans had not yet made that transformation and were still relegated to the lower classes, with all the moral, social, and economic ills that had made Elijah Muhammad's original message so potent and so attractive. Warith Deen Mohammed's reinterpretation would not have been particularly appealing for them. Moreover, with such drastic reinterpretations of the key tenets of the Nation of Islam, it is not surprising that more conservative adherents, many of whom had intense admiration for, loyalty to, and fervent belief in, Elijah Muhammad, would strongly object. The man who led that movement of objectors was Louis Farrakhan. In 1977 he reestablished the Nation of Islam with Elijah Muhammad's original teachings.

Louis Farrakhan was born Louis Eugene Walcott in the Bronx in 1933, though he was raised in Boston. He became one of the more educated leaders within the Nation of Islam, having earned a high school diploma and studied for two years at a teachers' college. Prior to joining the Nation of Islam, he worked as a professional musician, as a violinist, and as a calypso singer. When Elijah Muhammad ordered all musicians in the Nation of Islam to give up music or leave, Louis X gave up music even though he had been a member for only a few weeks. Later, his musical talent would be used on behalf of the Nation of Islam when he wrote their theme song, "A White Man's Heaven Is a Black Man's Hell." As we have seen, although Malcolm X helped to convert him and to train this equally charismatic speaker as a minister, Minister Louis X was among those who reported to Elijah Muhammad that Malcolm X was spreading rumors about the leader's adulterous activities. And after Malcolm X and the Nation of Islam parted ways, Louis X publicly and viciously attacked his former mentor.

With Malcolm X's removal, Louis X stepped into his shoes. He became the minister of the prestigious Temple No. 7 in New York City and was soon appointed the National Spokesman, whose duties included introducing Elijah Muhammad at the annual Saviour's Day rallies—both formerly Malcolm X's portfolios. Elijah Muhammad replaced his "X" with "Farrakhan" in the late 1960s as a sign of his new protégé's ascension to the inner circle. After Elijah Muhammad's death, Farrakhan initially supported Warith Deen Mohammed (then still called Wallace D. Muhammad) as the new Supreme Minister of the Nation of Islam. In 1975 he is quoted as saying, "There is no one wise enough to approach the shoelaces of Wallace D. Muhammad" and "The teachings of Wallace D. Muhammad are so right, so exact, so on time. . . ."[21] Furthermore, in the issue of *Muhammad Speaks* that announced the death of Elijah Muhammad and the acclamation of Wallace Muhammad as his successor, Louis Farrakhan is quoted as saying, "The Hon. Elijah Muhammad's life was the will of God: His son is the will of God. . . . Allah did not leave us comfortless. He knew we would need a comforter."[22] However, it is clear that he was seen as a threat within the Nation of Islam. In his first interview as the new leader of the Nation of Islam, Wallace Muhammad was asked about Louis Farrakhan specifically: "We understand he had pledged his allegiance to you just as he did to your Father before you, along with the other ministers of the Nation. Do you feel that you can depend on their loyalty if outside influences and inside influences try to bring about a split in the Nation of Islam?" Wallace Muhammad replied, "Their pledges of allegiance were received in all sincerity. I have nothing to say that would reflect anything else. One correction here: The title of Minister Louis Farrakhan is National Representative of the Supreme Minister."[23] He served as Wallace Muhammad's international spokesman until December 1977, when he announced his departure from the newly Sunni movement.

Louis Farrakhan formed another organization, the Nation of Islam, based on all the original doctrines of Elijah Muhammad, including the doctrines of Fard Muhammad's divinity, the story of Yakub, the Fall of America, a demand for a separate territory, and the claim that Whites are devils. He also reinitiated the defunct Fruit of Islam and the Muslim Girl's Training and General Civilization Class.

Louis Farrakhan had done much to bolster his position, from marrying his family into that of Elijah Muhammad's to attempting to parallel the latter's life.[24] It is clear that his followers came to see him as the rightful successor to Elijah Muhammad. They claim that Elijah Muhammad said to Louis Farrakhan, "As Allah made me to take His place among the people, I am making you to . . . take my place." And they claim that towards the end of his life Elijah Muhammad said that Farrakhan was the best minister he ever had.[25] Yet, even Farrakhan drifted in later years from some of the teachings of Elijah Muhammad. He too has introduced more Sunni practices into his second resurrection of the Nation of Islam,[26] and in the last decade made a rapprochement with Warith Deen Mohammed—for which he too has been criticized by even more conservative followers of Elijah Muhammad.[27]

Islamic Mythmaking in America[28]

The most prominent feature of Elijah Muhammad's formulation of Islam is his synthesis of much of traditional Islam with the racial teachings that he inherited from Fard Muhammad. Louis Farrakhan and Warith Deen Mohammed represent two different responses to Elijah Muhammad's forty years of mythmaking. Each of his successors tried to separate his race myth from his Islam myth by emphasizing one over the other. In so doing, they each introduced a false dichotomy into Elijah Muhammad's myth. He would not have seen Islam and his race teachings as in any way separate or even separable. The centrality of Islam (as a symbol) to his movement, his relation to other Muslims, his role within Islam, his use and interpretation of the Qur'an, and all the connections among these elements situate him firmly within the Islamic tradition and can be understood as the intertwined activities of social formation and mythmaking.

Myths and Mythmaking

Although anthropologists, psychologists, sociologists, mythologists, and scholars of religions have produced many definitions for the word "myth," most of them can be categorized in one of two ways. Those in the first category are similar to the popular definition of the word "myth": a false or implausible (and usually someone else's) belief or tale. Within this category fall those definitions that view myths as a product of euhemerism (which suggests that myths are based on exaggerated accounts of real people) or ancient savage philosophers trying to explain mysterious phenomena. In either case, the myths are false, though still interesting objects of study for the insights they provide into the minds of our ancestors. Certainly, there are euhemeristic qualities to the status accorded to Fard Muhammad, and perhaps even Elijah Muhammad. However, such an approach to the Nation of Islam's myths would prove pointless. Although people outside the Nation of Islam are unlikely to view their myths as anything but false, such an approach would bring us no closer to determining the reasons for the creation, appeal, and endurance of these myths among the members of these movements.

The second category of definitions for myth is that which tends to view myths as "true" in some sense. Of course, there are many ways for something to be true. A myth might be true in that it expresses something that is psychically real. For Sigmund Freud, myths are the social equivalent of dreams—both a product of repression. And, as the product of drives repressed for the sake of a harmonious civilization, myths could be seen as both true and false: they express a truth, but a truth that is not what it seems. (A similar claim might be made about Emile Durkheim, who would see myth as a true expression of group cohesiveness, but again a truth that is not what it seems.) For Carl Jung, myths also symbolically express a deep psychic reality. They are culturally determined manifestations of the universal archetypes that abide within the collective unconscious. Therefore, myths are true in the most crucial sense, albeit not ever literally true. Yet for some others, myths are products of a different mentality, one that is nonrational or beyond the rational (that is, mystical or emotional in nature). Once again, we have a different kind of "true." Closely related to Jung's and to mythopoeic definitions are those that suggest that myths are symbolically imbued with something that ultimately cannot be reduced or rationalized away. That is to say, myths express primordial truths, or the "sacred." Hence, they are true by definition. Although disguised in various forms, this kind of definition is espoused by such scholars as Mircea Eliade, Wendy Doniger-O'Flaherty, and Kees W. Bolle, to name only a few.

Accepting the myths of Elijah Muhammad as true, in whatever sense, seems even more problematic than dismissing them as false. That these myths were produced by individuals as opposed to groups is difficult to reconcile with some of the truth-definitions of myth, especially when the eclectic themes of Fard Muhammad's and Elijah Muhammad's myths seem to be borrowed from various sources.[29] Elijah Muhammad's myths also suffer from having been born less than a century ago. We know *how* and *when* the myths came to be. Furthermore, given the racial claims made by him, even the most open-minded and sanguine scholar might balk at seeing primordial truths or the sacred encapsulated within these myths. New myths are not as easily romanticized as their ancient cousins.

A third and more fruitful approach would be to examine these myths from a perspective that dismisses myths neither as impotent and largely irrelevant falsehoods nor as powerful and profound truths, but rather as the product of a surprisingly ordinary human activity. Russell McCutcheon redescribes the category of "myth" by suggesting

(1) that myths are not special (or "sacred") but ordinary human means of fashioning and authorizing their lived-in and believed-in "worlds,"

(2) that myth as an ordinary rhetorical device in social construction

and maintenance makes *this* rather than *that* social identity possible in the first place, and (3) that a people's use of the *label* "myth" reflects, expresses, explores and legitimizes their own self-image.[30]

The key words within his redescription are "ordinary," "identity," and "authorizing" (or "construction," "maintenance," and "legitimizing"). The term "ordinary" suggests that we are not dealing with some human activity that is beyond our ken. It is not extraordinary, unique, unknowable, or, in a word, "sacred." That is not to suggest that myths are therefore irrelevant; they deal with the critical human issue of self-identity. These rhetorical acts that construct and maintain identity are called mythmaking. Simply put, mythmaking is a social activity in which the group authorizes its identity and the role it sees for itself in the larger scheme of things.[31] It is one of the key ways in which a group forms and perpetuates itself. Consequently, myths have no inherent power or truth other than that bestowed upon them by the group that identifies itself through them.

One might well ask at this point what distinguishes mythmaking from other rhetorical acts of constructing and maintaining group identities. In a word, nothing. More elaborately stated, mythmaking can describe any rhetorical act whose goal is to create, renew, sustain, or radically reenvision a group identity—whether within a street gang, a nation, a religious community, or in this case a people identified by the color of their skin. What distinguishes "religious" mythmaking from "other" rhetorical acts (that some scholars might hesitate to call "mythmaking") is the tendency of the former type of acts "to speak of things eternal and transcendent with an authority equally transcendent and eternal."[32] The real question becomes whether this particular feature is sufficiently unique to demand that a distinction in terminology be made between rhetorical acts that have this feature and those that do not (but otherwise are similar in methods and outcomes). The answer to this question is, probably not. Nevertheless, mythmaking as practiced by Elijah Muhammad had this feature, and its presence explains the key, though seemingly odd, role that Islam plays within his mythmaking.

Elijah Muhammad's Mythmaking

The new and relatively recently created myths of Elijah Muhammad may seem strange and incredible at times, but these mythic ideas need to be viewed as plausible and appropriate to the self-understanding of a group of people, [33] in this case, Elijah Muhammad's followers. In other words, he was revising the past, "in light of present circumstances from a particular point of view to support a critical judgment about the present state of affairs."[34] The race myth provided a history that reversed the traditional account of the European and African contributions to civilization and so was a source of pride, inspiration, and revolutionary ideas to African Americans.[35] It would certainly appeal to people who saw the racist behavior of Whites as uncivilized. Moreover, the myth in positing an ancient golden age of black civilization not only appeals to the pride of African Americans but also dismisses all of the intervening and recent history as a departure from that ideal. The message is clear: to return to the greatness of old, one must return to (the Nation of) Islam. This is a common strategy in mythmaking: to seek or create a pristine moment in the past and bracket out the intervening and recent history as a failure to maintain that purity.[36]

At first glance it seems that Elijah Muhammad simply aligned the Nation of Islam with a slightly revised, more ancient, "black" Islam. Likewise, Jewish and Christian mythologies may seem as though they were reinterpreted in light of the antebellum and postbellum circumstances of African Americans. Most of his writings, after all, are laced with passages from the Bible—more than double the number from the Qur'an. But on closer inspection, it is clear that Elijah Muhammad built upon Fard Muhammad's race myth, which owed little to Judaism, Christianity, or Islam. The story of the tribe of Shabazz, of Yakub and his white race, of the enslavement of Blacks in America, and of the Fall of America could have been told without reference to the Bible or the Qur'an—*but they were not.* What Elijah Muhammad did was to reinterpret individual biblical and quranic passages (and sometimes their myths) to fit, substantiate, and elaborate his myth. This is particularly evident in the depictions of Moses, Jesus, and Muhammad, whose traditional biographies are ignored and for whom new roles are created within Elijah Muhammad's Islam.

In this way, he was able to dismiss Christianity, the religion from which his converts came, not as unnatural for African Americans (as Drew Ali had done) but as evil. Yet, at the same time, he could continue to appeal to the one scripture with which African Americans were familiar—the Bible—and in a way that left them utterly dependent on him for its interpretation. By employing Islam and its scripture, the Qur'an, within his mythmaking, Elijah Muhammad was able to develop new Islamic identities for his followers and a new Islamic authority for himself that could replace the ones he had just dismissed as evil.

The New Islamic Identities

At first sight the Islam of Elijah Muhammad and his myths may seem to be mere products of his overactive imagination. However, mythmaking is most frequently an organic activity that explains how a group sees itself and its place within the world; by its very nature mythmaking is not systematic but experimental. The key element in the myths created by Elijah Muhammad was their ability to present an identity that was appropriate for the circumstances of the group and so made sense and appealed to the members of that group. Otherwise, these myths would not have been understood, believed, and propagated.

A brief look at some of the more salient aspects of Elijah Muhammad's myths illustrates some of the myths' appropriateness for African Americans. Elijah Muhammad drew on Marcus Garvey and Drew Ali. The acceptability of a demand to return to Africa, spiritually and mentally in the case of Drew Ali, is deeply indebted to Garvey. Drew Ali simply found an eminently more feasible way to return to the homeland. The use of Islamic terminology and imagery was also made possible by vestiges of Islam among African Americans and the association of Islam as the enemy of Christianity. Elijah Muhammad also capitalized on these factors, but took the race consciousness of Drew Ali to the next level, race supremacy, and transformed the return to the homeland to a demand for the separation of Blacks and Whites, and for a separate nation within the continental United States. Islam was the evidence for supremacy, the means for transformation, and the motivation for separation.

The appeal of this greater militancy was no doubt heightened by the continued disparities between Whites and Blacks despite the economic growth after World War II. The practices and scripture of the Nation of Islam were far more Islamic than those of the Moorish Science Temple. Yet the role of traditional formulations of Islam in this new identity was somewhat limited. That was by design, or more accurately, by necessity. This new Islamic identity spoke directly to the racial problems faced by African Americans. It provided a past that reversed white supremacist myths, thereby declaring that the appalling situation was not how it was in the distant past, should be in the present, or would be in the future. It was a theodicy that said that such things were prophesied to end, thereby declaring that change was not only possible but *inevitable*— if only African Americans would adopt the right identity: the Islamic one.[37]

Elijah Muhammad's mythmaking was not simply a matter of arranging or rearranging ideas to produce a particular image, story, or set of symbols. Despite the apparently conscious production of these myths by an individual, it is clear that social circumstances and the appeal of new and noble identities motivated the production and adoption of these myths. Islam—as formulated by Elijah Muhammad—was absolutely essential to these new identities.

The New Islamic Authorities

The new Islamic identities included seeing Elijah Muhammad as the supreme authority within Islam. But what does it mean for a text or person to have authority? Authority can be contrasted usefully with coercion and persuasion, two additional but not unrelated ways in which a person may make other people do his or her will. However, the acts or threats of violence and the use of arguments or impassioned appeals are not same as authority. Authority is something people confer willingly:

> If authority involves the willingness of an audience to treat a given act of speech as credible because of its trust in the speaker, then under the sway of authority an audience acts *as if* it had been persuaded, *when in fact it has not*, while accepting the fact that its regard for the speaker obviates the need for persuasion. In contrast, when authority is asked to explain itself and responds to that request by arguing in earnest rather than simply reasserting itself, it ceases to be authority for the moment and becomes (an attempt at) persuasion.[38]

It is in this gray area between authority and persuasion that we find the roles assigned to Islam and the Qur'an by Elijah Muhammad. Islam and its Qur'an were used as insignia of authority. Insignia "announce the authority of the bearer for a given audience and within a circumscribed context or sphere of activity."[39] And they play an active role in the construction of that authority. Those who bear insignia will be granted authority: their words will be given respect.

The construction of an Islamic authority structure by Elijah Muhammad is most apparent in his use of the most tangible emblem of Islam, the Qur'an. For Noble Drew Ali, the actual Qur'an was of almost no importance. Even the *Circle Seven Koran* was not authoritative in and of itself; it was an insigne of authority. It need not, therefore, bear any resemblance to the actual Qur'an. It just needed to be a *Koran*—a scripture, the iconic emblem of prophethood—and in this case one associated with Islam, a non-Christian religion reflective of Drew Ali's conception of the Moors.[40] Not so for Elijah Muhammad. For him the Qur'an served several different roles. At first the Qur'an was unfamiliar, especially to his followers. The first time Elijah Muhammad wrote about the Qur'an, he had to describe its history, extol its virtues, and assert the need to respect it (in part by denigrating the Bible).[41] In short, he attempted to persuade his audience that the Qur'an was the proper and ancestral scripture for African Americans. Elijah Muhammad then employed the Qur'an as scripture, which meant for him that it was a text containing prayers, history, and, above all, *prophecies*. Its history was the history of the races and its prophecies were about the conflict between Blacks and Whites in America. For example, the theodicy most often employed by Elijah Muhammad to explain why the devils were permitted to make slaves of African Americans' "innocent, Righteous forefathers in Africa" is "Allah, our God, has revealed to us that it was all for a Divine Purpose—to fulfill the prophecies of the Scriptures."[42] From Elijah Muhammad's perspective, scripture's power, its authority, came largely from the historical and prophetic truths it contained. Once scriptural passages were understood properly, these truths would become manifest. His role as Messenger was to discover and propagate these truths. And in this way prophetic scripture, specifically the passages of the Bible or the Qur'an that he felt addressed his race myth and eschatology, served as the insignia of his prophethood. Because of the direction given to the movement by Fard Muhammad and the connections Elijah Muhammad thought Islam had with Africa, these insignia needed to be the actual Qur'an (not just "a Qur'an")—but in this case one subservient to Elijah Muhammad's racial message about the separation between Blacks and Whites.

The mere fact that Islam and the Qur'an served as insignia of authority for Elijah Muhammad does not mean that they were merely paraphernalia (as the Qur'an was for Drew Ali). Instead, they had a central and critical role for Elijah Muhammad. The Qur'an, as he understood it, was part of the politicization of Islam with himself as its Messenger—as the original and only appropriate religion for African Americans. The Qu'ran was central and critical, yes, but it was never meant to be ultimate authority: Elijah Muhammad gave primacy to the racial teachings that he had received directly from Allah, in the person of Fard Muhammad. Moreover, he maintained that the Qur'an would one day be superseded. In a strange twist of fate, he was wrong.

Elijah Muhammad was so successful at establishing himself as *the* Islamic authority that his insignia, Islam and the Qur'an, were also imbued with that authority. When he died in 1975, the authority he had created for himself died with him for the most part. (Vestiges remained, many of which transferred to his son Wallace Muhammad, and some of which would later be reclaimed by Louis Farrakhan.)[43] Islam and the Qur'an, not surprisingly, outlived Elijah Muhammad. As a result, Warith Deen Mohammed could move Elijah Muhammad's followers towards a fairly traditional Sunni understanding of Islam and the Qur'an with relative ease by simply invoking the remaining authorities within the Nation of Islam. Ironically, then, the very insignia Elijah Muhammad had first employed to bolster his own authority and to fashion the new identities for his followers—the Qur'an and Islam—came to supplant that authority and redefine those identities. "Islam" is, therefore, not only critical to understanding Elijah Muhammad and his Nation of Islam but also essential to understanding why both he—in the mind of Warith Deen Mohammed at least—and it could so easily be transformed.

Conclusion

Elijah Muhammad's formulation of Islam did not emerge in a vacuum. Vestiges of Islam from Muslim African forebears probably did not survive within Elijah Muhammad's African American contemporaries. The association of Islam with Africa and the depiction of Islam as the opponent of white Christianity—both of which may have made African Americans more receptive to Islam—were more likely derived from American islamicism. These factors assisted Drew Ali and Ahmadiyya Muslim missionaries as they sought to convert African Americans to their unique formulations of Islam. These new Islams in turn set the stage for the missionary activities of Elijah Muhammad. In other words, in many ways Elijah Muhammad and his followers had been prepared for this reintroduction of Islam into the African American community by their own ancestry, by islamicism, and by earlier Muslim missionaries.

The success of the Nation of Islam is, however, predicated primarily on the genius of Fard Muhammad and the devotion and dedication it inspired in Elijah Muhammad. His biography attests to the transformative and enduring power of this new formulation of Islam initiated by Fard Muhammad. The Nation of Islam founded by Fard Muhammad and developed by Elijah Muhammad taught that Islam was the original and inherent religion of African Americans. Part of their Islam included the myth that African Americans were the descendants of the original black humanity, who later produced the "wicked white race." Their unique formulation of Islam is a product of mythmaking and social formation, mutually reinforcing activities that are sped up in times of social disintegration and cultural change.[44] It is perhaps no surprise then that Elijah Muhammad was from the South and that many of the Nation of Islam's adherents, like himself, had recently moved to the North. Because of their experiences in the South, the willingness to move in search of a better life, and their disappointment in the North, these people were undoubtedly the most race conscious, the most courageous, and the most disillusioned.[45] To belong to a group whose myths, identities, and authority structures challenged the status quo and the traditional white characterizations of African Americans and proposed a radical alternative that promised to end and reverse current injustices would have been very attractive indeed.[46] Elijah Muhammad as the chief architect of these myths, authority structures, and identities may have produced his own formulation of Islam. But a formulation *of Islam* it was.

Elijah Muhammad's message—as he understood it—was not merely based on, or inextricably intertwined with, Islam. It was Islam. His understanding and exegesis of the Qur'an highlight that Islam and its scripture were essential features of his mission and movement. For almost every aspect of his message he found quranic support. His heavy reliance on the Bible, given that he saw it as a "poison book," did not diminish the centrality of the Qur'an. Moreover, Elijah Muhammad's need to find in the Qur'an the basis for most of his teachings not only was Islamic but also forced his followers, including his son Warith Deen Mohammed, to become intimately familiar with the Qur'an. This relationship led the son to Sunni Islam, and smoothed the way for most of Elijah Muhammad's Nation of Islam to follow him there.

Elijah Muhammad can thus only be understood within the context of Islam.[47] Even his willingness, perhaps even need, to engage Muslim opponents does not indicate that he stood outside of Islam; in fact, quite the opposite. It clearly demonstrates that his Muslim-ness was no mere façade for him. He was an active participant in that most traditional of Muslim debates, that is, the debate over who is a Muslim.

If the life, teachings, and legacy of Elijah Muhammad can only be understood properly within the context of Islam, then a troubling and interesting question presents itself: Why has Elijah Muhammad's Muslim-ness been so underemphasized by scholars? For those with a religious commitment to another formulation of Islam with a narrow set of acceptable beliefs and practices, it may be that Elijah Muhammad's formulation and theirs simply cannot be reconciled. But there may be another factor, especially for scholars who do not see themselves as apologists for more traditional forms of Islam. Despite the enormous legacy of Elijah Muhammad in terms of Islam in the United States, it is not his only legacy. Long before the Black Power movement of the 1960s, Elijah Muhammad had advocated that movement's key tenets: racial separation, black nationalism, economic independence, "black is beautiful," and even, at least in his rhetoric, the use of violence. Minimizing the role of Islam in these tenets allows Elijah Muhammad's less appealing ideas, such as the Mother Plane and his strange dietary regulations, to be overlooked and redirects focus on how for a quarter of a century embodied the ideals of black autonomy and black values better than anyone else. A similar revisioning took place with Malcolm X. His twelve-year adherence to and promulgation of Elijah Muhammad's teachings have been largely supplanted by his less than twelve months outside the Nation of Islam. Thus, he can be embraced by Sunni Muslim scholars as the paragon of acceptable African American Islam. For other scholars, and certainly within popular culture, this Muslim-ness (orthodox or otherwise) can be shorn from him completely. Thus, as historian Robin Kelley has pointed out,

> Malcolm X has been called many things: Pan-Africanist, father of Black Power, religious fanatic, closet conservative, incipient socialist, and a menace to society. . . . Malcolm has become a sort of *tabula rasa*, or blank slate, on which people of different positions can write their own interpretations of his politics and legacy. Chuck D of the rap group Public Enemy and Supreme Court Justice Clarence Thomas can both declare Malcolm X their hero.[48]

Interestingly, "Muslim" is not in the list. Similar forces seem to be at work on Elijah Muhammad's image. His great influence and numerous achievements are to be celebrated; his Islam and especially his novel formulation of it are to be quietly omitted. Given what this book has argued, such an enterprise is very problematic, if not impossible.

Moreover, it would be extremely ironic. Elijah Muhammad never got his autonomous black state and the racial separation that he desired. Even his enormous business empire was quickly dismantled. He did, however, despite being considered a heretic by so many other Muslims, do what these gainsayers could not: directly and indirectly Elijah Muhammad brought millions of African Americans into the Muslim world and Islam into the American world. This is his legacy—and it is an Islamic one.

Notes

INTRODUCTION

1. Muhammed's interview was published in three separate articles, and the preceding quotation was pieced together from these three articles: "Sixteen Journalists Obtain . . . Rare Interview," 3–4; "Muhammad Meets the Press!" (February 4, 1972): 3–4; and "Muhammad Meets the Press!" (February 11, 1972): 3–4.

2. Huntington, *The Clash of Civilizations and the Remaking of World Order*.

3. Smith, "Patterns of Muslim Immigration."

4. For more on this prejudice, see C. Eric Lincoln, *The Black Muslims in America*, 26 and chapter 6. Even Warith Deen Mohammed, Elijah Muhammad's son, shares this view. See chapter 5. For a discussion of a similar neglect by American historians, see Clegg, *An Original Man*, xi–xiii.

5. Muhammad, *Message to the Blackman in America*, 204.

6. See chapter 6.

7. McConkie, *Mormon Doctrine*, 513.

8. The term "orthodox" is extremely problematic since all Muslims believe they have "correct belief" regardless of the atypicality of their beliefs. It is a dangerous term for scholars of religion to employ, for it assumes a single articulation of Islam and implies a value judgment, perhaps even a theologically based judgment on what constitutes proper religious belief or practice and what does not. It is used, nevertheless, in this book because Elijah Muhammad himself employs the expression "orthodox Muslims" to describe his (usually Sunni) Muslim opponents.

CHAPTER 1

1. Wright, "Negro Companions of the Spanish Explorers," 226–28. See also Arrington, *Black Explorer in Spanish Texas*.

2. Wright, "Negro Companions of the Spanish Explorers," 228.

3. Hugh Thomas gives the figure of five hundred thousand in his *Slave Trade*, 804. Philip D. Curtin suggests 427,000 in his *Atlantic Slave Trade*, 71. Obviously, many more were brought to other countries in American ships.

4. Turner, "Mainstream Islam in the African-American Experience." Elsewhere, he cites Allan D. Austin's estimate of 7 to 8 percent. Turner, *Islam in the African-American Experience*, 12. Michael A. Gomez suggests that between 400,000 and 523,000 Africans were brought to British North America and "at least 200,000 came from areas influenced by Islam to varying degrees. Muslims may have come to America by the thousands, if not tens of thousands." Gomez, "Muslims in Early America," 682. See also Diouf, *Servants of Allah*, 45–48.

5. Diouf, *Servants of Allah*, 2.

6. Gomez, "Muslims in Early America," 672. The extent to which African American slaves were able to sustain their religions and cultures is a matter of some debate among scholars. Even when slaves seemingly adopted Christianity in lieu of their ancestral religions, it may not have been simply a matter of identity being erased. For instance, the adoption of Christianity and its message of spiritual equality may have resisted the dehumanization and self-destructive hatred engendered by slavery. R. L. Watson, "American Scholars and the Continuity of African Culture in the United States," 375–86, but especially 380.

7. Diouf, *Servants of Allah*, 6–8 and 107–44.

8. See Austin, *African Muslims in Antebellum America: Transatlantic Stories and Spiritual Struggles*, 32–156.

9. Gomez, "Muslims in Early America," 699.

10. Austin, *African Muslims in Antebellum America: A Sourcebook*, 29.

11. Diouf, *Servants of Allah*, 184–94.

12. Diouf, *Servants of Allah*, 185–90 and 205. In fact, Diouf suggests that the heretical beliefs of Elijah Muhammad (and Drew Ali) are such that "it is highly improbable that the last African Muslims in the Americas would have been involved in them." Diouf, *Servants of Allah*, 207. A similar conclusion is drawn by Sherman A. Jackson: it was "virtually impossible for African Muslim slaves to perpetuate their faith in America," and "[n]one of the distinct and palpable features of African Islam show up in the formative period of Blackamerican Islam." Jackson, *Islam and the Blackamerican*, 39.

13. Marr, *The Cultural Roots of American Islamicism*.

14. Jackson, *Islam and the Blackamerican*, 38.

15. Parts of this section have appeared in Berg, "Mythmaking in the American Muslim Context," 685–703.

16. Wilson, *Sacred Drift*, 15–16.

17. Robert Dannin points out that these activities were "reminiscent of early-nineteenth century attempts to commemorate the African-Islamic heritage of some slaves." Dannin, *Black Pilgrimage to Islam*, 27.

18. McCloud, *African American Islam*, 11; and Dannin, *Black Pilgrimage to Islam*, 28.

19. Fauset, *Black Gods of the Metropolis*, 72.

20. George Washington, who was a slave owner and aware of this Negro/Moor distinction, cut down the red banner of the Moors so as to hide this fact. This alleged event, incidentally, was said to have given rise to the "cherry-tree" legend. Wilson, *Sacred Drift*, 16–19.

21. For an analysis of this text, see chapter 3.

22. Ali, *The Holy* Koran, 57.

23. Fauset, *Black Gods of the Metropolis*, 47.

24. Dannin, *Black Pilgrimage to Islam*, 28. Emphasis added.

25. Fauset, *Black Gods of the Metropolis*, 47.

26. McCloud, *African American Islam*, 11.

27. See chapter 3.

28. In 1959, the *Chicago Defender*, an African American newspaper, explicitly linked the methods and teachings of Drew Ali with Elijah Muhammad. Both were accused of employing a strange religion and symbols to replace Christianity. Since the point was to criticize both Drew Ali and Elijah Muhammad, it is somewhat odd that the article also compared their respective efforts to create black businesses and enjoin a strict moral code that included no drinking, smoking, or foul language. Burley, "Pomp, Mysticism Key to Power," 1–2.

29. Abu Shouk, Hunwick, and O'Fahey, "A Sudanese Missionary to the United States," 137–91.

30. See McCloud, *African American Islam*, 21–24.

31. This list adapts and expands on the one found in Jackson, *Islam and the Blackamerican*, 44.

32. Ali, *The Holy* Koran, 59.

33. Muhammad, *The Supreme Wisdom: Volume Two*, 84.

34. Others say he was a black Jamaican, with a Syrian Muslim father. Yet others say he was a Palestinian Arab. C. Eric Lincoln, *The Black Muslims in America*, 12. In short, his origins remain a mystery, and so there is no clear indication of where Fard Muhammad acquired his understanding of Islam.

35. Muhammad, *The Supreme Wisdom: Solution*, 11.

36. Sahib, *The Nation of Islam*, 65.

37. Muhammad, *History of the Nation of Islam*, 3; Muhammad, "Nation of Islam Offers Hearst $100,000," 1–3; Shah, "Woe to Every Slanderer!" 2; and Sahib, *The Nation of Islam*, 69 and 94. Later writers said Fard Muhammad could even communicate with the animals and Martians! Toure Muhammad, *Chronology of Nation of Islam History*, 3–4; and Muhammad, "The Teachings of the Holy Qur'an" (July 4, 1969): 19.

38. Muhammad, "Mr. Muhammad Speaks" (July 23, 1956): 2. A slightly edited version appears also in Muhammad, *The Supreme Wisdom: Solution*, 15.

39. See chapter 4 for more on this theology.

40. For the development of this belief, see chapter 2.

41. Muhammad, *Message to the Blackman in America*, 17.

42. Muhammad, *The Supreme Wisdom: Solution*, 48. See also Muhammad, "Mr. Muhammad Speaks" (September 22, 1956): 2.

43. Muhammad, *Message to the Blackman in America*, 294.

44. According to an article entitled "History" in "Muhammad University of Islam = No. 2 – 1973: Year Book," 24, Fard Muhammad also "left 104 books for Messenger Muhammad to find." "Elijah Muhammad," 26 November, 1973, FBI file 105-24822, 6. These books or the reading list are also mentioned by Elijah Muhammad elsewhere: "Allah taught Me for 3 years and 4 months then He gave to Me 100 and 4 books to study. He gave Me the names of them and the places where I could find them, so I studied." Muhammad, *Theology of Time*, 379.

45. Muhammad, *History of the Nation of Islam*, 5.

46. Muhammad, *History of the Nation of Islam*, 5.

47. Elijah Muhammad claimed in 1963 that Fard Muhammad communicated with him. He did not appear in person but Elijah Muhammad said, "I hear him in my ears" when awake. "Muslim Cult of Islam," 30 July 1963, FBI file 105-63642-36. See also chapter 2.

48. Muhammad, *Message to the Blackman in America*, 142.

49. "Wallace D. Fard," FBI files 100-43165-15–17. The debate regarding the identity of Fard Muhammad continued into the 1980s, when he was rumored to be a Qadiyani Ahmadiyya from India living in California named Abdullah. He was also said to be a Turko-Persian. Turner, *Islam in the African-American Experience*, 164–65.

50. Clegg, *An Original Man*, 21. It has been claimed that he was known as David Ford-El. Moreover, according to some scholars, Fard Muhammad not only had contact with the Moorish Science Temple but also claimed to be Drew Ali reincarnated. Essien-Udom, *Black Nationalism*, 48; and Marsh, *From Black Muslims to Muslims*, 51. In an interview in 1965, however, Elijah Muhammad denied that Fard Muhammad was in any way associated with Drew Ali. Muhammad, *The True History of Master Fard Muhammad*, xvii.

51. "Wallace D. Fard," FBI file 100-43165-15.

52. Beynon, "The Voodoo Cult," 895–97; "Wallace D. Fard," FBI file 100-43165-1A(1); and Sahib, *The Nation of Islam*, 66–67.

53. Beynon reconstructed these teachings from three texts issued by Fard Muhammad: *Teaching for the Lost Found Nation of Islam in a Mathematical Way* and the *Secret Ritual of the Nation of Islam*, parts 1 and 2. Beynon, "The Voodoo Cult," 899–901.

54. Beynon, "The Voodoo Cult," 903.

55. Sahib, *The Nation of Islam*, 72.

56. In the *Secret Ritual*, part 1, Fard Muhammad stated that Muslims must sacrifice four "Caucasian devils" in order to return to Mecca. Beynon, "The Voodoo Cult," 903. For a discussion of this charge, see Essien-Udom, *Black Nationalism*, 248–52. See also chapter 1 and Sahib, *The Nation of Islam*, 95.

57. Sahib, *The Nation of Islam*, 70.

58. "Wallace D. Fard," FBI file 100-43165-15.

59. Sahib, *The Nation of Islam*, 71.

60. The reporter was Ed Montgomery, who wrote the article entitled "Black Muslim Fake" for the *San Francisco Examiner* (July 28, 1963) in "Wallace D. Fard," FBI file 100-43165-15.

61. Sahib, *The Nation of Islam*, 71.

62. "Wallace D. Fard," FBI file 100-43165-15.

63. Muhammad, "Nation of Islam Offers Hearst $100,000," 1. Similar charges and a claim that Fard Muhammad was Polynesian were made in 1972. The Nation of Islam again made the same offer. See Shah, "Minister Offers A.P. Writer Merv Block $100,000 Plus Two Lives to Prove His Charges!" 2; Shah, "Woe to Every Slanderer!" 2; and 3X and Majied, "Through Lies, Distortions, Misquotes: Seek to Turn Black Man against Muhammad," 15.

64. Beynon called the latter two pamphlets the *Secret Ritual of the Nation of Islam*, parts 1 and 2. Beynon, "The Voodoo Cult," 903.

65. Sahib, *The Nation of Islam*, 147–49.

66. "Muslim Cult of Islam," 21 February 1957, FBI file 105-63642, 50.

67. Muhammad, *The Supreme Wisdom: Solution*, 11.

68. Sahib, *The Nation of Islam*, 121.

69. Muhammad, *Message to the Blackman in America*, 112–21. See also Sahib, *The Nation of Islam*, 152–53. For Yakub's motivation and methods for selective breeding, see chapter 4.

70. Muhammad, *The Supreme Wisdom: Solution*, 15.

71. Muhammad, *Message to the Blackman in America*, 230.

72. Muhammad, *The Supreme Wisdom: Solution*, 17.

73. Compare with his statement in chapter 5, in which some Whites are said to survive.

74. Sahib, *The Nation of Islam*, 94–95; and Muhammad, "Mr. Muhammad Speaks" (December 21, 1957): 10. See also chapter 4 for a discussion of the changing date for the fulfillment of this prophecy.

75. Elijah Muhammad stated that Fard Muhammad taught the lives of Jesus and Moses, but especially that of the Prophet Muhammad. Sahib, *The Nation of Islam*, 97. For a sketch of the life of Jesus as interpreted by Elijah Muhammad, see chapter 4.

76. Muhammad, *Message to the Blackman in America*, 68 and 80.

77. Muhammad, *Message to the Blackman in America*, 70.

78. Muhammad, *Message to the Blackman in America*, 3. Elijah Muhammad is recorded in the early 1960s as predicting that the end must come before the year 2000, and that the year 1970 was likely. Essien-Udom, *Black Nationalism*, 155.

CHAPTER 2

1. C. Eric Lincoln, *The Black Muslims in America*, 257. Barboza says Elijah Muhammad's original name was Robert Poole. Barboza, *American Jihad*, 77. Marsh gives his date of birth as October 7, 1898. Marsh, *From Black Muslims to Muslims*, 53.

2. Diouf dismisses Gomez's assertion that Elijah Muhammad's father was named Wali and so the implication that he had Muslim ancestors. Diouf, *Servants of Allah*, 199–200.

3. Essien-Udom states that he was the seventh child of twelve. Essien-Udom, *Black Nationalism*, 8.

4. Malcolm X, *The Autobiography*, 204–5.

5. Sahib, *The Nation of Islam*, 88–89.

6. Toure Muhammad, *Chronology of Nation of Islam History*, 5.

7. Marsh, *From Black Muslims to Muslims*, 52.

8. Muhammad, *History of the Nation of Islam*, 2. Compare with the alternate versions of this encounter described below. This version may reflect an earlier recension of the story. Fard Muhammad is the Son of Man, not God, and Fard Muhammad's response does not (yet?) resemble Jesus' statement in Matthew 16:16–20. See also John 7:6. However, Sahib's version does contain a reference to Jesus. Sahib, *The Nation of Islam*, 91–92.

9. Sahib, *The Nation of Islam*, 93.

10. Muhammad, *History of the Nation of Islam*, 2; and Sahib, *The Nation of Islam*, 92.

11. Muhammad, *History of the Nation of Islam*, 2–3.

12. Muhammad, *Message to the Blackman in America*, 17. Yet another variation is provided by Malcolm X: "Mr. Muhammad told me that one evening he had a revelation that Master W. D. Fard represented the fulfillment of the prophecy. 'I asked Him,' said Mr. Muhammad, 'Who are you, and what is your real name?' And then He said, 'My name is Mahdi. I came to guide you into the right path.'" Malcolm X, *The Autobiography*, 208.

13. Sahib, *The Nation of Islam*, 71.

14. Toure Muhammad, *Chronology of Nation of Islam History*, 5–6. Elsewhere, Fard Muhammad is described as sitting Elijah Muhammad beside him and saying, "This is the man that I want. That is just what we need; we need someone who teaches what I tell him." Sahib, *The Nation of Islam*, 96.

15. At this point, both men spelled their last name "Mohammed." Muhammad, "A Warning to the Black Man of America," 1.

16. Malcolm X, *The Autobiography*, 206.

17. Sahib, *The Nation of Islam*, 93–94. Clegg also states that Elijah Muhammad and Fard Muhammad gradually "invented" this claim over the period of three years. Clegg, *An Original Man*, 36.

18. Muhammad, "A Warning to the Black Man of America," 1.

19. Clegg, *An Original Man*, 36.

20. Sahib, *The Nation of Islam*, 80.

21. Muhammad, "The Hypocrites," 12.

22. Sahib, *The Nation of Islam*, 77 and 81.

23. Malcolm X, *The Autobiography*, 196–97.

24. Essien-Udom, *Black Nationalism*, 82.

25. Malcolm X, *The Autobiography*, 185.

26. Essien-Udom, *Black Nationalism*, 82. The actual number of members was a closely guarded secret, and so estimates vary greatly.

27. Even some African American newspapers portrayed this event as an act of lawlessness: ". . . Muhammad . . . stirred thousands to descend upon a Harlem police precinct station where they threatened to break in to liberate two of their brothers under arrest." Burley, "Portrait of a Shrewd Cult Leader," 1.

28. For example, *Time* used the phrase "Muhammad's doctrine of total hate" and *U.S. News & World Report* used "hatred of the white man." *Time*, "The Black Supremacists," 25; and *U.S. News & World Report*, "Is New York Sitting on a 'Powderkeg'?" 50.

29. The executive secretary of the NAACP, Roy Wilkins, charged, "The so-called Moslems . . . preach black supremacy and hatred of all white people." "NAACP Attacks 'Moslem' Cult," 1. Burley, "Portrait of a Shrewd Cult Leader," 1–2. In the latter article, Elijah Muhammad is described as a "shrewd master of mob psychology," being "anti-white and anti-Christ" and living "like a Mid-East potentate in a pretentious mansion." See also, Burley, "Pomp, Mysticism Key to Power," 1–2.

30. See chapter 5 for an analysis of the criticism by Talib Ahmad Dawud and Jamil Diab of Elijah Muhammad.

31. The evolution in Elijah Muhammad's attitude toward "orthodox" Islam is examined in chapter 5. In his eulogy for Gamal Abdul Nasser, who died in 1970, Elijah Muhammad claimed that the Egyptian president had asked him to stay in Africa to teach black people there. He even offered him a 75-room palace in Cairo, or to build him one if it was not to his liking. Muhammad, "The Sudden Death of President Nasser of Egypt," 17.

32. Muhammad, "Mr. Muhammad Answers White Filth Crusader," 6.

33. Stoner, "Letter to Elijah Muhammad," 1.

34. The claim was even made that Stoner's letter was a "phony" because "Mr. Stoner is working hand in hand with Mr. Muhammad." "Muslim Leader Calls Moslem Leader 'Phony,'" 11. See also Clegg, *An Original Man*, 152–55.

35. See chapter 6 for a discussion of Elijah Muhammad's conservatism.

36. Malcolm X, *The Autobiography*, 265.

37. Malcolm X, *The Autobiography*, 289–93.

38. Muhammad, "Nation Still Mourns Death," 1.

39. Muhammad, "Mr. Muhammad's Statement on the President's Death," 3. Emphasis added to show how much Elijah Muhammad was concerned about any backlash Malcolm X's statement might provoke.

40. Malcolm X, *The Autobiography*, 294–309.

41. Despite his orthodoxy, Malcolm X still blamed "Muslims from the East" for not having "done enough to make real Islam known in the West." Malcolm X, *The Autobiography*, 168.

42. See Malcolm X, *The Autobiography*, 434–39; and Clegg, *An Original Man*, 228–30, for a discussion of the controversy surrounding the assassins.

43. Muhammad, "Victory of the Apostle," 3. Also, Elijah Muhammad had always insisted that his followers be unarmed, stating, "We are forbidden by Allah to carry weapons." Muhammad, "Right to Peaceful Assembly Denied Black Americans," 1. See also "Sixteen Journalists Obtain . . . Rare Interview with Messenger Muhammad!" 3. Nevertheless, Elijah Muhammad felt the need to have his innocence proclaimed within *Muhammad Speaks* by his "orthodox" Muslim mouthpiece, Abdul Basit Naeem. Naeem wrote that "I shudder at the thought that the 'extreme punishment' decreed for him [Malcolm X] (not by the Honorable Elijah Muhammad as presumed and preposterously alluded by the Muslim's enemies but) by Allah (God) when the insubordinate and increasingly defiant 'Mr. X' further attempted to deride and defame his own former mentor and leader." Naeem, "Malcolm's Doom Decreed by God, Not the Messenger," 10.

44. For the reaction within the Nation of Islam to these threats, see Louis X (Farrakhan), "Minister Condemns Press Threats," 3.

45. Muhammad, "The Teachings of the Holy Qur-an on Obedience," 3, which is an article that was reprinted nine months later. Elijah Muhammad even wrote to the Muslims in Harlem, many of whom supported Malcolm X, "Obedience to Allah's Messenger is Obedience to Allah." Muhammad, "Muhammad Thanks Harlem," 4. See also Naeem, "Obey Divine Leader," 1, 3, and 6. Even the column in *Muhammad Speaks* devoted to quotations from the Qur'an was employed in driving home the message of obedience. See "Holy Qur-an: Chapter 4, Section 9: The Prophet Must Be Obeyed," 8. On hypocrites, see Muhammad, "Beware of False Prophets," 1 and 3; Muhammad, "Victory of the Apostle," 1 and 3–4; and Muhammad, "Hypocrites Condemned," 8. The same column on the Qur'an is also enlisted several times in this campaign. One column simply listed over thirty characteristics and activities of hypocrites—all drawn directly from Muhammad Ali's index to his translation of the Qur'an with little editing. "The Holy Qur-an: The Hypocrites and Disbelievers," 8.

46. Muhammad, *Message to the Blackman in America*, 254.

47. Muhammad, "Victory of the Apostle," 3–4.

48. Shabbaz, "Open Letter: Muslim Minister Writes to Malcolm," 9. See also X and X, "Biography of a Hypocrite," 16; and X and X, "Minister Exposed by Those Who Knew Him through Life," 5.

49. Louis X, "Boston Minister Tells of Malcolm—Muhammad's Biggest Hypocrite," 14. See also chapter 5 for Abdul Basit Naeem's strident defense of Elijah Muhammad and persistent attacks on Malcolm X.

50. Muhammad, "Victory of the Apostle," 3–4.

51. John Ali, "Whiteman and the Hypocrites Love Malcolm," 20–21.

52. Muhammad, "The Hypocrites," 12.

53. "Muhammad Meets the Press!" (February 11, 1972), 4.

54. "Decree Akbar Muhammad," 9.

55. Muhammad, "TO: The Family of Dr. Martin Luther King," 3.

56. Elijah Muhammad was extremely grateful to Mr. DeMets and the members of the church for waiting for so many years for the money to be raised and for accepting a $2 million mortgage. Muhammad, "Messenger Thanks Greeks," 2.

57. See chapter 4 for a discussion of the December fast.

58. Barboza, *American Jihad*, 78; and Marsh, *From Black Muslims to Muslims*, 90–91.

59. Muhammad, "Clarification of Actions Taken by Messenger Muhammad against Muhammad Ali's Action," 2–3.

60. Muhammad, "Truth Has Always Triumphed: Sport and Play Is Condemned," 16. See also Muhammad, "Revelation Guides Aright," 18.

61. "Allah's Last Messenger Answers Questions You Have Always Wanted to Ask!" 4.

62. Clegg, *An Original Man*, 260–61.

63. Farrakhan, "Muslim 'Feud' a Hoax, Farrakhan Explains," 3.

64. Muhammad, "Hypocrites: Do Not Befriend Hypocrites," 15.

65. See chapter 4 for a more detailed discussion of the quranic term "hypocrite."

66. Rassoull, "Warning," 15; and Rassoull, "Holy Names," 3.

67. "Allah's Last Messenger Answers Questions You Have Always Wanted to Ask!" 4.

68. Clegg, *An Original Man*, 275.

69. 14X, "Fundraising Dinner a 'Quiet Success,'" 4.

70. "Chicago Mayor Proclaims Muslim Saviour's Day," 1; and Mary Eloise X, "Two Great Families Unite!" S1–S7.

71. "News of Messenger Muhammad's Illness Evokes Growing Expressions of Concern," 5; and "'Get Well' Sentiments Arrive in 'Avalanche,'" 5.

CHAPTER 3

1. Parts of this chapter have appeared in Berg, "Early African American Muslim Movements and the Qur'an," 22–37; and Berg, "Elijah Muhammad and the Qur'an," 42–55.

2. Wilson, *Sacred Drift*, 16.

3. This fact was, as far as I can tell, first noted in an FBI report from 1943. "Moorish Science Temple of America (Noble Drew Ali)," 2 April 1943, FBI file 62-25899-90. Editing included changing words such as "God" to "Allah."

4. Wilson, *Sacred Drift*, 21.

5. Noble Drew Ali, *The Holy Koran*, 57.

6. Drew Ali wrote, ". . . the Islamic Creed from the East was brought to the Asiatics of America by the Prophet, NOBLE DREW ALI. . . . [H]e has brought the only remedy for the nations. The remedy brought by Jesus, Mohammed, Confucius, and all the other prophets, which remedy is truth." Noble Drew Ali, *Moorish Literature*, 8–9.

7. Noble Drew Ali, *The Holy Koran*, 56.

8. McCloud, *African American Islam*, 11–12.

9. McCloud, *African American Islam*, 13.

10. Wilson, *The Sacred Drift*, 30.

11. Noble Drew Ali, *Moorish Literature*, 11.

12. Noble Drew Ali, *Moorish Literature*, 12. This exact phrase in his "Prophet Has Spoken" is repeated in "General Laws as Said by the Prophet." Noble Drew Ali, *Moorish Literature*, 15. His pamphlet entitled *"Humanity"* also contains these two statements. Both documents are dated "Friday, November 9, 1928." Noble Drew Ali, *Humanity*, 1 and 3–4. If these dates are accurate, they seem to support the later publication date for the *Circle Seven Koran*.

13. Noble Drew Ali, *Koran Questions*, 1, 3, and 5.

14. Noble Drew Ali, *Moorish Literature*, 16.

15. Noble Drew Ali, *Moorish Literature*, 10.

16. English translations of the Qur'an of that time translated *"dar al-salam"* differently: Alexander Ross (1649) used "Paradise"; George Sale (1734) used "dwelling of peace"; and J. M. Rodwell (1861), E. H. Palmer (1880), Mirza Abu'l Fadl (1912), and Maulana Muhammad Ali (1917) opted for "abode of peace." Mohammad Abdul Hakim Khan (1905) translated it as "home of peace." Only Ghulam Sarwar (1920) used "House of Peace," but his translation of 78:95 is quite different from Drew Ali's. I have only been able to find volume 1 of Mirza Hairat Dihlavi's three-volume *The Koran: Prepared by Various Oriental Learned Scholars* (Delhi: 1912) in the British Library. Volume 1 ends with Qur'an 9. Even so, I assume his translation was used by Drew Ali because (1) none of the other translations uses the same wording, and (2) the spelling of the Qur'an as "Koran" is the same. However, it is possible that Drew Ali received this translation directly

from an Arabic-speaking Muslim. Ahmadiyya Muslim missionaries were active in several of the cities that had Moorish Science Temples and the Sudanese Sunni missionary, Sāttī Mājid, made contact with Drew Ali (see chapter 1).

17. "Moorish Science Temple," 31 January 1944, FBI file 62-25899-260.

18. "Moorish Science Temple," 22 April 1944, FBI file 62-25899-265.

19. Members of the Moorish Science Temple described their Koran as "their Bible." However, the word "Bible" was being used as a synonym for "scripture." Elsewhere the Bible is described as having been "written to enslave the Negro." "Moorish Science Temple," 9 February 1943, FBI file 62-25899-66.

20. Noble Drew Ali, *Moorish Literature*, 20.

21. However, he did speak of a future book (for which, see below).

22. Sahib, *The Nation of Islam*, 70.

23. Muhammad, *The Supreme Wisdom: Solution*, 12, and *Message to the Blackman in America*, 94.

24. Muhammad, *The Supreme Wisdom: Solution*, 13.

25. Muhammad, *The Supreme Wisdom: Solution*, 13. Elsewhere, he described the Bible as a "beautiful book but you have to understand it's [sic] meaning." "W. D. Muhammad," 7 March 1958, FBI file 100-33683-55.

26. Muhammad, *Message to the Blackman in America*, 88.

27. John Ali, "Introduction," in Elijah Muhammad, *The Fall of America*, vi.

28. Muhammad, *Message to the Blackman in America*, 141.

29. Elijah Muhammad added, "There are many Muslims who do not care to read anything in the Bible. But those Muslims have not been given my job. Therefore, I ignore what they say and write!" Muhammad, *Message to the Blackman in America*, 82.

30. Beynon, "The Voodoo Cult," 900.

31. "Elijah Muhammad," 26 November, 1973, FBI file 105-24822.

32. Muhammad, *The Supreme Wisdom: Solution*, 51. In pictures of Elijah Muhammad holding a copy of the Qur'an, the cover appears to be that of the 1917 edition.

33. For an example of his use of footnotes, see Muhammad, *Message to the Blackman in America*, 23, in which he urges readers to examine note 2,276, which explains the expression "the days of Allah." See also Muhammad, *Message to the Blackman in America*, 254, where he refers the reader to note 2,794. For an example of his use of headings, compare Muhammad, *Message to the Blackman in America*, 255–56 and *The Holy Qur-an*, 231–32.

34. Muhammad, "The Teachings of the Holy Qur-an" (July 4, 1969), 19.

35. "Walking the Earth like Brothers," 67.

36. Muhammad, *The Supreme Wisdom: Solution*, 50–51; and Muhammad, *Message to the Blackman in America*, 92.

37. Muhammad, *The Theology of Time*, 379.

38. Muhammad, *Message to the Blackman in America*, 92.

39. Muhammad, *The Supreme Wisdom: Solution*, 20.

40. Muhammad, *The Supreme Wisdom: Solution*, 20.

41. See discussion of *The Supreme Wisdom: Solution* below.

42. Sahib, *The Nation of Islam*, 98.

43. Muhammad, *Message to the Blackman in America*, 52. My emphasis indicates the words drawn from Qur'an 1:2.

44. Muhammad, *The Supreme Wisdom: Solution*, 15.

45. Muhammad, *Theology of Time*, 379. An earlier version of this story has Fard Muhammad giving his minister two copies of the Qur'an but adding, "These are not the only books I have but I have another book that I made myself." Sahib, *The Nation of Islam*, 71.

46. Muhammad, *History of the Nation of Islam*, 38–39. All of this seems at odds with his statement that "[t]he Holy Qur'an will live forever."

47. Muhammad, *The Theology of Time*, 379.

48. Muhammad, "A Warning to the Black Man of America," 1.

49. See chapter 6 for a discussion of the critical role Islam played for Elijah Muhammad.

50. "W. D. Muhammad," 7 March 1958, FBI file 100-33683-55.

51. C. Eric Lincoln, *The Black Muslims in America*, 127. As Lincoln mentions, *The Supreme Wisdom: Solution* has been published in several editions. In fact, *The Supreme Wisdom: Volume Two* contains virtually all the material of the first volume, which appears verbatim in the second, and hence, the latter is more of a revised edition. This recycling of material also occurs between *The Supreme Wisdom: Volume Two* and *Message to the Blackman in America*.

52. The "simplicity of his speaking style and his improvised syntax" (Clegg, *An Original Man*, 117) are very much present in all three of the aforementioned books. Elijah Muhammad was primarily a preacher, as his father and grandfather before him had been. Being poorly educated, he dictated his writings and speeches to his secretaries. Even *Message to the Blackman in America* was less a monograph than a compilation of earlier columns and speeches. Clegg, *An Original Man*, 177–79.

53. Muhammad, *The Supreme Wisdom: Solution*, 21 and 50.

54. Muhammad, *The Supreme Wisdom: Solution*, 26.

55. Muhammad, *The Supreme Wisdom: Solution*, 31.

56. Elsewhere he wrote, "It (Islam) teaches an eternal heaven for the righteous. (Hell, according to Islam, is not eternal.)" Elijah Muhammad, *The Supreme Wisdom: Solution*, 44. Elijah Muhammad meant that hell is the period of the white race's rule and it will end, whereas heaven will endure forever thereafter.

57. See also his treatment of the *Sūrat al-fatiha* in the context of prayer. Muhammad, *The Supreme Wisdom: Solution*, 45–47.

58. Muhammad, *The Supreme Wisdom: Solution*, 43.

59. Muhammad, *The Supreme Wisdom: Solution*, 46.

60. For his discussion of the Judgment, see Muhammad, *The Supreme Wisdom: Solution*, 17. When Elijah Muhammad cited Qur'an 2:168, which commands people not to follow Satan, he explained, "The devils referred to are not other than the white people." Muhammad, *The Supreme Wisdom: Solution*, 23. For an additional and longer example of this exegetical technique, see Elijah Muhammad's discussion of Qur'an 30:41. Muhammad, *The Supreme Wisdom: Solution*, 28–29.

61. Those that are absent that have some relevance to the Qur'an include the passages entitled "The Future Holy Book" and "Be Yourself," the latter being called "Allah's greatest teaching and warning to . . . the so-called Negroes." Muhammad, *The Supreme Wisdom: Solution*, 12. Perhaps they were removed to bring the Nation of Islam more in line with orthodox Muslim views.

62. Muhammad, *The Supreme Wisdom: Volume Two*, 2.

63. Muhammad, *The Supreme Wisdom: Volume Two*, 65.

64. Muhammad, *The Supreme Wisdom: Volume Two*, 46. See also Muhammad, *The Supreme Wisdom: Volume Two*, 9, 20, 29, 35, 46, 69, 80, and 82–83.

65. Muhammad, *The Supreme Wisdom: Volume Two*, 67. For a longer exegesis of Qur'an 112, see the discussion of Allah. Muhammad, *The Supreme Wisdom: Volume Two*, 9. Even less explicit is the passage entitled "Firewood of Hell," which states, "The true One God is Allah, the author of Islam. The Holy Quran states that what you worship besides Allah is the Firewood of Hell." Muhammad, *The Supreme Wisdom: Volume Two*, 42. This seems to be a reference to Qur'an 111.

66. This technique is even more noticeable in Elijah Muhammad's next book. See, for example, Muhammad, *Message to the Blackman in America*, 155–56 and 294.

67. Muhammad, *Message to the Blackman in America*, 76.

68. For another example, see the discussion entitled "Islam, only true religion of God," which consists of the earlier pericopes "Allah, Our God, is one and self-independent God," "The Bible on Allah (One God)," "Jews and Christians set up rivals to Allah," "Insult to Allah," and "The 112th Chapter of the Holy Quran." Muhammad, *Message to the Blackman in America*, 73–75, and *The Supreme Wisdom: Volume Two*, 9, 13, 13, 11–12, and 67, respectively.

69. Clegg, *An Original Man*, 177–79.

70. Watson, "The Rise of the Moslems: Messenger Muhammad Leads Thousands to Clean Living through the Islamic Faith," 2.

71. See, for example, Muhammad, "Future of American So-Called Negroes," 3, 6, 8, and 16–17; and Muhammad, "12,000 Cheer Muhammad's History of Black Man's Role in Islam," 3–4.

72. Muhammad, *Message to the Blackman in America*, 187.

73. Muhammad, *Message to the Blackman in America*, 189. In a similar argument, Elijah Muhammad claimed that the Qur'an, when it states that Allah sends a messenger to each community He intends to warn, supports Elijah Muhammad's claim to be a "messenger." Muhammad, "Memo: From the Desk of Muhammad," 5 and 14.

74. Muhammad, *Message to the Blackman in America*, 189. Elijah Muhammad added later in the passage, "There are religious scientists in Islam who know these things to be true as I am saying, and there are those who do not understand their Holy Qur-an and the prophecy of Muhammad being the last among the dead, for the Bible teaches that God will use him to make Him himself known in the last days." Muhammad, *Message to the Blackman in America*, 189.

75. Muhammad, *The Supreme Wisdom: Solution*, 21.

76. See chapter 5 for a discussion of his break with "orthodox" Muslims.

CHAPTER 4

1. Parts of this chapter have appeared in Berg, "Elijah Muhammad: An African American Muslim *mufassir*?" 1–27.

2. Elijah Muhammad had many prominent themes, such as the need to protect African American women from Whites, economic self-sufficiency, the separation of the races, the "true" history of Jesus, and the vices of Christians and Christianity. The ones discussed here represent those that highlight his exegetical techniques and that bear some relation to his formulation of Islam. Other prominent "Islamic" themes such as the virtues of Islam and the Qur'an have been discussed in chapter 3 and the physical incarnation of Allah in Fard Muhammad has been discussed in chapter 2.

Elijah Muhammad, however, was not limited to these themes. He wrote missives about the dangers of jaywalking, the improved service at his Salaam Restaurant, the problem of air pollution (which he believed would be solved by using steam), the requirement for Muslims to pay their debts, the need to shun astrology, the danger of people going door-to-door pretending to collect donations on behalf of Elijah Muhammad, the need for donations, the gratitude he felt to the governor of Illinois and the mayor of Chicago for naming a day after him in 1974, and (somewhat ironically) the "crazy and nasty minded people" foolishly requesting permission to "take over other women and other men" whom he accuses of committing fornication and adultery. Muhammad, "'Daring Pedestrian' Who Challenges Motorist," 12–13; Muhammad, "The Daring Pedestrian: Part II," 12–13; Muhammad, "TO: The Patrons of Your Supermarket and Salaam Restaurant," 6; Muhammad, "Air Pollution Can Be Controlled," 2; Muhammad, "Pay Your Debts," 16; Muhammad, "Pay Your Debts!" 1; Muhammad, "Shun Astrology," 17; Muhammad, "Warning to Donors," 2; Muhammad, "Money Necessary," 6; Muhammad, "Thank You!" 1; and Muhammad, "Special: Read," 13.

3. Muhammad, "Old World Going Out with a Great Noise!" 16–17. Others eventually expanded on this theology. Near the end of his life, Elijah Muhammad was forced to deny the claim by some followers that he was Fard Muhammad. He also rejected teachings that gave Fard Muhammad an esoteric cosmological status (e.g., "Master Fard Muhammad represents substance, physical matter, the

reflector, that which is incomplete, invisible, transparent, white crystal.") and that spoke of his miraculous birth and meetings taking place on Mars. Nathaniel Muhammad, "October 15 Address: Muhammad Clarifies Truth! Condemns Liars," S8–S9.

4. "Muslim Cult of Islam," 21 February 1957, FBI file 105-63642. As noted above, the twenty-three scientists produce a scripture every twenty-five thousand years but then wait an additional ten thousand years before giving it to a prophet. Such was the case with the Torah, Bible, and Qur'an. Sahib, *The Nation of Islam*, 70.

5. This date is given in *Lost-Found Lesson 2*, question 26, which reads,

> 26. What year was that [that is, the grafting of the devil]?
>
> Ans.—It was in the year eight thousand four hundred, which means from the date of our present history or Koran, or about two thousand and six hundred years before the birth of the Prophet Mossa. "Muslim Cult of Islam," 21 February 1957, FBI file 105-63642.

Eighty-four hundred years, plus six hundred years of grafting, plus six thousand years of the white rule equals fifteen thousand years.

6. Muhammad, *The Supreme Wisdom: Volume Two*, 12.

7. Muhammad, *Message to the Blackman in America*, 237.

8. Muhammad, *Message to the Blackman in America*, 294.

9. Muhammad, *Message to the Blackman in America*, 31–32.

10. Muhammad, "What Was the Idea of God Making the Moon?" 21–22.

11. Muhammad, "Significance of the Moon," *Muhammad Speaks* (January 17, 1969): 21–22; and Muhammad, "Significance of the Moon." *Muhammad Speaks* (January 24, 1969): 3.

12. Muhammad, "Old World Going Out with a Great Noise!" 16–17.

13. Muhammad, "The Teachings of the Holy Qur-an" (July 4, 1969): 19.

14. Muhammad, "Old World Going Out with a Great Noise!" 17; and Muhammad, "Fasting" (December 10, 1971): 17.

15. Muhammad, "The Teachings of the Holy Qur-an" (July 4, 1969): 19. This interest in astronomy, however, did not translate into an interest in astrology. Elijah Muhammad condemned it: "Islam is not an Astrology believing Religion. Astrology often proves to be untrue! So, the Holy Qur-an Teaches against Astrology. It is a work of the Devil." Muhammad, "Shun Astrology," 17.

16. Muhammad, "Mr. Muhammad Speaks" (August 10, 1957): 10; (August 17, 1957): 10; (August 24, 1957): 10; (August 31, 1957): 10; (September 7, 1957): 10; and (October 19, 1957): 10. See also, Muhammad, "Christmas!" 15.

17. Muhammad, "Christmas!" 15.

18. "Muhammad Meets the Press!" (February 11, 1972): 3–4.

19. Muhammad, "Fasting" (December 10, 1971): 17.

20. Muhammad, *The Supreme Wisdom: Volume Two*, 53.

21. Muhammad, *The Supreme Wisdom: Solution*, 44.

22. Muhammad, *Message to the Blackman in America*, 58–61.

23. Muhammad, "Warning to M.G.T. and G.C. Class," 4.

24. See for example, Muhammad, "The Filth That Produces the Filth," 16–17.

25. Muhammad, "To the Black Woman in America," 16–17. See also Muhammad, "To My Beloved People: Warning," 14–15, in which he criticized both skirts and shorts that were above the knee.

26. Muhammad, "Why and How We Fast in December," 11.

27. Muhammad, "Fasting" (December 18, 1970): 15.

28. Muhammad, "Fasting" (December 10, 1971): 16–17.

29. "Tricknology" is the set of "superior tricks" that Yakub taught his newly created race to ensnare the original black race. For example, he had learned that unlike attracts and alike repels. "When Yakub, the Father (God) of this race of people (white Man) was six (6) years old, he was playing. Playing with two pieces of steel. He found in them an attraction. Yakub looked up at his uncle and said, 'Uncle, when I get to be an old man, I am going to make a man and he will rule you.'" Therefore, he had to make his new people unalike: pale-skinned and blue-eyed. He did so by separating the "black germ and brown germ" within the black man's sperm and only allowing the brown babies to live. He continued in this manner, making progressively lighter people until he was able to achieve the un-alike features he required. With these features they were attractive to the original black, brown, and yellow peoples and were thus able to "deceive the Black man, destroy him . . . and take over the earth." Not surprisingly, Elijah Muhammad commands, "Let alike unite and repel unalike. Accept your own!" Muhammad, "Unalike Attracts and Alike Repels," 3; and Muhammad, "Playing with Steel," 16–17.

30. Muhammad, *Message to the Blackman in America*, 128. Elijah Muhammad argued, "We created man (white race) from a small life germ. [T] the soft pronoun 'we' used nearly throughout the Holy Qur-an makes the knowledge of the Original Man much clearer and of a more intelligent knowledge of how the white race's creation took place." Muhammad, "Mr. Muhammad Speaks" (July 28, 1956), 2.

31. Muhammad, *Message to the Blackman in America*, 118.

32. Muhammad, "Mr. Muhammad Speaks" (June 29, 1957): 10.

33. Muhammad, *Message to the Blackman in America*, 133. Elijah Muhammad is not always consistent in his assigning of the symbols. Sometimes the white race is the serpent, the devil, and the tree of knowledge, while Adam and Eve are merely victims. Muhammad, *Message to the Blackman in America*, 126–27. Thus the devil can be Adam and Eve, the serpent, the tree, Yakub, and/or the white race as a whole.

34. Muhammad, *Message to the Blackman in America*, 104 and 119.

35. Muhammad, *Message to the Blackman in America*, 133. See also his *Supreme Wisdom: Solution*, 18, in which II Thessalonians 2:9 is adduced to

explain why the white race has been given free rein of the world for a period of time. Qur'an 2:36; 3:174; 7:12, 20, and 27; 8:48; 15:16–18 and 42; 16:99; 20:120; 22:3 and 26; 23:97; and 38:37 are all cited as describing the characteristics of the "devil white race." Muhammad, "Mr. Muhammad Speaks" (October 26, 1957): 10.

36. Muhammad, "The Holy Qur-An," 10. Only once is the devil white race identified with the *jinn*. In regard to Qur'an 72:5–6—"And we thought that men and jinn did not utter a lie against Allah; And persons from among men used to seek refuge with persons from among the jinn, so they increased them in evil doing"—Elijah Muhammad declared, "Jinn is the devil and men is the Black People." Muhammad, "The Teachings of the Holy Qur-an" (July 4, 1969): 19.

37. Muhammad, *Message to the Blackman in America*, 128.

38. On the basis of Revelation 14:1, Elijah Muhammad believed that only 144,000 Muslims would be saved: the other "16,856,000 would go down with the enemies of Allah (God)." Muhammad, "Mr. Muhammad Speaks" (August 11, 1956): 2. See also Muhammad, "Mr. Muhammad Speaks" (October 20, 1956): 2.

39. Muhammad, "The Mother Plane," 20–21; and Muhammad, "Continued: The Mother Plane," 20–21.

40. Muhammad, *Message to the Blackman in America*, 270. In the same book, which was published in 1965, he expects the end within twenty-four months. Muhammad, *Message to the Blackman in America*, 297. Elsewhere, he is even more urgent: "Do not expect ten more years, the fall will be within a few days." Muhammad, *The Fall of America*, 19. However, later (perhaps out of necessity), the date was moved to 1970.

41. Muhammad, *Our Saviour Has Arrived*, 60.

42. Muhammad, *Message to the Blackman in America*, 38.

43. Essien-Udom, *Black Nationalism*, 155.

44. Sahib, *The Nation of Islam*, 97.

45. Muhammad, *Message to the Blackman in America*, 18.

46. Muhammad, *Message to the Blackman in America*, 134.

47. Muhammad, *Message to the Blackman in America*, 125–26; and *The Supreme Wisdom: Solution*, 18.

48. Muhammad, *Message to the Blackman in America*, 276. The italics of the original have been removed, except in the case of Elijah Muhammad's comments and glosses, which have been retained for the sake of clarity. Likewise, his brackets have been replaced with parentheses so that my emendations will not be confused with his comments.

49. Muhammad, *Message to the Blackman in America*, 293–95.

50. Muhammad, *Message to the Blackman in America*, 293.

51. Muhammad, *The Supreme Wisdom: Solution*, 43.

52. Muhammad, *Message to the Blackman in America*, 273, 290–91, and 303.

53. Muhammad, *Message to the Blackman in America*, 303–5.

54. Muhammad, *Message to the Blackman in America*, 267–68. Italics were added to facilitate the distinction between the scriptural texts and Elijah Muhammad's comments within the scriptural quotations. Also, his brackets have been changed to parentheses for the sake of clarity and consistency.

55. "Muhammad Meets the Press!" (February 11, 1972): 4.

56. Muhammad, *How to Eat to Live*, 17.

57. Muhammad, *How to Eat to Live*, 24, 67, and 110. However, in his *Supreme Wisdom: Solution*, 23, Elijah Muhammad mentioned Qur'an 2:173, but did not reproduce it.

58. Muhammad, *How to Eat to Live*, 69–72 and 95–99. In his *Supreme Wisdom: Solution*, 23, the biblical passages Deuteronomy 14:8, Isaiah 66:2, 3, 5, and 18, and Mark 5:11–16 were mentioned.

59. Muhammad, *How to Eat to Live*, 61–62.

60. Muhammad, *How to Eat to Live*, 60.

61. Muhammad, *How to Eat to Live*, 70.

62. Muhammad, *How to Eat to Live*, 4–12.

63. Muhammad, *How to Eat to Live*, 36.

64. Muhammad, *How to Eat to Live*, 99–101. Italics added to facilitate the distinction between the biblical text and Elijah Muhammad's comments.

65. Muhammad, *The Supreme Wisdom: Volume Two*, 22.

66. Muhammad, "Mr. Muhammad Speaks" (May 23, 1959): 14. For the reasons for the reappearance of the term "hypocrite," see chapter 5.

67. Clegg, *An Original Man*, 209. In an interview in 1972, Elijah Muhammad spoke of assassination attempts "going on for forty years, ever since I was Missioned." However, he also felt that such attempts had to fail, for he was protected by Allah. "Sixteen Journalists Obtain . . . Rare Interview with Messenger Muhammad!" 3.

68. C. Eric Lincoln, *The Black Muslims in America*, 199.

69. *Message to the Blackman in America* was, of course, written after Malcolm X left the Nation of Islam. Later, in the early 1970s, the term would begin to appear again in his columns as he fought to control the various factions within the Nation of Islam. See also Muhammad, "Victory of the Apostle," 3–4.

70. Muhammad, "Beware of False Prophets," 3.

71. See, for example, Muhammad, "Hypocrites!" 18. In this full-page article, Elijah Muhammad wrote, "One Hypocrite among the Muslims, is worse than one hundred disbelievers who have never sought to come among the Muslims." He describes the hypocrite as "evil," "poisonous," and "not only hated by Allah (God) but . . . hated by all believers."

72. Muhammad, *Message to the Blackman in America*, 248–51.

73. Muhammad, *Message to the Blackman in America*, 252–59.

74. Elijah Muhammad followed this with similar analyses in this passage of Qur'an 5:53, 4:144 and 145, 47:23 and 25–27, 66:9 and 10, and Qur'an 104 without quoting the verses. Muhammad, *Message to the Blackman in America*, 252–53.

75. Muhammad, *Message to the Blackman in America*, 259–60.

76. Muhammad, *Message to the Blackman in America*, 269.

77. Muhammad, *Message to the Blackman in America*, 262–63.

78. See, for example, Muhammad, *Message to the Blackman in America*, 261–62.

79. Muhammad, *Message to the Blackman in America*, 263. See above where the cited passage from *The Fall of America* links the appearance of hypocrites and the end of the present world.

80. Muhammad, *Message to the Blackman in America*, 138 and 141.

81. Muhammad, *The Supreme Wisdom: Solution*, 45–47.

82. Muhammad, *The Supreme Wisdom: Volume Two*, 64–65.

83. Muhammad, *Message to the Blackman in America*, 135–37. Elijah Muhammad's italics have been removed and his brackets changed to parentheses for the sake of clarity.

84. Muhammad, *Message to the Blackman in America*, 135–37.

85. Muhammad, *Message to the Blackman in America*, 146–47.

86. Muhammad, *Message to the Blackman in America*, 135–60. For example, Elijah Muhammad includes the following translation of the "*duʿāʾ al-qunūt*":

O Allah, we beseech Thy help and ask Thy protection. We believe in Thee and trust in Thee. We worship Thee in the best manner and we thank Thee. We are not ungrateful to Thee and we cast off and forsake him who disobeys Thee. O Allah, Thee do we serve and to Thee do we pray and make obeisance. To Thee do we flee and we are quick. We hope for Thy mercy and we fear Thy chastisement, for surely Thy chastisement overtakes the unbelievers. Muhammad, *Message to the Blackman in America*, 155.

This exact translation was readily available in many prayer manuals. See, for example, Siddiqui, *Elementary Teachings of Islam*, 61. In this case, Elijah Muhammad seems to have slightly emended the version available in his Qur'an. Muhammad Ali, preface to *The Holy Qur-án*, xxv. Also, as early as 1957 Elijah Muhammad gave a detailed description of how to perform a standard prayer. Muhammad, "Mr. Muhammad Speaks" (February 15, 1957): 14; and Muhammad, "Mr. Muhammad Speaks" (February 22, 1957): 14.

87. Muhammad, *Message to the Blackman in America*, 143–44. In a 1965 column on prayer in *Muhammad Speaks*, Elijah Muhammad directly quoted the preface of Muhammad Ali's translation to describe the five daily prayers. He even quoted the notes appended by Ali. Muhammad, "Muslim Prayer Service," 10.

88. For a discussion of some Muslims' reaction to the Nation of Islam's less-than-orthodox prayers, see chapter 5.

89. See for example, Muhammad, "Revelation Guides Aright," 18.

90. See for example, Muhammad, "The Bursting Asunder," 20–21; and Muhammad, "Opposition to Truth Is Punished," 2.

91. Muhammad, *Message to the Blackman in America*, 161–205 and 220–47.

92. Muhammad, *Our Savior Has Arrived*, 6.

93. Wansbrough, *Quranic Studies*, 121.

94. Wansbrough, *The Sectarian Milieu*, 2.

95. Wansbrough, *The Sectarian Milieu*, 3.

96. The passage from Joel 3:2–3, 7, and 14 and Isaiah 65:1–5 was exegetical whereas the passage on the creation of the devils seems largely parabolic. Paraphrastic exegesis was evident in the ubiquitous allusions to biblical motifs and the adoption of quranic idioms, such as "Lord of the Worlds."

97. Wansbrough, *Quranic Studies*, 127.

98. Wansbrough, *Quranic Studies*, 142 and 148.

CHAPTER 5

1. Jackson, *Islam and the Blackamerican*, 43.

2. McCloud, *African American Islam*, 4, 37–38, and 169–70.

3. C. Eric Lincoln, *The Black Muslims in America*, 220–23.

4. Barboza, *American Jihad*, 4–6; and McCloud, *African American Islam*, 32.

5. Clegg, *An Original Man*, 69.

6. Even using a more complex definition, one that sees religion as discourse, such as that of Bruce Lincoln—"Religion, I submit, is that discourse whose defining characteristic is its desire to speak of things eternal and transcendent with an authority equally transcendent and eternal"—obviously makes the Nation of Islam a religion. Lincoln, *Theses on Method*, 225.

7. Curtis, *Black Muslim Religion*, 6.

8. The term "religion" and the determination of what makes something "religious" are themselves extremely problematic. See Arnal, "Definition," 21–34; and Braun, "Religion," 3–20.

9. Curtis, *Islam in Black America*, 6.

10. Baghdadi, "Who's behind the Splinter Group? Messenger's Attackers Exposed," 2.

11. See also al-Ghareeb ("Lauds Leader: Eastern Muslim Calls Nation of Islam 'Great,'" 15 and 18), who wished he could join the Nation of Islam and even accepted Allah in the person of Fard Muhammad. What also makes al-Ghareeb unusual is the relatively late date of his support for Elijah Muhammad: 1971.

12. For example he wrote "Inexcusable indeed . . . is the uncalled for criticism of the teachings of Mr. Elijah Muhammad by the (so-called) 'orthodox.' I am also convinced that Mr. Elijah Muhammad's mission is God-inspired." Naeem, "Pakistan Muslim Tells the Truth about the Honorable Elijah Muhammad," 3. See also Naeem's apologetics on behalf of the Nation of Islam: Naeem, "Pakistan Muslim Blasts Press Slander of Islam," 3; Naeem, "Rips Role of Lomax," 4; and Naeem, "Pakistan Muslim: Muhammad's Work, Not Words, True Test of Greatness,"

18–19. Naeem also leapt to the defense of Elijah Muhammad, attacking Malcolm X and warning people not to listen to rumors or spread gossip. Naeem, "Obey Divine Leader," 1, 3, and 6. He also wrote a four-part series for *Muhammad Speaks* harshly criticizing Malcolm X: Naeem, "How the Late Malcolm X Misrepresented Himself and the Divine Messenger," 9; Naeem, "Self-Publicity Motivated Malcolm, Not Devotion," 10; Naeem, "Pakistani Muslim Tells: Why, at Times, I Refused to Cooperate with Malcolm," 10 and 12; and Naeem, "Malcolm's Doom Decreed by God, Not the Messenger," 10. Even well after Malcolm X's death, Naeem maintained his assault on his character: "Malcolm . . . never did comprehend True Islam . . . [and was] devoid of Islamic characteristics." Naeem, "Pakistan Muslim: Rips Malcolm Statements Printed in Foreign Press," 10.

13. Naeem, "Introduction" to Muhammad, *The Supreme Wisdom: Solution*, 4.

14. Naeem, "Introduction" to Muhammad, *The Supreme Wisdom: Solution*, 4. In his introduction to *The Supreme Wisdom: Volume Two*, Naeem continued his support. He ironically critiqued the Christian belief that Jesus is God. (It seems unlikely that he was surreptitiously critiquing the most controversial of Elijah Muhammad's doctrines.) He then pointed to the many successes of Elijah Muhammad as proof "that most surely Allah, our Almighty God, *is* with him." Naeem, "Introduction," 3.

15. Naeem, "Says the Messenger and His Followers May Hold Key to Future of World Islam," 10.

16. Naeem, "Says the Messenger and His Followers May Hold Key to Future of World Islam," 10. See also Naeem, "Declares Messenger of Allah Deserves Support of Entire Muslim World," 10.

17. "Muslim Leader Calls Moslem Leader 'Phony,'" 11. The different spelling of "Muslim" for each group in the newspaper's heading may indicate the editor's bias.

18. DeCaro, *On the Side of My People*, 147–48; "Moslems Fill Rockland," 21; "White Man Is God for Cult of Islam," 1; and "Muslim Leader Calls Moslem Leader 'Phony,'" 11. When the "White Man" article in *The New Crusader* came out, members of the Nation of Islam in Chicago and New York attempted to buy every copy and publicly burn them all. Essien-Udom, *Black Nationalism*, 316.

19. "Dakota Says There's No Connection 'Tween Her Faith, Muhammed," 3; and "Muslim Leader Calls Moslem Leader 'Phony,'" 11.

20. "Fire New Blasts at Moslems," 1–2.

21. Clegg, *An Original Man*, 134.

22. Curtis, *Islam in Black America*, 90. This period also saw an increase in the Islamic literature available to African Americans. McCloud, *African American Islam*, 7. This increase may also have contributed to the need for Elijah Muhammad and Malcolm X to engage the claims of other Muslims.

23. Mughal, *Frequently Asked Questions*.

24. This sentiment is hardly unique. For a similar, but somewhat less polemic comparison, see also El-Amin, *The Religion of Islam and the Nation of Islam*.

25. Muhammad, "Mr. Muhammad Answers White Filth Crusader," 6. Elijah Muhammad was also concerned that scholars of the Qur'an overemphasized Allah as "spirit" in the same way Christians did. Muhammad, "Mr. Muhammad Speaks" (October 19, 1957): 10.

26. Muhammad, "Mr. Muhammad Speaks" (June 8, 1957): 10. Emphasis added.

27. Muhammad, *The Supreme Wisdom: Solution*, 29–30, 31, 33, and 35.

28. Muhammad, *The Supreme Wisdom: Solution*, 37.

29. Malcolm X, "Arabs Send Warm Greetings," 1.

30. Muhammad, "Mr. Muhammad Speaks" (August 15, 1959): 14.

31. Clegg, *An Original Man*, 133.

32. Essien-Udom, *Black Nationalism*, 203–4.

33. Elijah Muhammad cited in Abdul Basit Naeem, "Introduction" to Muhammad, *The Supreme Wisdom: Solution*, 4. See also C. Eric Lincoln, *The Black Muslims in America*, 220–21.

34. Naeem, "Explains Why U.S. Muslims Don't Pray in Orthodox Way," 10. Naeem also defended Elijah Muhammad's priorities in a series of articles about the five pillars of Islam within the Nation of Islam in his weekly column in *Muhammad Speaks*. Naeem argued that the Nation of Islam was in its infancy and not yet ready for the deeper, more spiritual meanings of prayer, but that their efforts to clothe, feed, and shelter others were a form of prayer; theirs was a prayer of action and service to others. Moreover, they did not have the linguistic skills to pray in Arabic, nor were they all morally prepared. Naeem, "Examines '5 Pillars of Islam' and Black Nation," 10; Naeem, "Explains Why U.S. Muslims Don't Pray in Orthodox Way," 10; and Naeem, "U.S. Muslims' Good Deeds Are Prayers in Action," 10 and 27. Similarly, Naeem argued that the time and energy of the Muslims of the Nation of Islam would be better spent spreading Islam in the United States than going on *hajj*. Not only would they there encounter peculiarities of "old world" Muslims that might perplex them, but technically these new world Muslims were also surrounded by a hostile (white) enemy; they were, therefore, in a state of jihad and exempt from performing the *hajj* based on Islamic law. Naeem, "Thinks U.S. Muslims Should Aid Islam at Home before Pilgrimage to Mecca," 10–11.

35. For an example of how Elijah Muhammad used his "*hajj*" experience, see Muhammad, *Theology of Time*, 22–23. His focus was on the health effects of the water from the Zamzam well. There was no mention of its connection to the traditional stories of Hagar and Ishmael or of its rediscovery by Muhammad's grandfather.

36. Clegg, *An Original Man*, 144.

37. Muhammad, "Mr. Muhammad Answers Critics," 3–4.

38. Muhammad, *Message to the Blackman in America*, 49–50.

39. Muhammad, *Message to the Blackman in America*, 187.

40. Muhammad, *Message to the Blackman in America*, 188–90.

41. Muhammad, "Black Man of U.S.A. and Africa," 20.

42. "Allah's Last Messenger Answers Questions You Have Always Wanted to Ask!" 4.

43. Muhammad, *Our Saviour Has Arrived*, 61.

44. Muhammad, *Message to the Blackman in America*, 289 and 264. Science too must take a back seat to this divine authority: "I do not make mistakes in what I write pertaining to these two races—black and white—and I do not need to study the theory of evolution to learn about them. Theories do not always prove to be the truth. I have the truth from the All-wise One (Allah), to Whom praise is due." Muhammad, *The Supreme Wisdom: Solution*, 21. Similarly, scientific discoveries about the moon (such as its age) and Mars (such as the presence of Martian life) were wrong or lies, for Elijah Muhammad got his information about such things from Allah. Muhammad, "Old World Going Out with a Great Noise!" 16–17. However, Elijah Muhammad did not oppose science. In fact, he strongly encouraged his followers to pursue higher education, particularly in technology, mathematics, and "higher science." For him, the advancement and independence of African Americans depended on obtaining this knowledge. Muhammad, "Qualification Is a Must: Advance Education," 16–17.

45. Muhammad, "The Hypocrites," 12.

46. Diouf, *Servants of Allah*, 207.

47. See Curtis, *Black Muslim Religion*, for a detailed examination of the critical and personal role Islam played for members of the Nation of Islam from 1960 to 1975.

48. C. Eric Lincoln, *Black Muslims*, 210.

49. C. Eric Lincoln, *Black Muslims*, 26.

50. Marsh, *From Black Muslims to Muslims*, 103–4.

51. A similar position is taken by Essien-Udom, who states,

> The Nation of Islam represents an esoteric, in-group struggle to provide standards by which the social, cultural and moral life of the Negro masses can be raised to a meaningful community fabric. It seeks an outlet for Negro striving and performance. The movement combines the attractions of religion, nationalism, and political "pies in the sky" with a peculiar sense of belonging and achievement, and proposes the possibility of "greater" achievement for its members. The Nation assists its members to strive for traditional American middle-class values while maintaining their identity with the Negro community. Essien-Udom, *Black Nationalism*, 362.

52. Muhammad, "Black Man of U.S.A. and Africa," 20.

53. Marsh, *From Black Muslims to Muslims*, 105.

54. Curtis, *Islam in Black America*, 2.

55. Ghareeb, "Lauds Leader: Eastern Muslim Calls Nation of Islam 'Great,'" 15.

56. Muhammad, *Message to the Blackman in America*, 204.

57. Curtis, *Black Muslim Religion*, 37.

58. Jackson, *Islam and the Blackamerican*, 44.

59. Jackson, *Islam and the Blackamerican*, 4, 29, and 31.

60. Jackson, *Islam and the Blackamerican*, 28.

61. Curtis, *Black Muslim Religion*.

62. Jackson, *Islam and the Blackamerican*, 44.

63. Jackson's concept of "Black Religion" is also problematic. There is no existence of Black Religion independent of the existence of religions such as Islam and Christianity. It seems possible, therefore, that Jackson has selected some salient characteristics of particularly politically active expressions of these religions among African Americans and reified them into a discernible religious movement. Jackson's Black Religion is brilliant as a descriptive category, but whether this abstraction can then be pressed into service as the active agent that, for instance, appropriates the vocabulary of Islam and so gives rise to the Nation of Islam is a somewhat more dubious claim. Furthermore, except for Jackson's use of the phrase "holy protest," it is not exactly clear what makes Black Religion religious. In other words, it seems just as plausible to suggest that there is black protest against white supremacy in the United States that appropriates religious language from Islam in the case of the Nation of Islam and political language from nationalism in the case of the Universal Negro Improvement Association.

64. Lee, *The Nation of Islam*, 2.

65. Turner, *Islam*, 4–5.

66. Muhammad, "Mr. Muhammad Speaks" (October 12, 1956): 2; and "Sixteen Journalists Obtain . . . Rare Interview with Messenger Muhammad!" 3.

67. (The use of "Surah" is also very unusual.) Muhammad, "Fight in the Cause of Allah with Those Who Fight You," 1.

68. Naeem did so to explain why *hajj* was not incumbent on members of the Nation of Islam. Naeem, "Thinks U.S. Muslims Should Aid Islam at Home before Pilgrimage to Mecca," 10.

69. Clegg, *An Original Man*, 282.

70. Marsh, *From Black Muslims to Muslims*, 107 and 110.

71. For instance, Fard Muhammad taught that whites were evil, but it was a black man, Yakub, who had created them. Also, God himself (i.e., Fard Muhammad) was the son of a black man and a white woman.

72. Mohammed, "Address to the University of North Carolina at Wilmington."

73. Sahib, *The Nation of Islam*, 71.

74. Muhammad, "Teachings of the Holy Quran," 18.

75. "First Official Interview with the Supreme Minister of the Nation of Islam, The Honorable Wallace D. Muhammad," 3.

76. Turner, *Islam*, 158.

77. Sherman A. Jackson also uses the term "proto-Islamic movement" for

both the Moorish Science Temple of America of Drew Ali and the Nation of Islam of Elijah Muhammad. However, in so doing he is not suggesting, as Warith Deen Mohammed does with regard to Fard Muhammad and as Muhammad Abdullah does with regard to Elijah Muhammad, that these men were consciously engaged in a secret effort to bring African Americans to Sunni Islam. His goal is to emphasize that these forms of Islam were not "interpretations" of Islam but "appropriations" of Islam. In other words, Drew Ali and Elijah Muhammad had little interest in the way other Muslims practiced Islam. Instead, they sought to use Islam to reject white supremacy and anti-Black racism. Jackson, *Islam and the Blackamerican*, 5 and 43–44.

78. Curtis, *Islam in Black America*, 18–19.

CHAPTER 6

1. Haddad, "Introduction: The Muslims of America," 4.

2. Clegg, *An Original Man*, 282.

3. Elijah Muhammad was certainly not theologically conservative in the context of Islam, but he "clung rather slavishly to Christian categories and antecedents." Jackson, *Islam and the Blackamerican*, 37. See also Ansari, "Aspects of Black Muslim Theology," 137–76.

4. See chapter 4 above for a discussion of women.

5. Having argued that the separation of the races is inevitable and mandated by God, Elijah Muhammad stated, "If you were forced to choose between segregation and integration you would be better off to ask the southern white people to give segregation back to you." Muhammad, "The Fatal Mistake," 17.

6. Elijah Muhammad warned his female followers that he opposed "adopting the African dress and hair styles . . . accepting traditional African tribal styles and garments with gay colors." Muhammad, "Warning to M.G.T. and G.C. Class," 4. With regard to men, beards, Afros, and traditional African "garb," these were dismissed as "jungle styles." He said, "I am against wearing beards. I am against men wearing long hair like women." His main issue with beards and long hair, besides their being "non-modern," was a matter of hygiene. He believed them to be "germ-carriers" and unsanitary. Even the "white man," who "came out of the cave . . . full of hair . . . [that] covered his whole body and face," shaves. Muhammad, "Beards," 5.

His issue with hygiene highlights his negative and condescending attitude towards Africa as well. Of beards or "hair worn down their backs like a woman," Elijah Muhammad noted, "This is the way the uncivilized white man went in the days when they lived in caves. It is the style of Black people of uncultured parts of Africa and the Islands of the Pacific, which was caused by the absence of the right guide, but they too will turn to the civilized way when they have the right guide." Muhammad, "To the Black Woman in America," 16–17.

After encouraging the "Black Man" to "wash and be clean," to refrain from using "filthy language" and from being loud, and to give up smoking, drinking, and drugs, Elijah Muhammad stated, "We must even teach Africa, and all other Black peoples, wherever they are on the earth, to have higher morals and more self-respect. We must get to them." After all, "The devil practices good manners. Why do not you and I do the same thing?" Muhammad, "Wash and Be Clean," 21.

Elijah Muhammad's conservative, perhaps even prejudiced attitude towards Africans is extended to Native Americans as well, even though he considered them descendants of "an old Ancient People, the Black Man of Asia." He taught that they originated in India and are therefore "so-called American Indians." They came to America because they had been exiled from India for their unbelief in Allah and refusal to worship in His religion, Islam. After reaching America on foot (as part of their punishment) via the Bering Strait, they worshiped gods that they had fashioned themselves (as they had done in India). Their near annihilation by the white man was therefore a punishment for rejecting Allah. Elijah Muhammad then made Native Americans an offer: "So if you desire to live, my once-brothers, the Indians of America, seek me and I will Seek God for you, that you may live, yet again. Allah taught me that we can get along with the Indians of America, for they yet have some blood of the aboriginal Black people." Muhammad, "Indians in America," 20.

7. C. Eric Lincoln, "The Muslim Mission," 286.

8. These two men head the two most influential movements that emerged from the Nation of Islam after Elijah Muhammad's death. There were about a dozen offshoots, with the third most influential being that of John Muhammad, Elijah Muhammad's brother.

9. Essien-Udom, *Black Nationalism*, 93.

10. Marsh, *From Black Muslims to Muslims*, 78.

11. Malcolm X, *Autobiography*, 297.

12. Malcolm X, *Autobiography*, 339.

13. Curtis, *Islam in Black America*, 111.

14. Marsh, *From Black Muslims to Muslims*, 91.

15. "He Lives On!" 1; Kashif, "Muslim Ministers Declare Support for New Leadership," 3 and 19; Wallace Muhammad, "Saviour's Day Address: Hon. Wallace Muhammad," 12–13; 67X, "He Lives On!" 2; and Baghdadi, "Middle East Report," 2. In subsequent issues, Wallace Muhammad's picture would become ubiquitous and he granted a long interview to make his case directly to his father's followers. "First Official Interview with the Supreme Minister of the Nation of Islam, The Honorable Wallace D. Muhammad," 3 and 11–14.

16. "First Official Interview with the Supreme Minister of the Nation of Islam, The Honorable Wallace D. Muhammad," 3.

17. Marsh, *From Black Muslims to Muslims*, 92.

18. "First Official Interview with the Supreme Minister of the Nation of Islam,

The Honorable Wallace D. Muhammad," 3. Wallace Muhammad also related that his mother and father had been told by Fard Muhammad that Wallace Muhammad would be a boy and would be "a helper to his father." Ibid., 13.

19. Mohammed, "Address to the University of North Carolina at Wilmington."

20. Mamiya, "From Black Muslim to Bilalian," 138–52.

21. "White Muslims?" 52; and Sullivan and Moore, "Cleveland Hosts Mass Elder Citizen Affair," 3.

22. Kashif, "Muslim Ministers Declare Support for New Leadership," 19.

23. "First Official Interview with the Supreme Minister of the Nation of Islam, The Honorable Wallace D. Muhammad," 12.

24. Curtis, *Islam in Black America*, 130. The double wedding of Louis Farrakhan's daughters Donna and Maria to Elijah Muhammad's nephew, Wali Muhammad, and his grandson, Alif Muhammad, occurred on January 28, 1975, less than a month prior to Elijah Muhammad's death. Mary Eloise X, "Two Great Families Unite!" S1–S7.

25. Toure Muhammad, *Chronology of Nation of Islam History*, 11–12.

26. Given Curtis's argument that between the years 1960 and 1975 the Nation of Islam was gradually islamicized by Elijah Muhammad, one could see Louis Farrakhan as merely continuing that process. Curtis, *Black Muslim Religion*.

27. If Mamiya's thesis is correct, perhaps part of Farrakhan's recent shift is due to his followers also moving into the middle class. As with the generation before, the racial separatist ideology of Elijah Muhammad is not as appropriate as it once was.

28. Parts of this section have appeared in Berg, "Mythmaking in the American Muslim Context," 685–703.

29. Clegg, *An Original Man*, 69–73.

30. McCutcheon, "Myth," 200.

31. Mack, *Who Wrote the New Testament?* 11.

32. Bruce Lincoln, "Theses on Method," 225.

33. Mack, *Who Wrote the New Testament?* 71.

34. Mack, *Who Wrote the New Testament?* 36.

35. A good example of this kind of reversal can be seen in Elijah Muhammad's treatment of the white racist claim that it is "obvious" that Africans are more closely related to other primates from which humans evolved. Elijah Muhammad reversed this claim by stating that Allah taught him that some Whites had tried to "graft themselves back into the black nation." They only got as far as turning themselves into gorillas. "In fact, all the monkey family are from this 2,000 year history of the white race in Europe." Muhammad, *Message to the Blackman in America*, 119.

36. Mack *Who Wrote the New Testament?* 118.

37. The importance of identity is made explicit in Elijah Muhammad's ubiquitous command "Be yourself!" and his emphasis on "knowledge of self" and

"do for self." The former is said to be "Allah's greatest teaching and warning to us (the so-called Negroes)." Muhammad, *Supreme Wisdom: Solution*, 12 and 18–19. "Be yourself" meant being proud of being black, seeing black as beautiful, and becoming Muslim. "Do for self" meant breaking one's economic, social, and religious dependence on Whites.

38. Bruce Lincoln, *Authority*, 6.

39. Bruce Lincoln, *Authority*, 7.

40. Drew Ali made his views on Christianity clear at the end of his *Circle Seven Koran*:

> We, as a clean and pure nation descended from the inhabitants of Africa, do not desire to amalgamate or marry into families of the pale skin nations of Europe. Neither serve the gods of their religion, because our forefathers are the true and divine founders of the first religious Creed, for the redemption and salvation of mankind on earth.
>
> Therefore we are returning the Church and Christianity back to the European Nations, as it was prepared by their forefathers for their earthly salvation.
>
> While we, the Moorish Americans are returning to Islam, which was founded by our forefathers for our earthly and divine salvation. Noble Drew Ali, *Circle Seven Koran*, 59.

Drew Ali saw a chronological priority and a spiritual superiority of Islam, but did not denigrate Christianity, "for every nation must worship under his own vine and fig tree." Noble Drew Ali, *Circle Seven Koran*, 59. However, it is wrong for people descended from Moors to follow anything else but Islam. Elijah Muhammad, in contrast, stated, "Christianity is a religion organized and backed by the devils for the purpose of making slaves of black mankind." Muhammad, *Supreme Wisdom: Solution*, 13.

For Drew Ali, the Qur'an (or at least its name) was central to his self-exoticizing claims of prophethood. For an excellent discussion of this "self-exoticizing" and its connection with African Americans' perception of Islam and the "East" in 1920s Chicago, see Nance, "Respectability and Representation," 623–59.

41. See, for example, Muhammad, "Mr. Muhammad Speaks" (June 30, 1956): 2; Muhammad, "Mr. Muhammad Speaks" (July 7, 1956): 2; and Muhammad, *The Supreme Wisdom: Solution*, 12 and 20.

42. Muhammad, *Supreme Wisdom: Volume Two*, back cover.

43. For those who refused to follow Warith Deen Mohammed, much of Elijah Muhammad's authority passed to his writings. Several organizations, such as the Coalition for the Remembrance of Elijah (CROE), United Brothers Communications Systems, and Messenger Elijah Muhammad Propagation Society, continue to preserve and propagate Elijah Muhammad's teachings.

44. Mack, *Who Wrote the New Testament?* 11.

45. Sherman A. Jackson lists a similar set of "four key facts." The spread of the Islams of Drew Ali and Elijah Muhammad was a twentieth-century, northern, urban, and underclass phenomenon. Prior to the twentieth century, the existential reality of African Americans precluded first preserving the Islam brought from Africa and then later resuscitating it. The migration of millions of African Americans to the cities of the post-Reconstruction North, where they remained poor, highlighted the "uneasy place" black Christianity occupied within an American Christianity dominated by Whites and the inability of black Christianity to adapt to this new cultural milieu. The result was a significant number of African Americans who were alienated from black Christianity and susceptible to the new black Islams. Jackson, *Islam and the Blackamerican*, 38–42.

46. Mack, *Who Wrote the New Testament?* 176.

47. As noted earlier, phenomenologically, if one brackets out theological prejudice, Elijah Muhammad must be treated as a Muslim on the basis of his own claims (see chapter 5). If one were to create a "minimal definition of Islam" (as discussed in chapter 5), the preeminence he accords to the Qur'an (see chapters 3 and 4) and even to the figure of Muhammad (if not his Sunna) suggests that Elijah Muhammad would fit such a definition. Of course, it is not for the scholar of Islam to adjudicate whether anyone is a Muslim. Rather, my point is that these aforementioned facts, along with the vital and essential role of the religion of Islam within the authorities and identities he created (see above) and his tremendous impact on "orthodox" Islam in America before and after his death (see above), highlight the need to study him within the larger Islamic tradition.

48. Kelley, "Malcolm X," 1,233.

Bibliography

3X, Allen and Eugene Majied. "Through Lies, Distortions, Misquotes: Seek to Turn Black Man against Muhammad." *Muhammad Speaks* (April 21, 1972): 15.

14X, Larry. "Fundraising Dinner a 'Quiet Success': Unity, Dominant Theme at Muhammad Hospital Fund Affair." *Muhammad Speaks* (January 31, 1975): 4.

67X, Charles. "He Lives On!" *Muhammad Speaks* (March 14, 1975): 2.

Abu Shouk, Ahmed I., J. O. Hunwick, and R. S. O'Fahey. "A Sudanese Missionary to the United States: Sāttī Mājid, 'Shaykh al-Islām in North America,' and His Encounter with Noble Drew Ali, Prophet of the Moorish Science Temple Movement." *Sudanic Africa* 8 (1997): 137–91.

Ali, John. "Whiteman and the Hypocrites Love Malcolm." *Muhammad Speaks* (October 3, 1969): 20–21.

Ali, Noble Drew. *The Holy Koran of the Moorish Science Temple of America.* N.d.

———. *Humanity.* N.d.

———. *Koran Questions for Moorish Americans.* N.d.

———. *Moorish Literature.* N.d.

"Allah's Last Messenger Answers Questions You Have Always Wanted to Ask! Muhammad Meets the Press!" *Muhammad Speaks* (February 4, 1972): 3–4.

Ansari, Z. I. "Aspects of Black Muslim Theology." *Studia Islamica* 53 (1981): 137–76.

Arnal, William E. "Definition." In *Guide to the Study of Religion*, 21–34. Edited by Willi Braun and Russell McCutcheon. New York: Cassell, 2000.

Arrington, Carolyn. *Black Explorer in Spanish Texas: Estevanico.* Austin, TX: Eakin Press, 1986.

Austin, Allan D. *African Muslims in Antebellum America: A Sourcebook.* New York: Garland Publishing, 1984.

———. *African Muslims in Antebellum America: Transatlantic Stories and Spiritual Struggles.* New York: Routledge, 1997.

Baghdadi, Ali. "Middle East Report." *Muhammad Speaks* (March 14, 1975): 2.

———. "Who's behind the Splinter Group? Messenger's Attackers Exposed." *Muhammad Speaks* (May 5, 1972): 2.

Barboza, Steven. *American Jihad: Islam after Malcolm X.* New York: Doubleday, 1994.

Berg, Herbert. "Early African American Muslim Movements and the Qur'an." *Journal of Qur'anic Studies* 8.1 (2006): 22–37.

———. "Elijah Muhammad: An African American Muslim *mufassir*?" *Arabica: Revue d'études Arabes* 44 (1997): 1–27.

———. "Elijah Muhammad and the Qur'an: The Evolution of His *tafsir*." *The Muslim World* 89.1 (January 1999): 40–55.

———. "Mythmaking in the American Muslim Context: The Moorish Science Temple, the Nation of Islam, and the American Society of Muslims." *Journal of the American Academy of Religion* 73.3 (September 2005): 685–703.

Beynon, Erdmann Doane. "The Voodoo Cult among Negro Migrants in Detroit." *American Journal of Sociology* 43 (July 1937–May 1938): 894–907.

"The Black Supremacists." *Time* (August 10, 1959): 24–25.

Braun, Willi. "Religion." In *Guide to the Study of Religion*, 3–20. Edited by Willi Braun and Russell McCutcheon. New York: Cassell, 2000.

Burley, Dan. "Pomp, Mysticism Key to Power: Elijah Muhammad Part II." *Chicago Defender* (August 22, 1959): 1–2.

———. "Portrait of a Shrewd Cult Leader." *Chicago Defender* (August 15, 1959): 1–2.

"Chicago Mayor Proclaims Muslim Saviour's Day: 'Nation of Islam Day' Feb. 26, 1975." *Muhammad Speaks* (February 14, 1975): 1.

Clegg, Claude Andrew, III. *An Original Man: The Life and Times of Elijah Muhammad.* New York: St. Martin's Press, 1997.

Curtin, Philip D. *The Atlantic Slave Trade: A Census.* Madison: University of Wisconsin Press, 1969.

Curtis, Edward E., IV. *Black Muslim Religion in the Nation of Islam, 1960–1975.* Chapel Hill: University of North Carolina Press, 2006.

———. *Islam in Black America: Identity, Liberation, and Difference in African-American Islamic Thought.* Albany: State University of New York Press, 2002.

"Dakota Says There's No Connection 'Tween Her Faith, Muhammed." *The Pittsburgh Courier* (August 1, 1959): 3.

Dannin, Robert. *Black Pilgrimage to Islam.* Oxford: Oxford University Press, 2002.

DeCaro, Louis A., Jr. *On the Side of My People: A Religious Life of Malcolm X.* New York: New York University Press, 1996.

"Decree Akbar Muhammad." *Muhammad Speaks* (January 1, 1965): 9.

Diouf, Sylviane A. *Servants of Allah: African Muslims Enslaved in the Americas.* New York: New York University Press, 1998.

Dowling, Levi H. *The Aquarian Gospel of Jesus the Christ: The Philosophical and Practical Basis of the Religion of the Aquarian Age of the World and of the Church Universal, Transcribed from the Book of God's Remembrances, Known as the Akashic Records.* London: Fowler, 1930 [1908].

El-Amin, Mustafa. *The Religion of Islam and the Nation of Islam: What Is the Difference?* Newark, NJ: El-Amin Productions, 1991.

Essien-Udom, E. U. *Black Nationalism: A Search for an Identity in America.* New York: Dell, 1962.

Farrakhan, Louis. "Muslim 'Feud' a Hoax, Farrakhan Explains." *Muhammad Speaks* (February 22, 1974): 3.

Fauset, Arthur Huff. *Black Gods of the Metropolis: Negro Religious Cults in the Urban North.* Philadelphia: University of Pennsylvania Press, 1944.

Federal Bureau of Investigation. "Elijah Muhammad." FBI file 105-24822.

———. "Fard, Wallace D." FBI files 100-33603; 100-43165; and 105-63642.

———. "Moorish Science Temple of America (Noble Drew Ali)." FBI file 62-25899.

"Fire New Blasts at Moslems: Leader Explains Role of 2 Groups." *Chicago Defender* (December 5, 1959): 1–2.

"First Official Interview with the Supreme Minister of the Nation of Islam, The Honorable Wallace D. Muhammad." *Muhammad Speaks* (March 21, 1975): 3 and 11–14.

"'Get Well' Sentiments Arrive in 'Avalanche.'" *Muhammad Speaks* (February 28, 1975): 5.

Ghareeb, Zahid Aziz al-. "Lauds Leader: Eastern Muslim Calls Nation of Islam 'Great.'" *Muhammad Speaks* (July 2, 1971): 15 and 18.

Gomez, Michael A. "Muslims in Early America." *The Journal of Southern History* 60.4 (November 1994): 671–710.

Haddad, Yvonne Yazbek. "Introduction: The Muslims of America." In *The Muslims of America*, 1–8. Edited by Yvonne Yazbek Haddad. New York: Oxford University Press, 1991.

"He Lives On!" *Muhammad Speaks* (March 14, 1975): 1.

The Holy Qur-an. Ali, Maulvi Muhammad, trans. 4th rev. ed. Lahore: Ahmadiyya Anjuman Ishaat Islam, 1951.

"The Holy Qur-an: Chapter 4, Section 9: The Prophet Must Be Obeyed." *Muhammad Speaks* (April 4, 1965): 8.

"The Holy Qur-an: The Hypocrites and Disbelievers." *Muhammad Speaks* (January 1, 1965): 8.

Huntington, Samuel P. *The Clash of Civilizations and the Remaking of World Order.* New York: Simon and Schuster, 1996.

"Is New York Sitting on a 'Powderkeg'? Racial Unrest Forces Its Way to the Surface." *U.S. News & World Report* (August 3, 1959): 48–51.

Jackson, Sherman A. *Islam and the Blackamerican: Looking toward the Third Resurrection.* Oxford: Oxford University Press, 2005.

Kashif, Lonnie. "Muslim Ministers Declare Support for New Leadership." *Muhammad Speaks* (March 14, 1975): 3 and 19.

Kelley, Robin D. G. "Malcolm X." In *Africana: The Encyclopedia of the African and African American Experience*, 1,233–36. Edited by Kwame Anthony Appiah and Henry Louis Gates, Jr. New York: Basic Civitas Books, 1999.

Lee, Martha F. *The Nation of Islam: An American Millenarian Movement*. Syracuse, NY: Syracuse University Press, 1996.

Lincoln, Bruce. *Authority: Construction and Corrosion*. Chicago: Chicago University Press, 1994.

——. "Theses on Method." *Method & Theory in the Study of Religion* 8.3 (1996): 225–27.

Lincoln, C. Eric. *The Black Muslims in America*. 3rd ed. Grand Rapids, MI: Eerdmans, 1994 [1961].

——. "The Muslim Mission in the Context of American Social History." In *African-American Religion: Interpretive Essays in History and Culture*, 279–94. Edited by Timothy E. Fulop and Albert J. Raboteau. New York: Routledge, 1997.

Mack, Burton L. "Social Formation." In *Guide to the Study of Religion*, 283–96. Edited by Willi Braun and Russell T. McCutcheon. London: Continuum, 2000.

——. *Who Wrote the New Testament? The Making of the Christian Myth*. New York: HarperCollins, 1995.

Mamiya, Lawrence H. "From Black Muslim to Bilalian: The Evolution of a Movement." *Journal for the Scientific Study of Religion* 21.2 (1982): 138–52.

Marr, Timothy. *The Cultural Roots of American Islamicism*. New York: Cambridge University Press, 2006.

Marsh, Clifton E. *From Black Muslims to Muslims: The Transition from Separation to Islam, 1930-1980*. Metuchen, NJ: Scarecrow Press, 1984.

McCloud, Aminah Beverly. *African American Islam*. New York: Routledge, 1995.

McConkie, Bruce R. *Mormon Doctrine*. Salt Lake City, UT: Bookcraft, 1958.

McCutcheon, Russell T. "Myth." In *Guide to the Study of Religion*, 199–207. Edited by Willi Braun and Russell T. McCutcheon. London: Continuum, 2000.

Mohammed, Warith Deen. "Address to the University of North Carolina at Wilmington." Paper presented on February 2, 2002.

"Moslems Fill Rockland, Leader Fails to Show." *The Amsterdam News* (August 22, 1959): 21.

Mughal, Asim. *Frequently Asked Questions: Part 10. Islam: Farrakhism & Malcolm X*. http://allanswers.org/religion/islam-faq/part10.htm, version 3.3, 1993.

Muhammad, Elijah. "Air Pollution Can Be Controlled." *Muhammad Speaks* (August 7, 1970): 2.

——. "Beards." *Muhammad Speaks* (July 4, 1969): 5.

——. "Beware of False Prophets." *Muhammad Speaks* (July 31, 1964): 1, 3, and 8.

——. "Black Man of U.S.A. and Africa." *Muhammad Speaks* (October 17, 1969): 20–21.

——. "The Bursting Asunder." *Muhammad Speaks* (September 26, 1969): 20–21.

——. "Christmas!" *Muhammad Speaks* (December 25, 1970): 15.

——. "Clarification of Actions Taken by Messenger Muhammad against Muhammad Ali's Action." *Muhammad Speaks* (April 11, 1969): 2–3.

———. "Continued: The Mother Plane." *Muhammad Speaks* (September 5, 1969): 20–21.

———. "'Daring Pedestrian' Who Challenges Motorist." *Muhammad Speaks* (August 11, 1967): 12–13.

———. "The Daring Pedestrian: Part II." *Muhammad Speaks* (August 25, 1967): 12–13.

———. *The Fall of America*. Chicago: Muhammad's Temple of Islam No. 2, 1973.

———. "Fasting." *Muhammad Speaks* (December 18, 1970): 15.

———. "Fasting." *Muhammad Speaks* (December 10, 1971): 16–17.

———. "The Fatal Mistake." *Muhammad Speaks* (January 23, 1970): 16–17.

———. "Fight in the Cause of Allah with Those Who Fight You." *Muhammad Speaks* (October 28, 1966): 1.

———. "The Filth That Produces the Filth." *Muhammad Speaks* (September 4, 1970): 16–17.

———. "Future of American So-Called Negroes. . . ." *Muhammad Speaks* (April 1962): 3, 6, 8, and 16–17.

———. *History of the Nation of Islam*. Atlanta: Secretarius Memps Publication, 1993.

———. "The Holy Qur-An." *Muhammad Speaks* (February 4, 1966): 10.

———. *How to Eat to Live*. Newport News, VA: National Newport News and Commentator, 1967.

———. "The Hypocrites." *Muhammad Speaks* (April 26, 1968): 12.

———. "Hypocrites!" *Muhammad Speaks* (May 14, 1971): 12.

———. "Hypocrites Condemned." *Muhammad Speaks* (October 23, 1964): 8.

———. "Hypocrites: Do Not Befriend Hypocrites." *Muhammad Speaks* (November 26, 1971): 15.

———. "Indians in America." *Muhammad Speaks* (March 28, 1969): 20.

———. "Memo: From the Desk of Muhammad; To: The Original Black People!" *Muhammad Speaks* (September 11, 1964): 5, 14, and 20.

———. *Message to the Blackman in America*. Newport News, VA: United Brothers Communications Systems, 1992 [1965].

———. "Messenger Thanks Greeks." *Muhammad Speaks* (March 3, 1972): 2.

———. "Money Necessary." *Muhammad Speaks* (August 3, 1973): 6.

———. "The Mother Plane." *Muhammad Speaks* (August 29, 1969): 20–21.

———. "Mr. Muhammad Answers Critics: Authority from Allah, None Other." *Muhammad Speaks* (August 2, 1963): 3–4.

———. "Mr. Muhammad Answers White Filth Crusader: Says So-called Negroes Will Soon Lose Love for Their White Oppressors." *The Pittsburgh Courier* (March 30, 1957): 6.

———. "Mr. Muhammad Speaks." *The Pittsburgh Courier* (June 30, 1956): 2 (Magazine Section).

———. "Mr. Muhammad Speaks." *The Pittsburgh Courier* (July 7, 1956): 2 (Magazine Section).

———. "Mr. Muhammad Speaks." *The Pittsburgh Courier* (July 23, 1956): 2 (Magazine Section).

———. "Mr. Muhammad Speaks." *The Pittsburgh Courier* (July 28, 1956): 2 (Magazine Section).

———. "Mr. Muhammad Speaks." *The Pittsburgh Courier* (August 11, 1956): 2 (Magazine Section).

———. "Mr. Muhammad Speaks." *The Pittsburgh Courier* (September 22, 1956): 2 (Magazine Section).

———. "Mr. Muhammad Speaks." *The Pittsburgh Courier* (October 12, 1956): 2 (Magazine Section).

———. "Mr. Muhammad Speaks." *The Pittsburgh Courier* (October 20, 1956): 2 (Magazine Section).

———. "Mr. Muhammad Speaks." *The Pittsburgh Courier* (February 15, 1957): 14.

———. "Mr. Muhammad Speaks." *The Pittsburgh Courier* (February 22, 1957): 14.

———. "Mr. Muhammad Speaks." *The Pittsburgh Courier* (June 8, 1957): 10.

———. "Mr. Muhammad Speaks." *The Pittsburgh Courier* (June 29, 1957): 10.

———. "Mr. Muhammad Speaks." *The Pittsburgh Courier* (August 10, 1957): 10.

———. "Mr. Muhammad Speaks." *The Pittsburgh Courier* (August 17, 1957): 10.

———. "Mr. Muhammad Speaks." *The Pittsburgh Courier* (August 24, 1957): 10.

———. "Mr. Muhammad Speaks." *The Pittsburgh Courier* (August 31, 1957): 10.

———. "Mr. Muhammad Speaks." *The Pittsburgh Courier* (September 7, 1957): 10.

———. "Mr. Muhammad Speaks." *The Pittsburgh Courier* (October 19, 1957): 10.

———. "Mr. Muhammad Speaks." *The Pittsburgh Courier* (October 26, 1957): 10.

———. "Mr. Muhammad Speaks." *The Pittsburgh Courier* (December 21, 1957): 10.

———. "Mr. Muhammad Speaks." *The Pittsburgh Courier* (May 23, 1959): 14.

———. "Mr. Muhammad Speaks." *The Pittsburgh Courier* (August 15, 1959): 14.

———. "Mr. Muhammad's Statement on the President's Death." *Muhammad Speaks* (December 20, 1963): 3.

———. "Muhammad Thanks Harlem: Wins Sweeping Support." *Muhammad Speaks* (July 17, 1964): 1 and 4.

———. "Muslim Prayer Service." *Muhammad Speaks* (June 4, 1965): 10.

———. "Nation of Islam Offers Hearst $100,000 to Prove Charge: Beware of Phony Claims." *Muhammad Speaks* (August 16, 1963): 1 and 3.

———. "Nation Still Mourns Death: When Abe Lincoln and J. F. Kennedy Spoke Out for Negroes. . . ." *Muhammad Speaks* (December 20, 1963): 1 and 3.

———. "Old World Going Out with a Great Noise! Disagreement Mounting." *Muhammad Speaks* (November 26, 1971): 16–17.

———. "Opposition to Truth Is Punished." *Muhammad Speaks* (January 2, 1970): 2.

———. *Our Saviour Has Arrived.* Chicago: Muhammad's Temple of Islam No. 2, 1974.

———. "Pay Your Debts." *Muhammad Speaks* (January 5, 1973): 16.

——. "Pay Your Debts!" *Muhammad Speaks* (September 20, 1974): 1.

——. "Playing with Steel." *Muhammad Speaks* (April 9, 1970): 16–17.

——. "Qualification Is a Must: Advance Education." *Muhammad Speaks* (November 21, 1969): 16–17.

——. "Revelation Guides Aright." *Muhammad Speaks* (December 25, 1970): 18.

——. "Right to Peaceful Assembly Denied Black Americans." *Muhammad Speaks* (November 22, 1963): 1, 3, and 9.

——. "Shun Astrology." *Muhammad Speaks* (January 5, 1973): 17.

——. "Significance of the Moon." *Muhammad Speaks* (January 17, 1969): 21–22.

——. "Significance of the Moon." *Muhammad Speaks* (January 24, 1969): 3.

——. "Special: Read." *Muhammad Speaks* (January 11, 1974): 13.

——. "The Sudden Death of President Nasser of Egypt." *Muhammad Speaks* (October 9, 1970): 17.

——. *The Supreme Wisdom: Solution to the So-Called Negroes' Problem.* Newport News, VA: National Newport News and Commentator, 1957.

——. *The Supreme Wisdom: Volume Two.* Hampton: U.B. & U.S. Communications Systems, n.d.

——. "The Teachings of the Holy Qur-an." *Muhammad Speaks* (July 4, 1969): 19.

——. "Teachings of the Holy Quran." *Muhammad Speaks* (August 15, 1969): 18.

——. "The Teachings of the Holy Qur-an on Obedience." *Muhammad Speaks* (April 24, 1964): 3.

——. "The Teachings of the Holy Qur-an on Obedience." *Muhammad Speaks* (January 15, 1965): 21.

——. "Thank You!" *Muhammad Speaks* (April 12, 1974): 1.

——. *The Theology of Time.* Transcribed by Abass Rassoull. Hampton, VA: U.S. Communications Systems, 1992.

——. "To My Beloved People: Warning." *Muhammad Speaks* (February 16, 1968): 14–15.

——. "To the Black Woman in America." *Muhammad Speaks* (September 4, 1970): 16–17.

——. "TO: The Family of Dr. Martin Luther King." *Muhammad Speaks* (April 12, 1968): 3.

——. "TO: The Patrons of Your Supermarket and Salaam Restaurant." *Muhammad Speaks* (April 26, 1968): 6.

——. *The True History of Master Fard Muhammad.* Compiled and edited by Nasir Makr Hakim. Atlanta: Messenger Elijah Muhammad Propagation Society, 1996.

——. "Truth Has Always Triumphed: Sport and Play Is Condemned." *Muhammad Speaks* (April 17, 1970): 16.

——. "12,000 Cheer Muhammad's History of Black Man's Role in Islam: Applies Prophesy to Today's World." *Muhammad Speaks* (October 31, 1962): 3–4.

———. "Unalike Attracts and Alike Repels." *Muhammad Speaks* (September 15, 1967): 3.

———. "Victory of the Apostle." *Muhammad Speaks* (January 15, 1965): 1 and 3–4.

———. "A Warning to the Black Man of America." *The Final Call to Islam* (August 18, 1934): 1–2.

———. "Warning to Donors." *Muhammad Speaks* (July 6, 1973): 2.

———. "Warning to M.G.T. and G.C. Class." *Muhammad Speaks* (June 28, 1968): 4.

———. "Wash and Be Clean." *Muhammad Speaks* (August 1, 1969): 21.

———. "What Was the Idea of God Making the Moon?" *Muhammad Speaks* (January 17, 1969): 21–22.

———. "Why and How We Fast in December." *Muhammad Speaks* (December 3, 1965): 11.

"Muhammad Meets the Press!" *Muhammad Speaks* (February 4, 1972): 3–4.

"Muhammad Meets the Press!" *Muhammad Speaks* (February 11, 1972): 3–4.

Muhammad, Nathaniel. "October 15 Address: Muhammad Clarifies Truth! Condemns Liars." *Muhammad Speaks* (October 27, 1972): S8–S9.

Muhammad, Toure. *Chronology of Nation of Islam History*. Chicago: Toure Muhammad, 1996.

Muhammad, Wallace. "Saviour's Day Address: Hon. Wallace Muhammad." *Muhammad Speaks* (March 14, 1975): 12–13.

"Muslim Leader Calls Moslem Leader 'Phony.'" *The Amsterdam News* (October 3, 1959): 11.

"NAACP Attacks 'Moslem' Cult: Roy Wilkins Hits Racists for Aid." *Chicago Defender* (August 8, 1959): 1–2.

Naeem, Abdul B. "Declares Messenger of Allah Deserves Support of Entire Muslim World." *Muhammad Speaks* (May 6, 1966): 10.

———. "Examines '5 Pillars of Islam' and Black Nation." *Muhammad Speaks* (June 24, 1966): 10.

———. "Explains Why U.S. Muslims Don't Pray in Orthodox Way." *Muhammad Speaks* (July 1, 1966): 10.

———. "How the Late Malcolm X Misrepresented Himself and the Divine Messenger." *Muhammad Speaks* (August 6, 1965): 9.

———. "Malcolm's Doom Decreed by God, Not the Messenger." *Muhammad Speaks* (August 27, 1965): 10.

———. "Obey Divine Leader." *Muhammad Speaks* (July 17, 1964): 1, 3, and 6.

———. "Pakistan Muslim Blasts Press Slander of Islam: Declares U.S. Muslims True Brothers in Islam." *Muhammad Speaks* (September 30, 1962): 3.

———. "Pakistan Muslim: Muhammad's Work, Not Words, True Test of Greatness." *Muhammad Speaks* (October 31, 1962): 18–19.

———. "Pakistan Muslim: Rips Malcolm Statements Printed in Foreign Press." *Muhammad Speaks* (December 24, 1965): 10.

———. "Pakistan Muslim Tells the Truth about the Honorable Elijah Muhammad." *Muhammad Speaks* (October 15, 1962): 3.

———. "Pakistani Muslim Tells: Why, at Times, I Refused to Cooperate with Malcolm." (August 20, 1965): 10 and 12.

———. "Rips Role of Lomax: Pakistani Muslim Blasts Handling of TV Interview with Messenger of Allah." *Muhammad Speaks* (January 1, 1965): 4.

———. "Says the Messenger and His Followers May Hold Key to Future of World Islam." *Muhammad Speaks* (April 22, 1965): 10.

———. "Self-Publicity Motivated Malcolm, Not Devotion." *Muhammad Speaks* (August 13, 1965): 10.

———. "Thinks U.S. Muslims Should Aid Islam at Home before Pilgrimage to Mecca." *Muhammad Speaks* (August 14, 1967): 10–11.

———. "U.S. Muslims' Good Deeds Are Prayers in Action." *Muhammad Speaks* (July 8, 1966): 10 and 27.

Nance, Susan. "Respectability and Representation: The Moorish Science Temple, Morocco, and Black Public Culture in 1920s Chicago." *American Quarterly* 54.4 (2002): 623–59.

"News of Messenger Muhammad's Illness Evokes Growing Expressions of Concern." *Muhammad Speaks* (February 28, 1975): 5.

Rassoull, Abass. "Holy Names." *Muhammad Speaks* (December 8, 1972): 3.

———. "Warning." *Muhammad Speaks* (June 1, 1973): 15.

Sahib, Hatim A. *The Nation of Islam.* M.A. thesis, University of Chicago, 1951.

Shabbaz, John. "Open Letter: Muslim Minister Writes to Malcolm." *Muhammad Speaks* (July 3, 1964): 9.

Shah, Yusuf. "Minister Offers A.P. Writer Merv Block $100,000 Plus Two Lives to Prove His Charges!" *Muhammad Speaks* (April 14, 1972): 2.

———. "Woe to Every Slanderer!" *Muhammad Speaks* (April 14, 1972): 2.

Sharif, Sidney R. *The African American (Bilalian) Image in Crisis.* Jersey City, NJ: New Mind Productions, 1985.

Siddiqui, Muhammad Abdul Aleem. *Elementary Teachings of Islam.* Islamic Call Society, n.d.

"Sixteen Journalists Obtain . . . Rare Interview with Messenger Muhammad!" *Muhammad Speaks* (January 28, 1972): 3–4.

Smith, Jane I., "Patterns of Muslim Immigration." http://usinfo.state.gov/products/ pubs/muslimlife/ immigrat.htm.

Stoner, J. B. "Letter to Elijah Muhammad." *The Amsterdam News* (September 19, 1959): 1 and 7.

Sullivan, Carl 2X and Constance 2X Moore, "Cleveland Hosts Mass Elder Citizen Affair." *Muhammad Speaks* (November 7, 1975): 3.

Thomas, Hugh. *The Slave Trade: The Story of the Atlantic Slave Trade, 1440-1870.* New York: Simon and Schuster, 1997.

Turner, Richard Brent. *Islam in the African-American Experience*. Bloomington: Indiana University Press, 1997.

———. "Mainstream Islam in the African-American Experience." *Muslim American Society* (August 25, 2004): http://www.masnet.org/history.asp?id=1572.

"Walking the Earth like Brothers." *The Economist* (August 24, 1996): 67–68.

Wansbrough, John. *Quranic Studies: Sources and Methods of Scriptural Interpretation*. Oxford: Oxford University Press, 1977.

———. *The Sectarian Milieu: Content and Composition of Islamic Salvation History*. Oxford: Oxford University Press, 1978.

Watson, R. L. "American Scholars and the Continuity of African Culture in the United States." *Journal of Negro History* 63.4 (October, 1978): 375–86.

Watson, Ted. "The Rise of the Moslems: Messenger Muhammad Leads Thousands to Clean Living through the Islamic Faith." *The Pittsburgh Courier* (April 21, 1956): 2 (Magazine Section),

"White Man Is God for Cult of Islam." *The New Crusader* (August 15, 1959): 1.

"White Muslims?" *Time* (June 30, 1975): 52.

Wilson, Peter Lamborn. *Sacred Drift: Essays on the Margins of Islam*. San Francisco: City Lights Books, 1993.

Wright, R. R. "Negro Companions of the Spanish Explorers." *American Anthropologist* N.S. 4.2 (April 1902): 217–28.

X, Jeremiah and Joseph X. "Biography of a Hypocrite: By Two Muslim Brothers Who Knew Him Best." *Muhammad Speaks* (September 25, 1964): 16.

———. "Minister Exposed by Those Who Knew Him through Life: He Was No 'Empire Builder.'" *Muhammad Speaks* (October 9, 1964): 5.

X, Louis. "Boston Minister Tells of Malcolm—Muhammad's Biggest Hypocrite." *Muhammad Speaks* (November 6, 1964): 11–15.

———. "Minister Condemns Press Threats: Let the Messenger of Truth Teach the World." *Muhammad Speaks* (April 16, 1965): 3.

X, Malcolm. "Arabs Send Warm Greetings to 'Our Brothers' of Color in U.S.A." *Pittsburgh Courier* (August 15, 1959): 1 (Magazine Section).

X, Malcolm, with Alex Haley. *The Autobiography of Malcolm X*. New York: Ballantine Books, 1973 [1964].

X, Mary Eloise. "Two Great Families Unite!" *Muhammad Speaks* (February 14, 1975): S1–S7.

Index

Abd ar-Rahman, Ibrahim, 11
Abdul Khaalis, Hamaas, 49
Abdullah, Muhammad, 124–125, 171n77
Abraham, 82, 97
Adam, 83, 86–87, 94, 162n33
Africa, 9–11, 14, 16, 20, 21, 53, 78, 80, 113, 117, 118, 128, 142, 143, 148n4, 171–172n6
Ahmad, Mirza Ghulam, 18, 78
Ahmadiyya, 5, 13, 18–19, 20, 25, 60, 61, 80, 101, 107, 109, 116, 125, 145, 150n49, 157n16
Alcohol, 13, 25, 46, 53, 171n6
Ali, John, 45, 48, 59
Ali, Duse Mohammed, 19
Ali, (Maulana) Muhammad (translator of Qur'an), 19, 60–61, 64, 101, 102, 154n45, 156n16, 157n32, 157n33, 165n87
Ali, Muhammad (Cassius Clay), 48, 131
Ali, Noble Drew, 2, 5, 6, 9, 14–18, 20, 21, 53–58, 60, 63, 71, 73, 116, 127, 139, 140, 141–142, 143, 148n12, 149n28, 150n50, 156–157n16, 170–171n77, 174n40, 174n45
Allah, 3, 21, 22, 24, 29–30, 54, 55, 57, 58, 62, 63–64, 75, 76–78, 105, 107, 110, 113,114, 115, 117, 118, 119, 122, 130–131, 132–133, 135, 142, 154n43, 156n3, 159n65, 159n68, 159n73, 163n36, 164n67, 164n71,

166n11, 167n14, 168n25, 169n44, 173n37. *See also* Muhammad, Wali Fard
American Nazi Party, 41
Armageddon, 30, 34, 88–92, 98, 121, 122, 135, 139, 163n40
Asiatics, 15, 54, 78, 128, 156n6

Barboza, Steven, 106
Ben Solomon, Job, 11
Beynon, Erdmann Doane, 25, 60, 150n53, 151n64
Bible, 32, 34, 40, 56, 58–60, 62–63, 64, 66, 67, 69, 70, 71, 75, 77, 85, 87, 89, 90, 91–92, 93–95, 99, 102, 110, 124, 137, 142, 144, 152n8, 157n19, 157n25, 157n29, 159n68, 161n4, 162n35, 164n58, 166n96
Bilal, 132
Bilali, Salih, 11
Blyden, Edward Wilmot, 14, 21
Buddhism, 70, 82

Canaanite Temple, The, 14–16, 18, 54
Cassius Clay. *See* Ali, Muhammad
Christians and Christianity, 4–5, 9, 10, 11, 12, 14, 15, 16–17, 18, 19, 20, 29–30, 31, 34, 34, 53, 59, 60, 66, 68, 69, 70, 71, 75, 77, 80, 81, 82, 84, 95, 96, 100, 107, 115, 118, 119–120, 128, 131, 139, 140, 143, 148n6, 159n68, 160n2, 167n14, 168n25m 171n3, 174n40, 175n45

About the Author

HERBERT BERG is Professor in the Department of Philosophy and Religion at the University of North Carolina–Wilmington. He is the author of *The Development of Exegesis in Early Islam: The Debate over the Authenticity of Muslim Literature from the Formative Period* and editor of *Methods and Theories in the Study of Islamic Origins*.